25 PLAYS

Jim Jennings (left) and Walter McGinn in Robert Heide's "The Bed" at the Caffè Cino, 1965

25 Plays
AND A SCREENPLAY

by Robert Heide

FAST BOOKS

Cover design by Barry Rowell
Cover photo by Edward Wallowitch
Back cover photo by George Bonanno

Copyright © 2017 by Robert Heide

ISBN 978-0-9982793-0-5

Fast Books are edited and published by Michael Smith
P. O. Box 1268, Silverton, OR 97381

CONTENTS

Preface by Michael Townsend Smith

Wordplay: an Introduction

Preface
by Michael Townsend Smith

Every serious conversation I have ever had with Robert Heide, my friend since the late 1950s when we were fellow students of Stella Adler, has come around at some point to Jean-Paul Sartre's *Being and Nothingness* and Søren Kierkegaard's *Fear and Trembling* and *The Sickness Unto Death*. Heide's iconic play *The Bed*, written in 1965, explicitly confronts the Sartrean dilemma. *Mr. Nobody*, written in 1982 but set in a MacDougal Street coffeehouse in 1963, talks about Sartre directly. Existentialism always rang true to Heide and crucially shaped his thinking, its potential bleakness offset by good humor and a pop sensibility.

Growing up in Irvington, New Jersey, Heide was inexorably drawn to Greenwich Village. He has lived in the same apartment on Christopher Street since the 1960s, sharing his life with John Gilman, who showed up in *Moon* at the Caffè Cino as the angelic visitor from upstairs who brings fresh-baked bread. Bob and John are recognized authorities on Mickey Mouse collectibles, Village history, and New Jersey diners and have written several books together. Heide to this day is a man about town in print and in person, generously sharing his memories of Joe Cino, Edward Albee, Andy Warhol, and other irreplaceable personalities he has known.

Robert Heide is one of the key first-generation playwrights of Off-Off-Broadway, a veteran of the Caffè Cino, La Mama, Theater for the New City, and other primary venues. He swims in the rich slurry of influences that formed our generation of playwrights, notably affected by Brecht, Sartre, Beckett, Genet, Ionesco, and Pinter as well as Tennessee Williams and William Inge. He is American to the core, his prolific output ranging widely over the sociological landscape. *Hector* is an ironic, heart-breaking tribute to his drama professor at Northwestern University. *The

Bed and *Moon* picture alienated young bohemians in 1960s New York. *West of the Moon* introduces an embittered gay hustler taking shelter in a doorway in the rain, explaining life to a naive young newcomer to the city. *Why Tuesday Never Has a Blue Monday* is a coming-apart star's session with her analyst. The two young people in *At War with the Mongols*, tripping on LSD, hallucinate a brutal Chinese invasion. *Suburban Tremens* is a nightmarish satire of family life. *Tropical Fever in Key West* is two plays: one gives us a Tennessee Williams in serious disrepair, the other a lost, aging couple across the street getting sloppily drunk as evening falls. There are many more plays with similarly louche characters, cruelly but affectionately stripped bare.

Like Kierkegaard, despairing of conventional consolations, Heide recognizes that all you can do is laugh.

WORDPLAY

AN INTRODUCTION

When did I first begin to write? Was it in kindergarten at Florence Avenue grade school in my hometown of Irvington, New Jersey, where accompanying a crude crayon drawing on paper I wrote the word "dog"? In later grades at this same school I began to contribute short and to-the-point poems as well as brief stories for the *Florenceonian Magazine*, grades one to eight. In print shop I looked on in awe as my words were replicated on an old-fashioned platen printing machine. Seeing one of my pieces in print in this school publication inspired me to continue writing.

By the seventh and eighth grades I wrote plays, my own versions of *Little Women* and *King Lear*. These were costumed with outfits borrowed from an antique shop owner who collected actual clothing from the nineteenth century. The vintage clothing – think hoop skirts and waistcoats made for smaller people – perfectly fit the boys and girls of the mid-twentieth century. These dramatic interpretations were put on, casting my friends, more in the sense of a fun romp than with serious intent. This same neighborhood group also presented garage and backyard shows based on the movies we saw at the Warner Bros. Sanford Theatre on Springfield Avenue, which offered Saturday afternoon matinees in addition to the regular double features. Our amateur theatricals were more like musical revues than dramas.

Once in high school, I forgot all about writing unless it was an assignment from the English teacher. At Irvington High, and later at the Carteret School for Boys in West Orange, I learned a good deal about sentence structure, and the required reading was everything from Shakespeare to Dickens and maybe a novel like *Fortitude* by Hugh Walpole. To increase vocabulary, students were required to learn "big" words, like verisimilitude or perspicacious, which had to be utilized in sentences at the end of the week.

Outside of school, like most teenagers in town, I was mainly concerned with becoming popular, going to dances, the movies, and, of course, struggling with painful awakening sexual urges and conflicts, bringing forth anxieties along with periods of depression and sometimes pent-up rage.

At the movies I identified with the method-actor rebels, particularly James Dean (*Rebel Without a Cause*) and Marlon Brando (*The Wild One*). At home I read movie magazines and dreamed of an escape to Hollywood, where I thought I might be able to live out my idea of a glamorous and carefree life. I read in *Confidential*, the popular gossip rag, that Marlon Brando was living with Wally Cox, who played a weird character called Mr. Peepers in a series on television. In their bohemian pad cluttered with newspapers, books, and clothes strewn all over the floor, they had begun painting the walls purple but never finished the job. Open cans of purple paint were now part of the messy décor. The article mentioned that Brando studied acting with Stella Adler. In my teenage mind I said to myself that one day I would live in Greenwich Village and I too would study with Stella Adler. The idea was that I could somehow follow in the footsteps of the great Marlon Brando.

Armed with this simple outline for my future, I headed off to Northwestern University in Evanston, Illinois, to study theatre with Alvina Krause, a professor in the drama department. I played Snobby Price in Shaw's *Major Barbara*, a small role in *Romeo and Juliet*, and the lead role of the tortured young man in *Tea and Sympathy*. Visiting speakers at the school included former Northwestern graduates Patricia Neal, Jennifer Jones, and Charlton Heston. Lee Strasberg showed up to conduct actor workshop seminars. Guided by an actor friend named Corky, I also discovered the Near North Side of Chicago and its notorious gay bars.

Following my stint at Northwestern, I moved to Greenwich Village, where I still live on Christopher Street. Think Leonard Bernstein's musical *Wonderful Town*, with the lyric, "Interesting people are living on Christopher Street" and ". . . this is the place for self-expression!" Once settled, I at last fulfilled my goal of studying with the grand and great Stella Adler, who upon first interviewing me said, "To be so young and to be in so much pain must be a terrible thing." At the time I was not sure what she meant, but she took me under her wing, later sending me off to apprentice (along with fellow student Peter Bogdanovitch) at the Stratford Shakespeare Festival in Connecticut, that season under the direction of John Houseman. There I was on stage with pros like Fritz Weaver, Mildred Dunnock, James Earl Jones, and John Emery, who played the lead in *King John*. One night at a party Emery introduced all of us to his ex-wife, Talullah Bankhead, who was appearing in a revue in Westport, Connecticut, called *Welcome Darlings*. The Festival's *Measure for Measure* starred movie/TV actress Nina Foch. Katherine Hepburn also showed up in preparation for one of her Shakespearian roles. I thought, "Wow! I'm in seventh heaven!" I was star-struck, and thanks to Stella, there I was! I should add here that one of the students I met at the Stella Adler Studio was Michael Smith, publisher of this book, former *Village Voice* chief theatre critic, Cino playwright cohort, and a no-nonsense friend.

At Lenny's Hideaway, a cellar dive gay bar on Tenth Street in the Village, I met Edward Albee, William Flanagan, Jerry Herman, Ned Rorem, and Jimmy Spicer. Jimmy Spicer, who became a close and intimate friend, took me to the San Remo Tavern on MacDougal Street, where we drank Black Russians and smashed the empty glasses onto the tile floor. Jimmy was general manager at The Living Theatre, where he introduced me to the charismatic Judith Malina and her genius husband Julian Beck. Judith asked me what I did, and I replied that I was working at becoming an actor, studying with Stella Adler for two years, then Uta Hagen at H. B. Studio . . . She interrupted me to say, "You should go home and write a play!" "What?" I answered. Surprised and puzzled, but instinctively knowing she was right, I did go home and wrote my first play, *Hector*, based on my college teacher Alvina Krause. A week later I handed it to Judith. After a Monday night performance at the Living Theatre, Jimmy Spicer with Lee Paton produced an evening of three plays at the Cherry Lane Theatre.

They were *Marriage on the Eiffel Tower* by Jean Cocteau, *Pericles* by the poet Kenneth Koch, and my play *Hector* with Jean Bruno, directed by Nick Cernovitch. A terrific review came in for me from Jerry Tallmer in *The Village Voice*.

Lee Paton asked me to write another one-act play for her New Playwrights Theatre on Third Street to accompany a new production of *Hector*, this time with the very accomplished actress Henrietta Strom, and an anti-war play called *The Blood Bugle* by Harry Tierney Jr. I wrote *West of the Moon*, a play about a down-and-out hustler who encounters an innocent young man newly arrived in the city in a doorway in the Village on a rainy night. Corruption, drugs, and sex for sale are integral elements of the play. Both Tierney and myself took a beating, yes, from six uptown critics. Wounded and feeling lower than low, I ran into Joe Cino in a bar. He had seen and liked *West of the Moon*. "I want you to write a play just like that one for the Caffè Cino. Make it for two young blonde men, and it better be good, and it better be sexy."

I came up with a time-warp existential play called *The Bed*, with the two men drinking and drugging and unable to get out of their bed of dissolution. This was somewhat autobiographical, based on my relationship with Jim Spicer, who later, to my dismay, became addicted to heroin after watching Jack Gelber's druggy jazz play *The Connection* night after night at the Living Theatre and hanging out till dawn at jazz clubs where shooting up was the norm.

The Bed opened after a fire at the Caffè Cino in 1965. Playwrights working at the little cafe/theatre on Cornelia Street at that time included Lanford Wilson, Sam Shepard, John Guare, Jean-Claude van Itallie, Robert Patrick, William M. Hoffman, Jeff Weiss, H.M. Koutoukas, David Starkweather, and Tom Eyen. Andy Warhol came many times to stare blankly at the boys in *The Bed* and decided to film it at the artist Richard Bernstein's loft on the Bowery. The film is now being digitized by the Museum of Modern Art along with other Andy movies.

The Bed and *Moon* at the Caffè Cino, *Why Tuesday Never Has a Blue Monday* at La Mama, *At War with the Mongols*, which opened at Brecht West in New Brunswick, New Jersey, and all the rest of my plays written after the decade of the 1960s are to be discovered here in this volume, along with *Lupe*, the scenario I wrote for Andy starring the wonderful Edie Sedgwick, which was adapted from Kenneth Anger's apocryphal account in *Hollywood Babylon* of the strange, dramatic suicide death of the "Mexican Spitfire," film star Lupe Vélez.

Robert Heide

This book is dedicated to
John Wright Gilman

HECTOR

A PLAY IN ONE ACT

Hector was first presented in December 1960 by James Spicer and Lee Paton on the Monday Night Series at the Cherry Lane Theatre in Greenwich Village, with Jean Bruno as Professor E. Grey Kraus. It was directed by Nicola Cernovich on a triple bill with *Pericles* by Kenneth Koch and *Marriage on the Eiffel Tower* by Jean Cocteau.

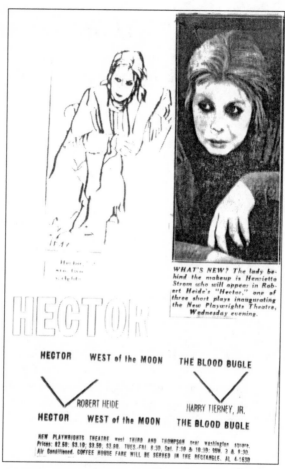

Newspaper ad and photo image of Henrietta Strom in "Hector," 1961

HECTOR

PROFESSOR E. GREY KRAUS, *a retired lady of letters, is seated (S.C.)*
on a soft cushion chair. Her head is in a reclining position; her arms
drooped.

It is a hot, sticky evening in summer; dusk.

PROFESSOR E. GREY KRAUS *is wearing a loosely fitted rose-beige-colored*
suit of some lightweight summer material such as linen or silk. No
shoes.

The small apartment room of PROFESSOR E. GREY KRAUS *is in*
Manhattan in a more or less dim sector. It is furnished, browns, grays
. . . . disconnected objects are scattered about indiscriminately,
newspapers, coffee cups, a paint bucket, a half-finished bottle of club
bourbon, glasses, books, and other debris . . . . It is clear
that this is the room of one who is quickly losing identity. It seems
untouched in its degenerate condition, the remains of an intellectual,
history certificates, trophies, books, books, books, collected dust. Dust.

PROFESSOR E. GREY KRAUS *had had moderate success in her past, as*
a lady poet; and, for most of her later life, taught at a private girls'
college in New England. She remained unattached, most of the time,
in that situation; and was often referred to by her adversaries as "the
old maid." Upon leaving her position as "English professor," having
come to the conclusion that it was time to retire, PROFESSOR E. GREY
KRAUS *— with some savings — also decided, in good faith, to depart,*
as much as was humanly possible, from an outside world that she had
never understood. In preparation for the death, there were: no more
relationships, no telephones, and no addresses given out — Some of her
former colleagues, speculating upon "the decision," chose to pass it off

as "schizophrenia." One associate, unable to locate the protagonist, had had her listed with the Bureau of Missing Persons. Professor E. Grey Kraus now employed a pseudonym; but not for literary purposes. No more identity. No relatives — — — — —

The most unusual object in the room is a large plaster dog statue obtained, once upon a time, from a game of chance at Coney Island. It is seated, throughout the entire play, directly left (S.C.) of PROFESSOR E. GREY KRAUS; and is lit, slightly before anything else, and throughout the play, by a white spot.

Darkness.

A sharp white spot on the dog statue; called HECTOR.

One moment.

A shaft of mauve light is projected from a window area (U.C.) onto the form of PROFESSOR E. GREY KRAUS.

A groan is uttered by PROFESSOR E. GREY KRAUS.

A long, silent moment.

A slight movement of PROFESSOR E. GREY KRAUS's right hand.

After another moment, PROFESSOR E. GREY KRAUS lifts her head up, slowly, as if she were coming out of a trance or a coma.

A sharp look toward the window.

The distant sound of traffic.

The distant sound of a baby crying.

A dog barks in a neighbor's apartment.

These sounds combine for a moment, and then recede.

Pause.

PROFESSOR E. GREY KRAUS groans. Standing up, she groans again, scratches her back, coughs, bends down, groaning, and picks up the bottle marked Club Bourbon. Sniffs it. Snorts. And Swallows. Places bottle back down. Sighs dejectedly . . . coughs; then, sits back down in the chair. A clock strikes seven times.

Her speech is melodic like a cantata, highs, lows, pauses, with many effects and efforts. It is almost, as it were, sung.

PROFESSOR E. GREY KRAUS Yes, yes, Mmmmm. Seven o'clock.
Indeed. Yes.

Dusk again.

Hot.

  (*Pause*)

Maybe if I got some ice things would not be so . . . . hot.
  Close.

  (*Coughs*)

God damn it! Breath! I'm . . . impossible to . . . breathe. It
  becomes necessary to keep on . . . (*breathing heavily*) talking.
  Ha ha . . . for some reason.

I forget now what it was that I was going to say.

For some reason . . . for some reason . . . I don't know why, I
  feel as if I ought to make a speech. Shit! About what? What
  now? Christ on the cross bleeding . . . or suffering.

History is dead; and futile.

  (*Coughs*)

God damn coughing.

History is dead; and futile.

  (*Coughs again*)

Mmmmmmm. Damn it!

History is dead; and futile.

  (*Coughs*)

History is dead; and futile.

Still busy with destruction, and hate.

The man on the radio said . . .

  (*Pause*)

Where was I? I seem to have lost my place.

Oh! Yes! The World War . . . and Elizabeth . . . and Essex . . .

and John Keats.

The perennial courage.

Perfervid performances in empty lecture halls.

The English language.

And England!

Phew! Sons of bitches.

(Pause)

The Earl of Shrewsberry.

The Boston Tea Party.

The Russians roaring; and running . . . after us *(excitedly)* with long spears, yes, yes and black woolly beards, ha ha, and . . . RED COATS!

Unbelievable!

(Pause – Transition)

Baby baby's fine yellow hair . . . the color of wheat. The color . . . of hay. A little baby bonnie Anglo-Saxon boy . . . mmm . . . oh God, well.

Never mind it.

(Pause)

(Singing now with an inner desperation, somewhat puzzled)

"Boys and girls together. Me and Mamie O'Rourke."

Ha ha.

(Pause – Deflation)

Me – rry-go-roun – d! There isn't any end to it

Maggie and Jiggs.

(Pause)

(Cryptically)

I know the answer . . ha ha . . I have evolved a solution.

Teacher! Teacher! Hey! Somebody! Mister!

Lord Jesus! I know the answer!

(No answer)

(*Pause – Deflation*)

I still have not lost the ability to think . . . or to . . . . feel.

I am getting old; and yet, I feel younger, except that, at the same time, feeling younger and younger, I am getting older and older; and I am dying . . . . in this room.

Sometimes I yell: like so – Ahhhhhheeeeeeeoooooo!

Like so; only, louder, pretending that I am dying here by myself . . . or that I am being . . . murdered.

Nobody comes . .

(*The sound of a baby crying*)

That is the sound of a baby crying. It is comforting.

Sometimes a dog barks . . . a clock strikes; and horns honk in the distance; and . . and . . that's the way it is.

Hmmmmmmmm.

Postcards from the postman.

One delivery a day . . . of . . . . . . milk!

No television; and no newspapers.

Ha ha. I am beginning to feel stupid . . . and giddy.

No grandeur.

No more calculations. Too many calculations.

A final . . . a final reckoning with the forces. Hmmmm.

Oh, dear! The dog! I forgot!

Him! *Him!*

(*Pointing a finger at* HECTOR, *the dog statue*)

I have taken the liberty of moving *him* to the middle of the room. His name is . . . Hector, a former door-stop; and he, ha ha ha, is without essence.

No essence. Poor thing. No blasted essence.

Too bad.

He only seems essential because of the light I have had arranged for him on the ceiling.

I decided he should have . . . . light.

Doesn't he look heavenly?

He used to be used by myself in the old days, and, also, in this apartment as a, ha ha, door-stop.

Yes. That was his function. Doorstopper!

Ridiculous!

I came to the decision that he ought to be relieved of that ugly function, and that he join me, functionless, a former professor, in my wait for DEATH!

Such an ugly word! DEATH!

I am waiting here for DEATH to move in on me!

No use making light of it.

Yes, indeed, he and I are waiting to enter the divine state of functionless . . . together.

Oh . . uh . . I have made arrangements for Hector here to go with me since I have always been, more or less, responsible for his existence. I would hate to leave him behind with the possibility of having him dumped, for instance, in an old garbage can.

Yes.

Arrangements have been made by myself to have Hector buried with me at Rosebridge Cemetery in Union, New Jersey. I think he will like that. I wonder what I will look like at my funeral with a dog statue beside me . . . in a casket. Most likely they will say that the executors of the estate were following the wishes of an idiot child. Well, I do feel younger.

I do . . . . in spite of . . . the cough.

Yes, they will say that I had become senile. Ha ha.

Poor old Hector.

He is my last sentimental possession on this earth, my last . . . attachment.

He was won many many years ago, yes, at Coney Island . . . it was.

I was with a man who wore a straw hat and a seersucker suit, grey, with white buttons.

Handsome, long black, black hair.

We had been in, well, ha ha . . . love for a period of time. Engaged. He and I. Ha ha.

The World War: I had been in college: yes.

Eighteen.

A telegram came: WE REGRET TO INFORM YOU . . . and that's the way it went.

Another story.

Death and . . . war. Hmmm. Anyhow, I decided that I would hold onto Hector here . . . always. That's what I decided. Hmmm.

So many decisions.

See Hector, how nice he sits.

He simply sits.

He just sits.

  (*Coughs*)

  (*Pause*)

  (*Holding her head*)

Oh my God! God damn! Hold it. Hold it. Phew.

Blackouts. Blacking out again. No. No. Blackout, coming on.

I have to fight it off.

Talk. Talk.

Oh, yes. A drink.

(*She stumbles over to the bottle marked Club Bourbon and takes a swig.*)

Ah! Ah! Good! Hmmmm.

  (*Sitting again*)

Wonderful dog!

  (*Resuming a train of thought*)

Nobody is holding doors open these days.

Too symbolic.

Too sentimental!

I . . uh . . could have had a bed-doll, you know with false eyelashes and a satin dress.

Too bizarre!

(*Slight pause*)

Later I became, or rather, finally, I became a Professor of English Literature at a fashionable girls' school . . . after THE DEATH . . . and I indulged in writing some mediocre poetry.

Many years have passed away.

Many years.

It all seems so far away. So distant.

I seem to be coming upon a new kind of awakening now . . . into . . . I don't know where.

I seem to be heading someplace else, that is . . . . (*coughing*) in terms of . . . . life!

And yet I know that the destructive forces are finally moving in on me.

It is so confusing . . . this duality of light and dark!

Oh God, my head!

I watch . . . I watch things more intently now.

In the city parks. Old people . . . such as myself, can barely walk.

I walk quite swiftly.

In the daytime, the city trees swaying.

The old men, as old as myself, sit on the park benches all day long scratching their groins.

Yellow teeth.

Thin white hair.

And pink faces.

I still manage to go out every day to purchase, for instance, a loaf of raisin bread, or cottage cheese, or, maybe, a head of lettuce.

I am dying, yes, dying you see; and can't eat too much. It puts a strain on the heart.

Old people, such as *I* am, can't, ha ha, eat too much.

I never never talk to strangers, or to anyone for that matter.

Oh, now and again, I will nod to one of the neighbors staring out of the windows or sitting on the stoop, or to the man in the store who sells me my raisin bread.

That's what I eat, mostly, these days . . . raisin bread.

I never say but two words to anyone; and no one says more than two words to me.

These days, more and more, I find myself mostly talking, talking too much, to myself, or to the dog, Hector, or to . . . the building . . . or to the audience, the world, at large.

You see, ha ha, I am dying to *live!*

. . . and talking is one of the ways that keeps me going.

I hold onto images like an . . . actress.

While I am talking I am not so . . . scared. Ha. Ha.

I mail in a monthly rent . . . yes.

No more sex.

There never was . . . much . . . in the past, long ago; but all of that belongs to a practically dead past – and, when I die I will take that past with me.

Yes, most of me belongs now to an ever dissolving . . . past.

And when we are buried it goes along with us.

That is one of the reasons Hector . . . and I . . . .

In my former identity, old-maid schoolteacher, lady, ha ha, of letters, I avoided it, for the most part, in favor of THE PROFESSION . . . ha . . . ha.

Instead I became familiar with poetry, Lord Byron, George

Gordon Byron, Geoffrey Chaucer, all the dead poets. Those
were my *special* companions, yes.

Hmmmmm . . . with flowers, the yellow daffodil . . . the sedgy
rivers of old England.

Yes.

Poetry.

Such grief to talk only, ha ha, of daffodil.

The academic existence. It has all been, ha ha, ridiculous.
Hmmm.

(*Slight pause*)

Yes. Some old ladies you see around this city walk dogs –
(*Coughing*) – damn it! . . . walk dogs through the park; and, at
other times, may be seen picking garbage out of trash cans.

Yes.

That's all they do, all day long, walk their dogs; and collect old
trash out of garbage cans.

Their dogs, usually, are fat, hideous drooling beasts, that have
begun to have trouble with . . . breathing . . . and can . . .
hardly walk.

Sometimes children throw stones at their dogs . . ha.

That is why . . .

That is one reason why old ladies carry . . . sticks.

To ward off the stone-throwers.

Hmmmm.

Old people watch things more and more intently –

They watch for . . . signs . . .

They are . . aware of danger . . . and cruelty.

They watch also for what is familiar – – like park benches, like
the garbage.

. . . a pair of shoes . .

. . . like their shriveling groins, like their dogs, how they
are moving now, how they are breathing . . . their dogs:

as hideous and as old as they are themselves, how they are moving, how they are breathing!

These are their signs of . . . ha . . ha . . life, the familiar.

Familiar safe attachments like, well . . . old, ha ha, Hector here.

Mmmmmm.

(*Slight pause*)

Oh dear . . . . my eyes . . . my head . . . My eyes are beginning to hurt with tired. I have been talking too . . .

Oh, yes: Hector and I.

We are nearing the end.

He is such a marvelous beast.

So grand.

Yes, sits perfectly still all the time.

He has . . . a manner . . . of . . . grace and of dignity that is seldom found these days.

He is like a sort of mother to us all.

Hector!

Absolute.

Tranquil.

Peaceful.

Hmmmm.

Just stares, continuously, softly, into space.

Yes.

Hmmmm.

Purple.

The sky is a sort of purple tonight, a strange luminous purple . . . or is it, perhaps . . . blue?

My eyesight is not too good anymore.

Mmmmm.

(*Pause*)

Do you suppose, Hector old dear, that it will rain tonight?

Yesterday, the man on the radio said . . . rain . . . for today. He was wrong. Maybe he meant this evening.

It is so hot!

It is possible that he meant rain for this evening.

That would relieve us of this unbearable heat.

Hector doesn't mind heat. Very little affects his composure.

. . . oh, once, his left ear . . . yes . . . (*touching it*) yes, right here, got chipped.

Someone had kicked him going through the doorway.

He fell . . . and had this accident. Ha ha. I had to repair the ear with glue.

It was like a minor surgical operation; it was playing nurse to Hector.

I played nurse to Hector here; didn't I, Hector?

Oh, yes.

(*Weary*)

Ah, if it would only rain.

I love the smell of rain in the city, don't you.

Gets rid of a lot of the stench . . . of old rubbish.

(*Pause*)

(*In a coy childlike tone*)

Hector.

Hector.

Hector.

Boo. Boo.

Oh, dear old Hector, bow wow, looks so sad sitting there. Mmmmm.

All lit.

Hector has been moved to the middle of the room . . . in preparation for . . ha. Ha.

Money is still left in the bank.

Maybe we can still last it for a while . . . Yes?

To go on.

My eyes.

Maybe if I close my eyes the heat will not be so . . . intense.

Identity belongs to a dead past.

I am almost in my grave . . . with Hector beside me.

Fading.

Drifting.

No mask.

Names.

Names.

So many names . . . . and people and none shall live.

Ha.

Identity belongs to the past.

I have moved you to the middle of the room.

Oh, God.

Images!

Hot.

Heat.

Sleep.

Heat.

Sleep.

Heat.

Sleep.

Oh, Hector, beloved Hector, I am getting so sleepy . . . . all of the time.

Sleep.

Desirable amiable sleep coming on . . .

Black void.

Nothingness.

And death.

And sleep.

Death and sleep.

Hmmmmmm.

Yes.

I think I will move onto the floor . . . where it will be . . .
cooler . . . next to old Hector here.

Oh, Hector, Hector!

I can't fight . . . .

(PROFESSOR E. GREY KRAUS *gets up, very slowly; and, then, falls,*
quickly, onto her knees. Remaining in that position for a moment, as
if in prayer, she begins to sing:)

"Boys and girls together. Me and Mamie O'Rourke."

(*Her body sways back and forth, to and fro, with great effort.*)

Oh God. Oh, God. Oh, God!

(*A cry is uttered._*

PROFESSOR E. GREY KRAUS *finally collapses; in a heap, like a rag doll,*
into a sleep, one arm around HECTOR, *the dog statue.*

The distant sound of a baby crying.

The sound of traffic.

The sound of a dog barking. These sounds recede.

Blackout on HECTOR. *Just afterward, quickly, window light out.*

Curtain.

Notes (in original script)

Time:

The play runs approximately 45 minutes. It is essential that the pacing of time be slow in accordance with the play's structure (pauses, silences, transitions, etc.). One aspect of the play to be considered by the audience is that IT *(life-living-stage or otherwise) is interminable, infinite, and perpetual; filled with many waitings, silences, emptinesses. Professor E. Grey Kraus, in this play, is re-acting against these things, as well as she is the death that is moving in on her. She is afraid of the unknown; and she is afraid of death. That is the direction of the play. Solitariness. One individual, singular, against and in direct relationship to the forces.*

The Set:

*The set should be somewhat surreal (i.e., lighting). The illusory-intermediate-sense of reality-concrete-fantasy, physical-metaphysical, life-death-unknown, is to be indicated in the stage circumstances--------
---mainly, of course, by the presence of the dog statue, Hector.*

Casting:

Hector is a plaster dog statue, white, of the cheap variety that is found at amusement parks. Hector is meant to represent, perhaps, physical attachment, or, for that matter, metaphysical attachments, God, Art, Love, Life, Absurdity. The silent. The non-communicable. Limitation. Whatever. Hector is abstract and, at the same time, not abstract. Hector has no commitment.

It is not necessary to have Professor E. Grey Kraus played by an old-woman-character-actress. The stage purpose of the character, among other things, is that it should represent old age. *Professor E. Grey Kraus, therefore, may be attempted by a younger actress, a younger actor, or anything (human) within reason of the ridiculous. Furthermore, it is essential that the role be enacted by an actor-actress-clown, capable of maintaining silence and inactions as well as words and actions, transformations, transitions, abstractions; and by one who has a flair for the absurd and the futile in this life (stage or otherwise).*

MAKEUP:

Makeup should be exaggerated, whitened, chalky, for the Professor, not unlike the pallor of Hector. There should be the suggestion of similarity between the two, a kind of grotesque parallel, the way things-related (lovers, dogs, cats, etc.) begin, after a while together, to bear resemblance.

WEST OF THE MOON

A ONE–ACT PLAY

West of the Moon was first presented in June 1961 by Lee Paton at the New Playwrights Theatre in Greenwich Village. It was directed by Lee Paton on a triple bill with *Hector* by Robert Heide, starring Henrietta Strom, and *The Blood Bugle* by Harry Tierney Jr.

LUCK	Paul Giovanni
BILLY	Joe Ponazecki

New York Times ad for New Playwrights Theatre premiere of "West of the Moon," 1961. Historian and activist Martin Duberman in his book "Stonewall" (E. P. Dutton, 1993) identifies "West of the Moon" as "one of the very first off-Broadway gay-themed plays ever done in New York."

WEST OF THE MOON

SCENE:

A street in any teeming city; this one happens to be New York. The set is a series of shop windows and doorways. In a doorway (stage center) the drifter, LUCK, *is waiting for the rain to stop, or perhaps . . . . just waiting.*

The rain, primarily symbolic, is to be indicated by rushing blue lights moving in circular patterns which are to be interrupted, occasionally, by cries of bolt lighting − brilliant pink lights, drums, and electronic effects.

It is a late evening in spring.

Over a center doorway, a neon sign reads with the usual audacity − JESUS SAVES UPSTAIRS. *A gypsy store window suspiciously invites* A LOOK INTO THE FUTURE *while still another suggests that, two flights down, a steam bath might do the trick.*

It is a lower section of town.

Horns honk.

The sound of rain.

The set itself, as a whole, should be non-realistic and somewhat transparent, revealing other light areas and space relationships.

Grays. Blues.

Rain ensues.

As the play begins, the waiting drifter is puffing wildly and nervously on a cigarette butt. He paces up and down the enclosure. Disgusted, finally, after a moment, he squeezes the butt out with his fingers. He begins to look intently across the street (toward the fourth wall), holding his hands up to his eyes, straining, watching something on the other side of the street. After a long moment, there is a flash of lightning, loud. At this instant BILLY, *running, bolts into the same doorway. The rain continues. There is a moment of silence, caution, hesitation, and then . . .*

LUCK (*annoyed at the sudden intrusion, behaves as if punctured out of a dream. Dazed. Dizzy. Angered.*) You, uh, always uh jump in on people like that?

BILLY (*embarrassed*) Oh . . . I'm . . . I'm sorry . . . – Frighten you?

LUCK (*defensive. Quick. The braggart in him slightly aroused. "A new victim" perhaps?*) You kidding, buddy? (*He gazes once again in the direction of the fourth wall, this time with a little more deliberation. To himself, more or less.*) Lights out now. (*Pretending at being absorbed.*) Lights . . . ss!

BILLY (*genuinely vague – he has not heard the last remark*) What? . . . Say somethin'?

LUCK (*emphatic: he is going to hold on to this one*) Lights out! I mean, a colored chickie was like . . . undressing. Crazy. I was hoping, you might say, to *attract* her *attention*. (*He waits to see the reaction of his prey.*)

BILLY From here?

LUCK Yaaa! (*He has got it. Now he can perk up and perform. His suspicions have been confirmed. A remark like "from here?" surely is a suggestion to go ahead with it.*) Yeah: I kinda dig down, way down, deep inside – like, you know, and dig up this energy which I kinda radiate forward, out; and then I usually whistle, like . . . (*He demonstrates a loud shrill note. Pause.*) Yes; and that is called the bird call of the forest primeval. *The Call of the Wild.* In a word . . . SEX. Mmmm. That is known as a sex call. Yes. Dig, baby? Do you know what I mean, buddy boy? Sex? (*Singing.*) 'When I'm calling you . . . hoo . . . hoo . . . hoo . . . hoo . . . hoo . . . hoooo . . . !

BILLY Why didn't you whistle then while she had her lights on?

LUCK (*hesitant*) Well, you know, it's a sort of dangerous bit. Just the direct action approach . . . I mean . . . a broad might call the, you know, *screws* or something; and well, in sex, in sex, there has to be some kind of a sign from the opposite party, THE OTHER. Yeah, buddy boy, there has got to be some kind of sign. I know that from experience. Heh. Ha. You know, once, once, I sold Life magazine, door to door. I . . . uh . . . got laid lots like that. I would get the eye and . . . you know, before I knew what was happening . . . Well . . . a hand pressed against the crotch. Before I knew what was happening . . . You know, some broads can be pretty aggressive. Lotta nonsense about female passivity. Man, the stories I could tell you . . . phew . . . about women. Yeah. Other times, I'll even follow broads into their hallways from the street; but only because they themselves wanted me to, only because I was *given* the sign. Yes. There has always got to be some sign, a word, or something . . . That is the way the game of sex works. Yeah. Instinct. Once in a while, I might take to knocking directly on doors if I'm hung up, no sex in a while, and ask, oh . . . maybe . . . street directions or the like till I find some broad friendly enough, attractive enough, who gives THE SIGN. Ya. Good way. Knock on doors. Knock on enough, make the pitch; and one is bound to open. You can get laid lots that way if you want. Ya. Why not! Sex happens in many ways. Kicks. More interesting. Adventurous. Sort of like Don Quixote. But there must *always* be a sign, something, hell, yes . . . a look, a kind of energy between two people, two people who are able to make the release . . . together. In that respect people are not altogether dogs sniffing one another. Yes, if sex is to be interesting, there must always be a sign. A sign.

BILLY This sign you speak of happens, I take it, with some regularity . . . I mean, it happens often for you?

LUCK Sure. Yes. That's 'cause I concentrate less on looks and more on quality . . . that elusive something. European-like. Earthy. Not these painted American-type dolls . . . Ah,

Christ! Shit. Rain keeps up . . . What time you got, buddy?

BILLY Time? Late, I guess . . . I don't know.

LUCK Doesn't matter . . . really. (*Pause.*) You . . . uh . . . are not . . . uh . . . heading anywhere in particular then, I gather?

BILLY What? Oh, no. just out walking when I got caught . . . in the rain. I should go back to my room, maybe. YMCA. (LUCK *has not heard this last remark. He seems to be preoccupied with something outside of the situation itself.*)

LUCK Think it will stop?

BILLY What?

LUCK The rain.

BILLY Eventually, I would suppose, wouldn't you?

LUCK Ya. Eventually, all things come to a stop. (*Slight pause.*) I was on my way to the park when I got caught. Thunderstorms. Boom. Boom. They say it's gonna go on all night. Heh. Heh.

BILLY Is it? (*Vague.*) Maybe, I suppose, I should make a run for it. Shoes are soaked, sonovabitch. Nothing like wet shoes.

LUCK (*with abandon*) Rain, rain, rain, glorious, glad rain. (*Singing.*) "Just singing in the rain." (*Quick transition – in a Shakespearian manner.*) Ah, the clean washed smell of rain in the city. (*Thoughtful. Suddenly this outburst of pseudo – exhilaration sinks into a stark unromantic moment – quickly then.*) Live close by, buddy? Around here?

BILLY (*suspicious*) Not really. Why?

LUCK No reason. Just curious. No offence, buddy. Just curious. I . . . uh . . . always like to be onto where people live, how they have sex, you know . . . people. Curious. Curious the Cat, that's me. Ha.

BILLY Is that always healthy?

LUCK Healthy? What in the hell is healthy in this world? A carrot, maybe, How many people do what's healthy?

BILLY Yes. (*A long pause in which* LUCK *and* BILLY *remain completely motionless. They seem to be stranded in space, each isolated and with themselves, a kind of desperate aloneness.* BILLY *moves a step toward the audience. The following lines are a repetition of something deep within his unconscious. In a semi-catatonic trance and in a slow droning liturgical manner then . . .*) Yes. Are you . . . are you saved brother from the sin of your existence? The Lord Jesus suffered, bled, died upon the cross so that you might be free. Nails were driven through his wrists and his ankles; and blood poured forth deep and red like a rose against the white of skin . . . Are you . . . free . . . from guilt . . . . . saved from pain?

LUCK (*tugging at him*) Hey, man, is there something the matter with you?

BILLY What?

LUCK What were you just saying?

BILLY Oh . . . I don't know . . . . . . sorry. I have this tendency to blurt out things . . . to myself . . . at times . . . to uh . . . daydream kinduv . . . .

LUCK Well, I can understand that.

BILLY Can you?

LUCK You seemed to be saying a prayer . . . about salvation or . . .

BILLY . . . being saved. Yes, now it is clear . . . saved. I have these visions which . . .

LUCK Saved? That's one. Ha ha. Not this boy. No sir. Not me. Not saved. Stuck to this earth. Held down by a gravitational force. Always on the move. Running. Creeping. On the move again. That's me! Yes, just an old cat prowling around back alleys, rain or shine. Like it that way. No mother, no father. No *nothing*. Held down. Just a stinking old alley cat crawling, cruising, creeping, looking for trouble . . .

BILLY No job?

LUCK Ha-ho-heh . . . me? Doing what, man? I've got at this miserable point fifty cents to my name; and my landlady just kicked me out on my ass. No rent, no room. Ha. You know what? I couldn't care less. I mean, things can't get any worse. I really don't give a damn, buddy! Thought maybe I'd sleep in the park until the rain . . . . . .

BILLY (*lightly*) It's a black life.

LUCK Blacker and blacker . . yup, blacker than a coon's ass, black. I don't even try to do nothin' no more! Just creep around, like you say, being unhealthy.

BILLY (*sarcastic, trying to maintain his own*) You sound a little tired . . . beat, a little bitter maybe, weighted down . . . by this world.

LUCK Tired is not the word for it, buddy. Not bitter either, and not beat . . . . . . emptied! (*Dramatically.*) Just living the best I can, empty as that tin can over there.

BILLY (*bold*) You seem to be hopped up on sex a bit, nevertheless, peeping in on black pussy cats.

LUCK Sure, yeah, sex, a whiff of pot, some horse, boo, or whatever. That is it, boy! There just ain't nothin' else. No sir.

BILLY You sure about that?

LUCK Maybe yes; maybe no. For the present that's my philosophy. The future? The future is still a black hole or a back alley. Suits me fine. No questions, no answers. Just an old back alley full of tin cans and garbage. That's life, buddy. Yes sir. That's the truth. Yup. That has become my unconditional attitude toward my environment. Society. Ha. Ha. Yes. For the record you can put it down that I'm a cop-hater, yes, and a hater of the square society – THE SYSTEM. "You must conform." Never! Not this boy. Yeah. Why burden you with all this malarkey? You know all about it, eh? Why say anything, I guess . . . except that, well, me, I'm kinduva talker by nature; and here you are . . and it's raining so why not . . . talk. You're hip, ain't yah? Yeah. Take this city, for instance: in this city . . . . Don't you feel honestly like you're always finding yourself at a ninety degree angle? I do, man! Yes. Kind of like all the time at a goddamned ninety degree angle. Dig? Walled in by skyscrapers. Geometric.

That's it. Ha ha. Ha ha. Yeah. Unable to escape or to find
rest . . . . . anywhere . . or . . sleep. Ha ha. Take yesterday: I
am in this dingy third-rate-type movie house on the square
attempting to catch some shuteye. Yeah. Sleep. Ha! A tap on
the shoulder, a flashlight glaring in my face. "Wake up, sonny
boy! This ain't no fleabag hotel. Wake up. Wake up." Wake
up to what? My eyes are killing me, burning, sore. Two hard-
boiled eggs, my eyes, yes. The panoramic screen is a blur.
Vague sexy images. Yes. For a moment, I wonder if I'm not
maybe back in my old lady's womb. My goddamned hand is
asleep. Christ. I wish to myself that I was dead. Stone dead.
Maybe I am dead, I say to myself. I am not. At least, I think
I'm not. I pinch myself. It hurts. I am in a goddamned movie
theatre. How did I get there? I don't remember. Obviously,
I've wandered in, off the goddamned street. What's the matter
with me? Oh yes . . . drinking . . . I'd had a bottle. Gin. My
stomach feels sort of tight. Yes. The cat next to me is making
it, playing with some chick. She is moaning. The picture.
It occurs to me that I've seen it before. Somebody is being
pushed down an elevator shaft. A scream. I run out. Where?
Where to now? The streets again. The eyes of people on
New York sidewalks, staring, looking, searching. People. Ha.
Going nowhere. Seemingly drifting . . . somewhere. Where?
It makes me feel crazy. Thousands of them. Times Square.
The five o'clock crush. Ha. Office workers. A Spanish chick
approaching me says I can have her for two bucks. I keep
on walking. The crowd, like a herd of wild horses, heading
toward you . . then away, toward you, then away. Where the
hell am I? Eyes staring, searching, some accusing, making . . .
making fast judgments. Cops in blue uniforms carrying sticks,
carrying guns. Ready to lock you up if yah wear the wrong
goddamned expression on yahr puss. Yeah! Paranoid. That's
the word. That's what you're forced to become in this set-up.
Yeah. Locked up. That's why you find me in this doorway.
Hiding. It's a risk to appear in a public place. Easier to get
nabbed; but if you need sleep or . . . . Ha. I am wanted for
. . . to pay a debt to society. Ha. Why should I tell you that?

You know what most people are in this city, man? Destroyers.
Most people you see walking around this goddamned city
are *destructive*. You better believe it. *Destructive*. Don't forget
it. People everywhere are that . . . destructive. Yes. Didn't
have to read no book by Freud to figure that one out.
Degeneration. There's another word I've learned a little bit
about in my experiences. No sir. I ain't quite stupid. Not for
a minute. Just 'cause yah have no education doesn't make a
person stupid. I know, man. I know what it's all about. This
planet. "Life on our fair planet is doomed!" I heard that
shouted on the streets just last night by a colored lady with a
Bible in her hand. "I am the voice of God," she says, "and you
are all doomed." Doomed. She spoke of hydrogen bombs and
of a great holocaust. Yes. And death, death . . . "Just like the
dinosaur of old you shall be extinct!" Kaput! Yes, a bomb.
Imagine that!? One big old bomb. Created a chain reaction.
Boom. Boom. Boom. Oh, well. Who the hell cares? Not me
anyhow. Ah, yes, uh huh. (*Pause.*) And here we are still alive
at this moment and watching rain. Rain. Even that ain't pure
no more. Fallout. Atomic particles. Yes. And radioactivity.
Too much. Gives yah the creeps. (*Pause.*) I'm called Luck, pal.
I mean that's my name. Luck. That is . . . that is what I *call
myself* . . . I mean, because that is what I've always lived by . .
. . . luck. You may as well know my name . . . . that is at least
– my nickname. I sure have been talking a blue streak here
in the old rain; but I'm apt to do that . . . talk . . . part of my
character. (*He extends his right hand.*) What do they call you,
kid?

BILLY I'm Billy.

LUCK See what's written in tattoo ink on his hand. (*To* BILLY.)
Read it.

BILLY Let's see. L★O★V★E. The word . . "love."

LUCK Right! Yes. Love. I've extended to you my friendship
hand . . reading . . in tattoo ink . . . "love." (*Pause. He looks
intently at* BILLY *now for a long moment.*) You look like maybe
you went to college somewhere. Yes?

BILLY (*nervous*) You guessed. Two years. Midwestern . . .
university. That was as much as I could take of it. The
academic system.

LUCK What didja study, man?

BILLY Study? Oh . . . . . philosophy . . . . mostly. That was my
main interest.

LUCK Philosophy?! What for?

BILLY (*laughing slightly*) Why not? Why anything? I suppose
that was my way at that time of manifesting *my* curiosity. The
study of philosophy.

LUCK I thought you looked a little, well, a little queer! I mean,
a little far out. Studious. Me? I've learned what I know from
the streets. Hard knocks. That stuff. You know . . . "an eye
for an eye."

BILLY (*embarrassed*) Well, I don't know. Maybe I'd better make
a run for it.

LUCK Ah, Christ, man, stick around man. No hurry. We're
friends now, ain't we? What's to be afraid of? Didn't I give
you this here hand which has "love" tattooed on it. See
the other hand here. Ha. Ha. On it is written the word . . .
"hate." See? Hate. See these bruises? See this here scar? (*He
gives him his left hand.*) Hate. Yes. Indeedy. This hand is used
for the purpose of protection. Yes, I have used this old hand
quite a bit for the purpose of protection. Ha. Not everyone in
this world is, well, exactly friendly.

BILLY You don't have to tell me about that.

LUCK I dig you kiddo. You're okay. Smooth. Yeah. Are we
friends or not then?

BILLY (*nodding*) Well . . . I . . . I guess so . . .

LUCK Shake again. (*They shake.*) Yeah. I never got no
goddamned college education. Left home at about the age of
sixteen. New York. I was dying to get to New York City. Ha!
"Go ahead and go," the old man says, my father. The lousy
bum. You know what my old man is?

BILLY (*annoyed at the confessional turn happening in the conversation*)
What?

LUCK   A lush! Yeah. A goddamned lush. Hmmph. Bastard!
He was, yes, himself responsible for the death of my old lady.
Yeah. She died when I was eighteen. You know where I was
when she died? (BILLY *does not answer.*) . . . . . Farmington
Prison, New Jersey! The bastards. They wouldn't even let
me out to see my old lady as she lay dying. Yeah. Physical
exhaustion. Death from physical exhaustion. Scrubbing floors
keeping the old man on alcohol. Ha. I wanted to give her a
decent funeral at least . . . anyway I could. She didn't even
have the dignity of a goddamned funeral. She was buried
without a headstone for the goddamned grave. Oh, well .
. . . . rest to her anyway. Ha. The old man! I would have
killed him when I got out if he wasn't such a goddamned
pathetic drunk. Yeah, he's still over there in Newark across
the river bumming drinks, I suppose. That's where I lived
. . . . . . Newark. A rotten city. The city of my beautiful
childhood. I have a brother somewhere too. Older. I ain't
never heard from him. Don't even know where he is. He just
skipped out . . . too. Oh, well . . . I think he went out west
somewhere. (*Pause.*) You know why I was in Farmington
boys' penitentiary?

BILLY (*stiffly*) Yeah?

LUCK   I was picked up. Forty-Second Street. Hustling. That was
the only way I could make it at that time. I must have slept
with five thousand queens in my time. For a price, naturally.
Usually Madison Avenue types . . . grey flannels. They went
for me. I was invited by old Colonel Whiting – that's what he
was called, I mean, before he was mysteriously bumped off in
a Broadway back alley – I was invited to join the syndicate.
He said I was a good-looker. Male prostitution. I refused.
I guess I was a little scared. You know, once you get in it's
damned hard to get the hell out. Like one buddy I knew on
the street who became a syndicate boy, got his arms broke
with a crowbar for making a deal with some rich old auntie

on the outside. They also gave him a railroad ticket back
to Atlanta, which is where he came from in the first place.
Anyhow, to make a long story short, I was, well, mysteriously,
picked up by two fuzz detectives as a j.d., juvenile delinquent.
My old drunk father was called in. At that time he had an
address . . . and he was stoned! I spit right in his lousy puss
then and there. They hauled me off. Gave me the hot and
cold shower treatment; beat on me till I was unconscious;
and when I woke up I was in this goddamned Farmington
Prison. All the way down there I screamed like crazy, which
got me a week of solitary confinement with bread and water
to live on. Ha. A vicious life. That's not the half of it either.
You should've been in that goddamned prison. Y'know,
sometimes I wish I was a literary so's I could write about my
experiences in that prison. Does all this scare you? You look a
little pale.

BILLY   Hardly. Talk away. I . . I don't mind hearing it.

LUCK   Well, why not! Prison! Well, first, I can tell you that
everybody down in that place was homosexual, queer, the
wardens, the guards. Prison. Sex houses. This was what was
known as social rehabilitation! Mutual masturbation. Oral
hygiene. Kinsey should've interviewed me. I could have given
him some pretty cool case histories. Ah! What's the use of it
all?

BILLY   It's all in the game.

LUCK   I guess. How about you? What's your story? Got any?

BILLY   Not much to tell. I mean . . I'm not really very good
about inventing dialogue about myself . . talking. That is . . .
I am *still trying* to formulate a . . character for myself that I
will be able to . . act out . . . in the world. This may sound
peculiar but I somehow don't feel related to . . to anything . . .
on this earth . . . to anything at all.

LUCK   (*softly*)   I dig.

BILLY   I believe I am in search of . . yes . . . in search of . . . uh
. . . . religious experience. (*Pause.*) My father. He was . . he

was . . a minister . . Baptist, a fanatic . . . Always preaching
the gospel of salvation . . . preaching about things he never
really . . . actually . . . ever understood. I don't believe he
ever experienced *anything* in his entire life. Yet he ranted and
yelled on and on. "Are you free brother from guilt? . . . . . .
Saved from pain?" "Hallelujah!," everyone would holler, and
nobody seemed to know what it was they were saying . . or
doing . . . or what it was they were looking for. To him, my
father, it was just, well . . . sort of like one continuous kind of
monologue. Maybe that's the way it is for most people . . . . a
repetition beginning nowhere and ending in the same place.
I was an only child. My mother . . . . always hated the role of
being a reverend's wife; but never, I guess, had the courage to
escape from it to anything else. Once she told me . . in secret
. . I was about fourteen then I think . . . that he, the minister,
had only had intercourse with her five times. I'd always
wondered why there'd always been arguments and then . . .
tension. Sexual frustration. Me. I was one of *those* five times.
What a joke. Impotent he was . . . having a love affair with
. . . God . . . . with Jesus too. (*Pause.*) My escape from the
whole damn situation came when it was decided, by the
two of them . . after much bickering . . that I should attend
college. The minister of course wanted me to study religion. I
wouldn't give in to that so finally they let me choose a school
just outside of Chicago where I studied . . philosophy . . .
and then after two years there I became disgusted with the
academic system and I joined the navy to see the world. It was
there, in the navy, that I learned all about . . . . . Has Kinsey
ever done a study of the boys in blue?

LUCK (*laughing*) I'm sure somebody has.

BILLY I wonder what time it is. I've lost all sense of time
standing here.

LUCK Time! That's another joke.

BILLY What do you mean?

LUCK Well, a watch . . . I swiped a couple of days back from
some guy's apartment where I spent the night. An Omega.

Good. Worth, I figure, about a hundred bucks. I take it to a pawn shop . . . . where the guy gives me twenty plus a ticket. Later, as it goes, I'm broke again; so, anyhow, I get a tip from somebody about places where people will buy pawn tickets. So this guy, a complete stranger – I mean, I never seen this guy before – gives me this address where I can sell the ticket. So I like go to this address uptown which turns out to be an apartment building. Yup. So I ring the designated doorbell and go upstairs. Inside the joint I see this short guy and this old bleached blonde whore type. The guy is a wheel. He is playing with a gun . . . twirling it casually on his forefinger. So the bitch says, "Make it fast buster what've yah got?" "A pawn ticket," I says, feeling like I'm in a Mickey Spillane novel. She says, "Lemme see it." "Okay." I give it to her! "Louie," she says, "give the kid a fin." "Five bucks," I says, "take my ticket for fifteen or not at all!" She grabs five out of a drawer, shoves it in my hand; and says, "Beat it, buster. Don't waste my time." Meanwhile this Louie character is grinning like a cat and clicking the barrel of his gun. "Quit bothering the lady, sonny boy, before you find a piece of lead up your ass." I was robbed. No kidding! Five bucks. So they'll buy the watch back and sell it for seventy-five. What the hell do you do? Run to a cop? Ha. Nobody is straight anymore. You can't run to a screw.

BILLY (*joking*) How about the Legal Aid Society?

LUCK Nah! Not me. I can't go there. I'd just wind up in the friggin' pen. People just look at me and got me pegged, pigeon-holed. I mean anybody law-abiding . . . you know . . . square.

BILLY Then how do you live . . . now? How do you get along?

LUCK I told you, man . . luck. Well, not all luck. I certainly can't make the Forty-Second Street scene. The place is crawling with cops. A clean-up campaign is going on in this city. They're pulling everyone in on morals charges of one kind or another. How do I live? . . Stealing, sometimes, books, records, which I then sell so I can buy . . . . . oh

. . something to get high on You know. Take me out of
this existence. (BILLY *begins to laugh.*) Why the hell are you
laughing, man?

BILLY (*laughing*) Books. Books. I work part-time in a
bookstore. That's what hit me as being funny.

LUCK Oh, I see. Square. You don't dig boosting.

BILLY No, not that. Not square. I mean I boost myself. These
two books. I stole them from the store where I work tonight
as a clerk. When I locked up by myself, well, I got this
impulse . . .

LUCK Wanna sell 'em?

BILLY What?

LUCK Sell. Cash. Cash.

BILLY Oh, heck, no . . . not yet. Maybe later on . . . First I'll
read them anyway.

LUCK (*looking puzzled by something*) Oh . . uh . . . okay. Boy, the
rain never lets up, does it?

BILLY It was the first time I really ever stole anything. That's a
joke.

LUCK There's a first time for everything, man. Take tonight.
Here we are in a doorway. We talk. Make a scene. Me cause I
have no place to go. You . . . . well, who cares about reasons
for a thing? Rain. Yeah. I guess I'll never make the straight
scene anymore. Oh, broads, yeah, occasionally . . . but even
them . . . take 'em or leave 'em. And, well, you know, for a
living. I still do that even . . sometimes . . . and in prison?
Well, that's somethin' else. Circumstantial. What book you
reading there?

BILLY Oh, this. (*Indicating the larger of the two books.*) This one
here, the big one is called *The Decline and Fall of Western
Civilization* . . . .

LUCK What?! Man! Where are you from?

BILLY Originally from the state of Wyoming – you know . . .
the desert country.

LUCK *The Decline and Fall of Western Civilization.* Man, I dig
that. You know, a friend of mine, a junkie, gave me a book by
this French artist bug . . . . *Opium.* Ever read it?

BILLY Yeah. I looked at it once . . . in the bookstore. Jean
Cocteau.

LUCK Did'jah ever smoke it?

BILLY What?

LUCK Opium, man!

BILLY (*faking it*) Yeah, once . . in the navy . . . a while ago.
Heh. Heh.

LUCK Man, I sure could go for some stuff tonight. Yeah. It was
Black Jake gimme that book. Crazy. That cat is up the river
now. Yeah, that black nigger is doing time in the pen. The
screws – found a whole goddamned barrel of grass in his pad.
Imagine that. Man, we used to have some wild old times up
at Black Jake's. No more. The author – ities are cleaning up
this town; and that is why I am crouched in this doorway
like a cockroach. I don't want to get picked up. I got needle
marks on my arm, man, that would send me up the river till
doomsday. Yeah, Jake is gone. Ha. The nigger. He was great.
I loved him. He gave me anything I needed, dexies, bennies,
pot, jazz, parties, women, dough, the white horse powder
which he pumped into my veins; but he is like – gone. Yeah!
We'd fly high, high as a kite, man . . . right off this earth.
Yeah, Black Jake tried to make it out the window when he
sees the law coming in. Suicide. Ha. He didn't even make it
to the sill. The fuzz beat on him something awful. Blood . . .
all over, blood. Yes. That was the end of Black Jake. Boy, I
sure would like to get high on something tonight; get out of
this world. Got any money, buddy?

BILLY Wish to Christ I did tonight. I wouldn't be standing here
if I did.

LUCK Yeah, it sure is black. And the rain keeps coming down
harder and harder, all the time harder. Man, I wish I were in
France right now smoking some goddamned opium with . . .

. . . . . . Who was it now that wrote that book?

BILLY Cocteau.

LUCK Yeah! Yeah. (*Dreamy.*) He said in this book which Black
Jake gimme to read that opium was the awakening to a new
life, a new part of yourself, yeah, new eyes, new hands,
wowie, new colors. I sure could go crazy for some stuff now .
. . I'd like to ride up in the sky high as a rocket.

BILLY (*somewhat hesitant, but beginning to move with the ecstasy*) I
. . . I wouldn't mind getting high myself on something, I'd
like . . . I'd . . like to get out on something, yes, that I'd like
. . . out on something. I'd like to get out of this lousy world .
. . . for a while! Some music . . . colors. Way out of this lousy
world.

LUCK (*excited*) And this lousy skin, brother. Out of this lousy
white skin, out, out, up, up, to the moon!

BILLY . . . And it is raining, raining, harder and harder . . . all
the time . . . harder!

LUCK Yes, sir. Yes, sir, buddy. Up . . up . . up . . phew . . . and
back down again. (*Pause. Breathless.* BILLY *and* LUCK *remain
motionless.*)

BILLY (*quietly*) I am looking for *something*. I don't know what.

LUCK What? . . . Oh, yeah. Well, I know of one chance. You
like lesbians?

BILLY What?

LUCK Lesbians. Female queers, man.

BILLY What has that got to do with . . . . .

LUCK Well, like man, about five blocks from here is a dyke
friend of mine, Freda . . . . . . if you don't mind a swim
through the rain . . . . . Freda is strictly a butch lesbian – a
bull – in other words she does not dig sex with men. Period.
Okay? Got that? Any objections to that?

BILLY Me? No. Why should I care about how people go for
sex?

LUCK Freda's okay. A good egg. A buddy. Well, I mean she

sometimes has some grass, *maryjane!* Get me?

BILLY Yeah.

LUCK Freda, usually, always has somethin' going at her pad. Something.

BILLY You're sure it's all right? No fuzz breaking down doors?

LUCK Ah, Christ . . . . no fuzz. Right. Let's go, buddy boy. You and me are both going out of this world. You stick with me and something will go. Wheels will turn. Yes, sir . . . . . we'll hit Mars!

BILLY Should we make a run for it then?

LUCK Okay. Yeah. Let's go. Yes. Make a run for it. One . . two . . . three . . Follow me. Let's go . . . . . .

They do not move. Forward stare. Loud sound of rain.

Blackout.

EAST OF THE SUN

AN EXISTENTIAL PLAY

East of the Sun was first presented in 1963 at Cafe La Mama as part of a benefit for Ellen Stewart's second space, at 82 Second Avenue.

Richard Craven and Gordon Ramsey as Shem and Sam in "East of the Sun" at Howl! Arts October 2016 benefit for the Actors Fund

East of the Sun

for Judith Malina

CHARACTERS:

SHEM — *An old man with a beard — work clothes*

SAM — *A thin wiry old man — long stringy hair — a great coat — smokes corn pipe*

SCENE:

A tool shed. Winter. White sunlight

OBJECTS:

Table with tools — a model windmill with north-south-east-west directional points connected to its base. An old coal stove.

SHEM *hits model windmill with small hammer consistently, with studied agitation.*

SAM *sits perched on a high stool over stove, rubs hand, chews, sucks corn pipe incessantly, nervously. Next to him on the floor is a large wicker basket covered with a checked kitchen towel.*

SHEM (*pounding — shouting — angry*) (*eyes fixed on windmill*) East! East! East!

SAM (*rubbing hands throughout*) (*staring straight front*) I say West!

SHEM (*more hysterical*) East. I say East! East!

SAM Nothing. Exactly nothing. East indeed. Hands getting warmer. I say hands . . . warmer.

(*Pause*)

Cracking up.

SHEM Nothing. Not a thing. As expected . . . as predicted. Just the same.

SAM Not one doughnut. Not able . . . not able to peddle off one holy-friggin' doughnut. What luck!

SHEM East and West. It doesn't work. Not working! Nothing working!

SAM On the endless plain – in the wheat field. A coming together. A coming . . . a coming together. Yes. Together. I say . . . she says – and get this – she says this! Your days are numbered, damn old fool. Numbered. Into the state nut house with you. Finally receeding . . my mind into . . . . or . . .

SHEM And so . . . and so . . . . so . .

SAM And so nothing! Again nothing. And again, again. Not-a-thing. Sick of your pee-stained underwear. (*Pause*) Into . . . (*Pause*) God, the sun. The sun. Into the sun . .

SHEM I say East. I say into . . . the . . .

SAM Southwest. And so nothing and . . then

SHEM . . . and so and . . so . . .

SAM Anxiety. Madness. A black noon-day. Starts at me with an axe. Mad mad like a dog. I scream. I run. No. No. No. I remember now it is she. It is all clear that she is gone berserk. Wednesday. She sets fire to the chicken coop on the excuse that she was smokin' out a fox. A fox? Her eyes are wild. Next day . . no the day after . . at sundown she is throwin' apples into space. Hurling green apples into . . space. What are yah doin', I says? Nothing. No answer. Only a stupid grin. Then back to her old self again. And not a word mentioned. Food placed on the table. Here are the doughnuts made, put in this basket . . . .

SHEM So, so, so . . . . what are we out to prove?

SAM Prove what? (*Eats a doughnut.*)

SHEM Where was the boy at this time?

SAM What do yah think yahr doin' tah me – I says. Don't hit so hard. COLD! I'm cold.

SHEM Direction! In what direction is it heading?

SAM Carrying a monkey on his back. Claiming not to
understand a word; but knowing all the time . . . knowing.
Pretending not to notice − her youngster running amok.
Wild geese are flying high in the sky in a V formation. He
. . the boy has a rifle . . . firing gunshots. Boom. Boom.
Boom (*As he says this we hear shots in the distance.*) Shooting . . .
trying to kill . . reckless . . aiming not like a sportsman . . or
sharpshooter but . . . wild . . crazy . . and out of control.

SHEM The East into . . out of the East.

SAM But what is happening now? What is . . . this fever . . .

SHEM What . . . is . . . what?

SAM Happening . . I'm burning up . . .

SHEM And so . . . and so.

SAM Oh . . oh . . and so you said to the East . . .

SHEM No. (*Sobs*) Not.

SAM The wind. Roar. Roar.

   (*Roaring loudly.*)

   Out. Out. There is nothing do you hear me. Late at night. I
am calling loud. There never was nothing! I run out of the
house . . and she is sobbing. I scream. It is night now. I look
up at the heavens, fall down, fall, fall, I say fall down. I fall
down on my knees, my knees. I am dying! I am dying you
see. Snow, snow is on the ground. I put my head into it . .
into the cold snow . . . and the tears. I tell you.

SHEM (*agitated*) And East. And East. And East. Yes. East.

SAM No sun. No nothing. Only a cold sun-moon.
   Interplanetary exploration. Inter − about to happen . .

SHEM And . . . and . . . and?

SAM The same thing.

SHEM Oh.

SAM Oh, oh, yes the same thing. No one can save us now.
   Now only ourselves to live for. Ourselves. And that? I try to

say something but she again just stares. I have the feeling that maybe now she knows, finally begins to recognize. I would like to escape, but there she is – staring at me, and seemingly knowing at long last, staring too as if she had just seen me masturbate for the first time in our life together. You are a liar, she says. I will be dead soon, gone, but she just laughs. There is no communication now. Perhaps there was . . . no not anything.

SHEM   . . . and

SAM   Silence. Time to be silent.

SHEM   To what end?

SAM   In the East. There is a light.

SHEM   And . . .

SAM   To . . . to . . . to – going into the light . . out of the darkness.

Blackout

Zoe's Letter

Zoe's Letter was first presented in 1964 at La Mama Experimental Theatre Club on a benefit for Cafe La Mama's third space at 122 Second Avenue

Joyce Miller and Oryan West in "Zoe's Letter"
at Howl! Arts, October 2016

Zoe's Letter

CHARACTERS:

ZALLEY — *a teenage boy wearing a high school football letter sweater, dungarees, and sneakers*

ZOEY — *a teenage girl sporting a pony-tail hairdo who wears a white angora sweater and a cheerleader's satin jacket*

SCENE:

A 1960s style ice cream parlor — two chrome-naugahyde chairs are set by a small circular formica-top table — an oversized jukebox is ablaze with rainbow colored panels — the table is covered with an assortment of movie and sports magazines.

Play opens to a record on the jukebox — Bob Dylan singing "I Want You."

Music fades.

ZALLEY *and* ZOEY *sit across from one another.* ZOE *is drinking an egg cream and* ZAL *is nursing a Coke. They stare at one another in silence.* ZOE, *in a state of anxiety, rifles through her large purse.*

ZOE Got a quarter?

ZAL What for?

ZOE The jukebox. I can't stand the silence in here. There is a tenseness . . . a heaviness in the air. I don't know. I just feel nervous.

ZAL (*looking in his pocket*) No. No change. You'll have to hear silence. (*Pause*) Whatsa matter? Feel guilty? Are you angry? Pissed off . . .

ZOE About what?

ZAL I don't know. I just wondered if there was some problem.

ZOE What do you think we should do? Do you still think we should break up?

ZAL What the Christ are you bringing that up for now? Forget it. I don't want to talk about it . . . today. We'll figure it out at another time.

(*Pause*)

ZOE I guess . . . I feel . . I can't take it anymore.

ZAL What?

ZOE The silence! The shutting down. Your withdrawals. What is happening here?

ZAL Hungover. My head hurts . . is pounding. Too much beer – last night.

ZOE You mean you can't . . . you won't talk? (*Pause*) Maybe you'd rather be alone . . . I'm leaving. I gotta get outa here.

ZAL Are we going to go through that stuff again? You're always running away. You see too many movies.

ZOE I mean it.

ZAL (*Gets up. Pulls her down.*) Sit down. Calm down. Drink some coffee. I'll order it. Later . . . we'll try to understand . . go into whatever it is you think it is. We'll go lie on the grass somewhere in the park. Smoke. Watch the sky.

(*Pause*)

ZOE Do you want to order a sundae – a banana split?

(*Pause*)

ZAL Nah! What the hell time is it?

(*No reply*)

ZOE I don't like being here in this place. The walls are painted flesh pink . . the color of . . .

ZAL What did the letter say?

ZOE What letter?

ZAL From your mother? You said you got it today? That's why you're so down? What is in it?

ZOE Oh . . . . I . . . . haven't read it yet.

ZAL Let me see it? I'll read it to you.

ZOE What?

ZAL The letter – give it to me.

ZOE (*looking in her purse*) I don't know where I put it . . . . (*Terrified.*) I . . . uh . . .

ZAL You took it out of the mailbox. It's in your purse. Give it . . . (*Grabs her bag pulling out a blue handwritten letter.*) Here it is. (*He reads it.* ZOE *doesn't look up.*) It says . . .

ZOE She needs shoes. She had to get away . . think things out . . something like that . . took a trip. Left us . . my father and me too. It's a big mess, I guess. She was in Salinas . . . now she's visiting . . . staying with an old high school girlfriend in the Napa Valley.

ZAL Way out West in wine country. I'd like to go there. Is she . . . will she come back?

ZOE I don't know . . but . . . things are not . . .

ZAL What about the old man?

ZOE He don't care. He's drunk most of the time again and now there's a new girlfriend named Hedy who drinks with him in the kitchen and sometimes at the corner bar . . . she's practically moved in . . sometimes I hear them moaning in the night . . . but he manages to get to work. We're okay. We'll be okay.

ZAL Want to take a walk . . the park? A movie?

ZOE No. I gotta go . . home . . face the goddamn music. I'll be all right.

(*She rushes out.*)

ZAL Wait. Oh, Jesus Christ.

*He goes to jukebox. Drops in a quarter. Jukebox lights up. He sits
down. Lights up a cigarette. Takes a puff and puts out cigarette. Stares
straight out blankly.*

*The same record heard at play's beginning – "I Want You" – plays
again.*

Lights slowly dim.

THE BED

A PLAY IN ONE ACT

The Bed was first presented in June-July 1965 by Joe Cino at the Caffè Cino, 31 Cornelia Street in Greenwich Village. Bed set by Ron Link. It was directed by Robert Dahdah with the following cast:

JIM	Jim Jennings
JACK	Larry Burns

The production was revived for a second run at the Cino in November 1965 with the same cast.

Note: Walter McGinn played the role of Jack for several performances at the Cino. He went on to Broadway and eventually became a Hollywood movie star before dying at a young age in a car crash.

1965 poster for "The Bed"

Larry Burns and Jim Jennings in the Caffè Cino production of "The Bed"

Jim Jennings and Walter McGinn in fetal position in "The Bed" at the Caffè Cino

THE BED

CHARACTERS:

JIM – *A young man*

JACK – *A young man*

SCENE:

A medium-sized apartment in a large American city.

The suggestion of a lavatory (down right), sink, etc.

The suggestion of a phonograph machine.

Scattered clothing.

Liquor bottles.

A clock.

Books.

Sunlight.

A great white double bed on a raised-tilted-slightly-forward-toward-the-audience platform.

JACK *(on one side of the bed),* JIM *(on the other), asleep.*

Silence.

JIM's *left hand moves slightly.*

Pause.

JIM *breaks suddenly out of a nightmare. Sits up. Moans. Twitches. Scratches his head. Looks slowly about the room as if trying to connect*

*one object with another: attempting, perhaps, to make the pieces merge
into one whole.*

Anguish.

Stares for a long moment at figure of JACK, *who is curled up into the
position of the womb.*

Alienation.

JIM *pokes* JACK.

JACK *groans.*

Long silence.

JIM (*groggy*) Think we should get up?

JACK (*not moving*) Drop dead!

   (*Pause*)

JIM What time do you think it is?

JACK (*slowly*) Look at the clock . . . . .

   (*Pause*)

JIM I think it stopped . . . . working.

JACK Throw it out of the window.

   (*Pause*)

JIM How long have we been lying in this bed? When was it
that we were last seen . . . for instance . . . out . . . on the
street?

JACK You're not getting me into one of those conversations.

JIM What conversations?

   (*Pause*)

Sun seems to be out.

   (*Pause*)

I . . . . I've been having difficulty with my breathing again.
My lungs. During the night I almost suffocated. I . . .

   (*Pause*)

. . . I had a nightmare.

(*Pause*)

JACK What about?

JIM I don't remember.

JACK That's good. Ha. Ha.

(*Pause*)

JIM Do you think we should . . . both of us . . . make an attempt to get out of this bed?

JACK (*tossing slightly, clutching pillow*) I want to sleep.

JIM For how long?

JACK Do whateer you like. Get up if you want to. Go. Leave me alone.

JIM I've lost time. How long have we been in . . . this time?

JACK Two days . . . about. Have a drink or something. Go to the refrigerator-box. Get something to eat if it pleases you. Live it up. Then . . . .

JIM I feel hung over.

(*Pause*)

I'm tired of sleep, fed up with eating, of drowning myself in drink into a coma.

JACK Quit intellectualizing.

JIM Where . . . where . . . are we getting this way?

JACK What difference could it possibly make. Get this through your thick skull. I'm tired. Bored.

(*Slight pause*)

I don't know. Try reading again . . . or maybe you could take up yoga or something. Didn't you used to study yoga?

JIM I'm getting up. Are you

JACK Eventually I'll have to . . . I guess.

JIM Do you want to go out . . . . . .

JACK No.

JIM . . . for a walk?

JACK Where?

JIM Anywhere.

(As JACK delivers the following lines he counts his fingers over and over again, almost as if to reassure himself of their existence.)

JACK Uh . . . . This week one of us will probably have to go to the bank. Draw money out of the account. Pay the rent. Get in some booze. Some food.

(Pause)

Food.

JIM When?

JACK Later this week. Ha ha! I guess. Ha ha!

JIM What're you laughing about?

JACK *(happily)* Money. Filthy-God-damn-money. A silver slab of a spoon stuck in my mouth since the day I was born . . . blasted out of my mother's bloody womb. Thinking of the old-man-dead-rotting-a-grinning-skeleton-dead-rotting in black earth six feet underground. Papa no longer with us. What does any of it mean to the old bastard now? What does it mean to the old lady guzzling booze uptown? What does it mean to me? Money . . . . deposited for me in the Bank of America . . . so that I can go on living . . . or some such thing. Did you hear me? *Go on living* . . . this beauteous tawdry tortuous existence . . . . so you can go on living-guzzling with me. Very feasible arrangement. You. Me. In the morning. In the evening. One day we'll be under earth too, just like the old man. I wonder which one of us will go first? Ha ha! Hey, you listening to this story of my life? Think it's amusing?

JIM Stinks.

(Pause)

Ah . . . . there's just something wrong . . . wrong . . . with this . . . this entire set-up.

(Pause)

With you. With me. With both of us together. Something's not working. I can't go on. I've just about passed the point of endurance. I am not up to this. I'm thinking of maybe pushing off. Out.

JACK What? (JIM *buries his head in his hands.*) Take a walk, and come back later.

JIM We don't do anything. We're . . . . we're like two objects frozen in time, in space, not even on earth, really . . . . suspended. Weightless being. Occasionally we go to the john to pee or to take a crap. We shove food down our throats . . pizza pie, hamburgers . . sent up from the corner; chocolate puff pastries, ice cream. Basic functionalism. Eating.

(*Short pause*)

I feel nauseated. This process going on like some great senseless flux. On and on and on. You. Me. Sex is dead. No, it's God. God is dead. No, it's Nietzsche. Nietzsche is dead. No, I am alive, here, and yet . . .

JACK Why don't you just drop dead?

JIM Maybe we're already dead and don't know it . . haven't been fully aware of it. Dead. Non-existent. Living-dying. Maybe . . . .

JACK Why in the hell don't you stop trying to figure the whole thing out? What's to explain?

JIM Nothing . . . I guess.

(*Pause.*)

(*Shakes* JACK.)

Get up already . . . . slob!

JACK No. Leave me alone. I just want to lie here . . . lie here and . . .

JIM . . . and?

JACK . . . stare into space . . . until something happens in my head . . . . inside my lunatic head . . . maybe an idea . . .

JIM What idea?

JACK I don't know yet what idea . . . . or if there will even be any. But I'm going to lie here. Maybe an idea will turn up . . . maybe . . . something from the past. Lie still. Somehow even if I wanted to now . . . I couldn't move . . . couldn't budge . . . out of this bed. I have to just lie still here. Still.

JIM I can't anymore. I'm getting up. I am . . . going to get up . . . (*Gets up quickly*.) . . . up and out!

(*He begins to move his arms wildly and to pace around the floor in a circle. Pause.*)

Mind if I play a record?

JACK Do whatever you like. (*Almost an offstage aside.*) You're lucky you have a sucker like me who lets you do whatever you like, who supports your miserable existence. You're lucky.

JIM (*having heard perhaps only the word "support"*) I'm not about to argue about your filthy lucre . . . to discuss economic problems with you. Your poor-little-rich-boy-guilt-problem act makes me sick. It's getting to be a drag.

JACK Cut it! Cut it!

JIM Your wealthy-overbearing-father-complex-complexities . . .

JACK All right. Cut the . . . bull . . psychology today. Cut the role you're playing down to half. I don't like these blanket judgment-assumptions of yours. It just *ain't* that easy.

(*Short pause*)

Play some music. Brush your teeth. Wash your armpits. Go out. Bring me back . . . . . .

JIM What?

JACK I don't know.

(*Pause*)

(JIM *goes over to the window ledge area: gets up onto ledge on all fours.*)

What're yah doing now?

JIM Thinking of jumping out.

(*Pause*)

Playing a game. Think it would make any difference . . . to . .
. . any . . .

JACK (*speaking objectively, reciting factual data*) You might not
make it. I mean, finish yourself off all the way. We're only
four floors up off the ground. Maybe you'd just break a leg or
something. You know. If you're gonna make the Big Blackout
there are ways that aren't quite as messy. Pills for instance. A
good way.

JIM How would you know?

(*Gets down.*)

Mmmmmm. Yeah.

(*Walks to phonograph machine. Turns it on. Song: "Any Way You
Want It" – Dave Clark 5 – Epic Records). Very loud. Blasting. As
in a discotheque. This is the monotonous drone of the "outer" world
bombarding the situation.*)

Neither JIM *nor* JACK *moves throughout the length of the recording.
They wear blank expressions on their faces and appear not to be
listening to the sound. At record's end,* JIM *makes it to the bathroom
area.*

Brushes teeth,

Washes armpits.

Puts on trousers,

Puts on shirt,

      socks,

      shoes.

*Gazes at himself for a long moment in mirror (front), not quite sure
that the apparition he sees in the glass is actually himself.*

Walks slowly toward bed.

Sits on bed.

Arms drooped, between legs.

Head down.

Head up.
Stares vacatly at fixed point (front).

Silence

JACK (*hand over face*) What are you thinking about?
JIM (*as if relieved of an intolerable burden*) Nothing.
   (Pause)
   Are you coming out with me or . . . staying?
   (*No answer.*)

JIM *proceeds to leave.*
Stop. Halt at doorway.
A long, tense staring at figure of JACK.
JACK *pulls himself into a ball and refrains from eye contact or gestures.*

JACK (*soft*) Where are you going?
JIM I don't know.
   (*Slight pause*)
   Out . . . maybe . . . for a . . cup of coffee . . To . . uh . . get
   some cigarettes. I just don't . . . I wish that . . .
   (*Hold moment.*)

Slow exit − JIM.

Door slam.

JACK *up quickly out of bed*
*Wanders around the room looking at objects − at anything − with no
specific intention.*
Finally picks up clock.
Shakes clock.
*Indicates throwing of object-clock out of window − image: shortstop
hurling a baseball.*

Looks at object-clock. Studies it for a moment.

Laughs.

Puts clock back in its place.

Goes to phonograph. Plays "Any Way You Want It."

Sits on bed. Stares out front with a blank, bewildered expression on his face. Looks at audience faces. Toward the middle of the record he slowly places his hands over his face.

Record end: reject.

Blackout.

NOTES ON TIME (in original script)

The Bed, in its essence, is dealing with the problem of inverted time-that-is-timelessness. The two characters have what might be called in technical circles a time-space problem – closely identified with schizophrenic time, non-time, or irrational time. Any director or reader should bear in mind that, while the play reads quickly, time is being dealt with in an acausal manner; that is, the performance time is slowed down by dramatic time intervals.

In no way is the time element in *The Bed* pushed forward into activity or into measured time; rather, time is paradoxical, neither here nor there. Many gaps. Actor movement should occur only when indicated – and at other times should be physically constricted . . . as opposed to explosive-outer-directed-emotion that is implosive (inner-directed) and, almost, catatonic-waiting-to-break-through. (It never does in this instance.)

Actual playing time may be anywhere between thirty and forty-five minutes to one hour. The play shold appear to be happening in space. We might think of a space capsule. (In performance, the bed was almost the entire stage. As a symbol it could represent gravity-pull-limitation, a death slab in a morgue, a "padded cell," a coffin, sleep, sexuality, whatever problem the bed might represent itself to be to an audience.) Like the mime who is walking forward in visual time but who is actually physically walking backward, time, herewith, has become non-conceptual. In this non-conceptual time, movement and emotional intention-actions must be emphasized and strained to an exaggerated point. For instance, while in conceptual time it may take two minutes to cross a street, in non-conceptual time it could take two-four-six-eight-nine and so forth.

Example –

JACK Do whatever you like. Get up if you want to. Go. Leave me alone.

JIM I have lost time. How long have we been in . . . this time?

Verbal delivery can be normal. Duration points between lines are optional, so that reactive periods in terms of their own experience of meaninglessness and emptiness would be quite long.

WHY TUESDAY NEVER HAS A BLUE MONDAY

Why Tuesday Never Has a Blue Monday was first presented on February 10, 1966 by Ellen Stewart at La Mama E.T.C., 122 Second Avenue. It was directed by Ron Link, with sets by Paul Hamlin, costumes by Ellen Stewart, and original music by Elliot Kirkland.

.

| THE MAN | Patrick Sullivan |
| LOIS WEST | Marilyn Roberts |

Patrick Sullivan and Marilyn Roberts in "Why
Tuesday Never Has a Blue Monday"

The poster for the La
Mama production of
"Why Tuesday Never
Has a Blue Monday"
featured a photo by
Edward Wallowitch

Why Tuesday Never Has a Blue Monday

The Room:

A room that is not an office and not a living room. Perhaps it is a study. There is something surreal about it. There is the feeling of screens and windows that have no end (d.c.) There are floor-to-ceiling windows that might lead onto a penthouse garden.

We are very high up.

A great number of plants, some tall, some hanging. Two Danish modern or Bauhaus chairs face one another from a distance of at least six feet.

A telephone that does not ring.

Papers.

Books. Shelves.

Radio-phono-tape recorder (described later in the play). A large picture or rug of an Egyptian cat hangs ominously over the room to one side. It gives the impresssion of being a Buddha that stares or watches over the entire scene.

There is an Oriental rug on the floor.

Colors are of the earth, trees, and sky.

Characters:

LOIS WEST — *a rising star of the theatre and cinema.* LOIS *is a young woman in her middle or late twenties who is extremely attractive.*

*No makeup, or the use of makeup to create a natural look. In
other situations, we might have the feeling that this is a woman
heavily adorned. She breathes an awareness of such an appearance —
sophistication by virtue of now-in-this-situation-shirking-it — as if to
emphasize it. The idea of appearances (particularly of her own and
things-as-they-appear) has become abhorrent to the creature since she
has discovered the devious ways in which appearance might be used to
distract, to manipulate without thought or intention toward a coming
through in any real emotional sense.*

The Image: LOIS *wears a shabby raincoat, slacks, a loose drab sweater,
and dark sun-glasses in the manner of one who avoids crowds — isolated
— alien — wherever she goes among the strangers that follow a star. This
muted costume is as if the antithesis of the dazzling image — an image
manufactured out of cynicism for the pleasure and approval of others.*

There is as well an infinite sadness, a forlorness.

THE MAN — *Fortyish, tall, solid, introspective, direct, a mustache,
loose-fitted corduroy pants such as a janitor might wear, a plaid shirt
open at the neck, slipping socks, steel cold intense eyes — he is too
preoccupied with ideas and their structures and superstructures to concern
himself with mode of dress. He dresses to be warm. At times the man
should act the part of a Greek chorus — delving into the inner life of
a heroine caught in a modern dilemma, the dilemma of self-exile and
alienation from what is seen to be — the outer world — the world outside
of ourselves. It is the man's role to bring the heroine back from her path
of self-torment, death, and destruction onto a path more committed to
life — to the life role — feeling, existing, and being responsible for actions
— the ability to discover others as a frame of reference — other than
herself.*

AT RISE — *As the lights come up through the windows and from the
skylight above, we see* THE MAN *slowly meandering about the room
looking from object to object, perhaps considering a rearrangement of
some kind.*

A long hard stare into space.

*A provoked look as if some anxiety had taken hold, thinking, perhaps,
about some disorganization, a forgotten event or some "going"*

relationship.

Behind a plant is a small watering can. THE MAN *picks it up, begins watering his plants and seemingly contemplating their growth.*

In the midst of the watering, the man goes over to an area where there are some shelves with books and other paraphernalia. He picks up a child's drawing of a house, a rooster, and some flowers crayoned sketchily over the paper. He examines it for a long moment. Puts it down. In the same area again. He switches on what is either a phonograph or a radio or a phono-radio combination. (We hear about two minutes of "Surfin' Bird" by the Trashmen.)

THE MAN *stares straight ahead. A kind of pensive anger crosses his face. The bombardment of music is felt to be some kind of social phenomenon from an outer world whose frenzy seems to be near — headed toward disaster with each ensuing beat. The sound grows louder, the lights slightly brighter, as if to emphasize this thought.*

Quickly, THE MAN *switches the machine off.*

He goes back to the plants, continues watering, touching the roots, the soil.

Enter, suddenly, LOIS WEST.

She sits hurriedly in one of the identical chairs. She seems in a chaotic state of mind. Digging into a large hand-bag, she pulls out a package of cigarettes. Nervously, she drops the package just as she takes out a cigarette.

Her hands are shaking. The man picks up the cigarette package, handing it to her. LOIS *looks at the package for a moment as if she were not sure what it was. It could be a dead flower or, perhaps, a giant spider. She grabs it like a vindictive child, shoving it quickly into her purse. Lighting her cigarette with a silver lighter, puffing wildly,* LOIS *fixes her gaze to the floor. She fumbles with her dark glasses as if she were unsure of whether to leave them on or off.*

Finally, taking them off, LOIS *continues to stare at the floor, rigid, almost seemingly hypnotized.*

Finishing his business with the plants, THE MAN *moves to the other chair.*

He sits and stares at the subject before him for a long moment.

*There is a wry look on his face. There is also — in his look — an
intensity — as if he were one who might have x-ray vision, as if he were
capable of reading the mind of another in his presence, anticipating their
behavior, their every gesture. He himself remains sturdy like some elk
that watches over a herd.*

*Both are frozen statues, two beasts stalking one another, each waiting
for the other to make a move.*

MAN You're late. (*There is no reply. Pause. Quietly, an aside.*)
You're cheating yourself, you know.

LOIS What?

MAN   . . . of time. (*Slight pause.*) Of being here. Of realizing
. . . .

LOIS Oh . . . subways . . the subway . . . got mixed up. I forgot
where to get off. I couldn't get a cab. I got off at the wrong
stop. I had to get back on. I didn't know which side to go up
. . . up or down . . . except there was no down. I thought . .
. There was this man . . . a Negro . . . he was staring at me. I
think he . . . (*Pause.*)

MAN He what?

LOIS   . . . has followed me . . . here.

MAN   Oh. (*Slight pause. A scrutinizing look as if the truth of the
matter might be elsewhere.*) Is he waiting . . . downstairs . . .
outside? Where . . . .

LOIS I . . . I . . . don't know. Maybe he's in the hall. (*Angry.*)
Let's drop it. I really don't care . . .

MAN What about?

LOIS Anything . . . I mean . . . if I'm murdered . . . or . . .

MAN What made you think of that?

LOIS (*nervous*) A look. He looked at me . . . on the train . . .
in a particular . . . peculiar way. I tried to avert his look; but
. . . in trying to avoid it . . . it almost seemed to promulge
. . . to encourage . . . to intensify his . . . looking at me. I

was reading the paper . . . the newspaper . . . someone . . . in the paper . . . I was reading . . . a young girl jumped . . . or had been pushed out of a window . . . from a terrace twenty stories high off the ground.

MAN Yes?

LOIS (*continuing a train of thought*) No explanation was given as to why she had . . . why she had done it . . . was dead. She had left a girl's boarding school . . . in the middle of a term . . . for no reason known to . . . just left . . . abruptly . . . came home to where her grandmother lives . . . wait . . . I'll show you. (LOIS *takes a newspaper out of her bag. Hands it to him.*)

MAN (*takes paper, looks at it, but does not read it*) Do you want me to read it . . . (*Slight pause.*) . . . now?

LOIS No.

(*Pause.*)

MAN (*puts newspaper down*) Would you like a drink?

LOIS Of what?

MAN Gin . . . vodka . . . whatever . . . you . . . like . . . Or . . .

LOIS (*quick*) I don't drink.

MAN But you told me . . . the last time you were here that you were frightened of the bottle . . . of becoming an alcoholic . . .

LOIS (*defensive, withdrawing, hostile*) Did I? Well, I've given all that up. Anyhow, why would you solicit my problem . . . anyhow . . . if I had one . . . a problem with drinking.

MAN There isn't any reason why . . . well, I'll get you something else.

(*He leaves room. LOIS gets up. Whistles. Moves about the room. Gazes stage front. Picks up a book. Looks at it for a moment. Rushes to her chair. Puts book in her bag. THE MAN returns carrying two glasses filled with a red liquid.*)

LOIS What's that?

MAN Punch. Hawaiian . . . from the A & P. Good? (*Hands her glass. He sits and drinks. LOIS takes a sip, putting her drink down on the floor. Pause.*) Where did you put the book?

LOIS What book?

MAN A book is missing . . . Kierkegaard . . . What did you do
with it?

LOIS I hid it.

MAN Where?

(*Pause.*)

LOIS Here. (*She reaches into her purse. Hands him the book.*)

MAN Why did you take this book?

LOIS I liked the title . . . *Fear and Trembling – The Sickness Unto
Death.* It said something . . . about . . . existence . . . about the
way I feel. Maybe I thought I'd find a clue to something . . .
about the problem of my existence . . . of finding myself . . .
alive . . .

MAN You thought you could find something . . . some answer
. . . in this book?

LOIS Don't you read books . . . find solutions . . . in order to go
on?

MAN Not in a book. It's not . . . in . . . a . . . (LOIS *goes into
herself. Her body becomes rigid, catatonic. Pause. Finally.*) What are
you thinking? (*No answer.*) What are you feeling?

LOIS (*softly*) Nothing. Empty.

MAN What did you say?

LOIS (*angrily*) I said I felt emptied out. I feel nothing. I'm sick
today. I have a pounding headache . . . heartbeat. I don't want
to talk to you or to anyone. I'm stifled with talk . . . with
word symbols – with communications. What is there to say? I
just don't . . .

MAN There is no choice . . .

LOIS What do you mean?

man (*louder, moving closer*)   . . . but to talk. I am saying that the
one thing we must continue to do . . . is to talk. (*Slight pause.*)
What are you feeling right now?

LOIS Stop asking me that question! I said nothing. I felt nothing.

MAN That's a feeling.

LOIS What is? What are you talking about? Stop asking me . . .

MAN Not feeling is a feeling. I mean something might be being avoided. (*Slight pause.*) What happened to you . . . the last time you left here?

LOIS (*after a moment*) Last time I felt . . . when I left . . . I sat outside . . . on the stairwell . . . and began to cry . . . at first just a little, then . . . more loudly, violently. I wanted to scream . . . simply scream . . . I ran to the window. (*At this point* LOIS *goes toward stage area which represents windows and screens, moving about, gripped by the same feeling she is describing having had after her last visit.*) . . . like right now . . . I wanted to . . . I looked out the window . . . down . . . down . . . onto the street. The people, the cars, were tiny specks. I thought about jumping . . . falling . . . falling to the ground. I got dizzy. Every time I come here . . . inside . . . that's what I feel . . . like . . . (*Pause.*)

MAN Yes?

LOIS Those doors! I feel like pushing them open and . . . oh, Christ!

MAN Why don't you?

LOIS Don't I . . . what?

MAN Jump . . . Now?

LOIS (*with consideration*) Why are you saying that to . . . (*Slight pause.*) Because I stop . . . and . . . (*Quickly.*) Because I know . . . somewhere . . . in my mind that I don't know yet who I am. I am somewhere trying to formulate a character that I can act out in life . . . in the world. Do you know who I am? Who, looking at me, would you say I was?

MAN (*slowly, as if he were solving*) I would say . . . . . . knowing you . . . that you are a famous . . . a well-known actress.

LOIS A what?

MAN A very good . . . actress . . . that you have a talent . . . a gift.

LOIS Why bring that up?

MAN Who you are. The identity that you made, are responsible for having made.

LOIS That's just it. That all seems . . . all seems to be . . . outside. Like someone else. The image that I created. I am someone else . . . somewhere else . . . misplaced . . . a misfit. Oh, God, we've been through all this before.

MAN Tell it again.

LOIS (*dizzily*) An image . . . a performance. But lately . . . my mind . . . that conception . . . the conception of The Image . . . has been . . . collapsing . . .

MAN   . . . and what is left?

LOIS Left?

MAN After the broken concepts and . . . ideologies?

LOIS I don't know. Damn it! I don't know! There seems to be no me . . . inside . . . a blank. I feel so often these days that I am . . . blanking out. After the disease and the symptoms have disappeared I say to myself, perhaps there will remain . . . nothing. Another emptiness . . . to fill with more and more empty words . . . to project onto faceless audiences . . . or perhaps I could establish some concrete meaning to put behind them . . . the words. Something is breaking down. I am confused . . . alone. I'm frightened . . . I remain frightened . . . in a state of terror most of the time. (*Slight pause.*) Last night . . . after . . . the play . . . after I left my dressing room . . . I was expected to attend a supper party with . . . instead I just ran . . . off by myself . . . alone . . . ran for blocks, not knowing where I was going . . . where I was running to. I just ran . . . as if . . . someone recognized me. They called my name. I continued to run. Then, suddenly, I was in a bar . . . a dark run-down bar somewhere in the East Forties . . . old wretched-demented-lecherous faces . . . hollow men . . . painted prostitutes . . . sailors . . . faggots . . . a blaring juke box. I ordered a drink. I sat alone. I thought . . . I began to

become . . . seductive. I thought I might find someone . . .
but they all stared at me with dead eyes . . . forgotten men.
Yet . . . in their look it seemed . . . they seemed to know . . .
they could see that . . . I was suffering from an illness . . .
some atrocious illness. Before long they all began to show
hideous smirks on their faces. I started to feel panic for no
real or apparent reason. I heard laughter. I tried to lift my
drink up to my mouth. I could not. I ran out . . . onto the
sidewalks. I walked. I walked faster, faster, as if . . . pursued
– but by whom? I was . . . I said to myself . . . completely
. . . utterly alone . . . but so what? My body felt heavy . . .
tight . . . stuck to the earth . . . yet I was . . . had entered into
. . . had been for some time in . . . another atmosphere. I felt
maybe I should be confined . . . hospitalized – (*To* THE MAN.)
I think I want to be put away again. My sense of time . . .
that is, of past, present, and future, seems to swim in space
. . . to evaporate . . . dissolve into blackness. Did I go home
and sleep? Did I become dizzy and faint? Did I dream . . . last
night . . . or had it actually happened earlier that evening?

MAN Had what happened?

LOIS (*as if broken out of a trance; and, then, picking it up again*)
Perhaps it had been a hallucination . . . consciousness
expanding . . . like LSD. It seemed I was in front of an
audience . . . perhaps it had been earlier that evening. It all
seemed to unfold before me as in a dream. I was in it . . . and,
yet, outside – watching . . . in a window . . . or doorway.
There I was . . . as usual . . . in the play that I appear in . . .
that I begin each evening at 7:30 . . . the play . . . we have
talked about . . .

MAN (*loud, quick, intense*) Go into it . . . as an experience . . . a
sense-memory. What happened to you?

LOIS A . . . the play . . . that I am in . . . as I told you, concerns
itself . . . that is . . . has a central theme . . . as I told you . . .
in which . . . which involves some kind of trial . . . the trial of
a girl who feels that she does not exist . . . and yet somehow
through some act of terror is made to feel that she does exist

by virtue of being on trial for life for a murder that she did
or did not commit at one time. She does not or . . . cannot
. . . remember . . . anything . . . previous to this. A judge
with a Nowhere Man face gazes at her. A horrible event has
happened. The judge speaks of . . . He says . . .

MAN (*flatly as if the line had been repeated a dozen times – hypnotic*)
"You are on trial for the murder of a child pushed out of a
window!"

LOIS "Who does he mean?" she says. "Perhaps" she says, "he
means myself; but how can that be . . . if I still . . . am . . .
Breathing heavily.) able to breathe . . . air. I am still alive,
awake." Perhaps it is my innocence that he is talking about
which I killed or which was killed . . .

MAN . . . By . . .

LOIS . . . By me . . . myself . . . at some early age. The girl
cannot remember. (*Slight pause.*) It was a day when somehow
from that day on . . . the girl assumes the outward shape of
reality . . . physical reality . . . (*Demonstrating this to the man
as well as to the present audience*) . . . she has hands, arms . . .
feet . . . a face that wears any expression it chooses. (*This is
also demonstrated.*) . . . and yet she knows that she has become
a monster, capable of anything . . . of murder. No longer in
the dimension of human. Smiles. Cajoling . . . lust . . . and
murder . . .

MAN (*underneath, suggestive, like a chant*) For didn't you murder
yourself?

LOIS It is a dream. An image of a self projected on an outer
world that . . . here . . . in this play . . . has become . . . a
nightmare without beginning, middle or . . .

MAN . . . end.

LOIS Yes, The Play has no end. The audience comes and
goes at regular intervals. Intermissions are provided for in
which people sip coffee . . . or some orange drink. The real
intermingles like some coitus with the . . .

MAN (*a bizarre expression*) . . . abstract?

LOIS Yes, it is abstract . . . and yet she is real somehow in it
. . . the play . . . the scene. Yet it seems as if it had not yet
begun. Yet she is being held responsible for a murder. Logic
plays against the illogical. A gigantic mirror confronts her in
which she sees the image of herself. Yet she is outside looking
at herself looking at herself as if existence were nothing more
than a hall of mirrors in which the image of ourselves is
continuously projected. There is no end . . . and yet it goes
nowhere into infinity. Perhaps there is something . . some
element beyond . . . that we do not yet understand. Where?
Can I . . . dare I ask that question . . . and which image
. . . which extension will be the real me? There can be no
adjustment to any prevailing patterns . . . only a swimming
into a sea of . . . madness from which there can be no return.
A death. A blackness. (*Slight pause. A mood change: matter of
fact.*) In any event something was . . . or had . . . collapsed.
What once seemed so huge, so authoritative, so wealthy, was a
structure – abstraction – that was collapsing – outwardly and
inwardly as well. A bomb had fallen. The city . . . the entire
land . . . had surrendered to a hostile enemy. Newspapers
and radio announcements spoke of continuous disasters. One
event was worse than the other – yet they all ended the same
way: A murder. A death. Others went on eating and grabbing
what they could out of garbage dumps. The enemy, however
. . . this enemy . . . was never specific . . . never even showed
its face. If only it were some foreign red or yellow aggressor.
It was a mute nothing that never spoke. There was a surrender
. . . an accusation . . . a mock trial . . . and a sentence to death.
The lights go out. (*On this line there should be an actual dimming
of lights to very diffuse point.*) There was nothing and yet . . . out
of the nothing . . .

MAN What?

LOIS (*moving forward, slightly dreamy*) A landscape – flat – vacant
– and I am walking on it. (*She begins to walk and move her arms
wildly.*) I-am-walking-on-it! This time it is like a movie . . .
like I am in a movie . . . except . . . it is also like I am walking

down a street . . . or here . . . or anywhere. A huge Eye appears. It focuses onto myself. A voice says . . .

MAN (*behind her now as if talking through her – into her*) "You are in the Territory of Death!"

LOIS If only I could see Death – confront it – as though it were some cloaked figure in an Everyman play. (*Her body begins to freeze.*) There is no one. I scream – "Return! Return!" I gasp . . . desperately fighting against the weight of my own body (*She re-experiences this.*) . . . trying to . . . get . . . out . . . out . . . of . . . the . . . dream.

MAN What happens?

LOIS (*more relaxed – lightens up*) Nothing. The same thing. A hand is held up. (*Holds her hand in front of her staring at it – caressing her arm with her other hand.*) It-is-a-hand. It-is-my-hand. I look-at-it. I sing a little song at the audience about peace and love.

(*She sings like a child, a note of irony, of sarcasm, as if the song had been sung many times to no avail. Vaguely to the tune of "My Country 'Tis of Thee."*)

> On and on and on we go.
>
> We can find a way.
>
> To a brighter Destiny.
>
> Oh, let it be today.
>
> Oh, let it be today.

(*Pause, deflated.*) . . . only there is no today. No one is left on stage . . . in the dream . . . the play . . . except myself. But that is a kind of victory.

MAN (*suggestive*) The audience . . .

LOIS (*picking up her cue*) . . . is onto its feet. The clap-clapping of hands. A great rushing about . . . in a turmoil. Someone fainted . . . or had died . . . in the audience. A call for the doctor . . . for help. (*Yelling.*) Help! The people think it is part of the play. I go off to . . . (*Switch of mood and pace.*) Would you mind opening the window? I can't breathe. I . . .

(THE MAN *opens a window. There is quite a long pause as if the "game" of fear and terror were over for the time being. The two characters smile at one another like Cheshire cats, like children who have been playing a naughty game like "doctor" or "man and wife."*)

MAN (*finally breaking the silence as they face one another*) What would you like to do now?

LOIS (*coyly*) Now I would like to . . .

MAN (*smiling*) What?

LOIS . . . do my animal act . . . my animal role.

MAN What animal?

LOIS . . . myself . . . as an . . . ha ha . . . as a wild animal. I will get onto the floor (*She does.*) and revert to . . . and become an animal (*On all fours.*) . . . and attack you! (*On all fours heading at her partner. The following attitudes should be played for animal voraciousness and hostility – never for cuteness.*) OOooowwrowww! Oooorow! Ooowrow!

MAN (*sexual*) And I will attack you! I will be the tiger-lion-king-male of the species!

LOIS We will play . . . ATTACK! (*She charges at THE MAN with the fervor of a combat soldier. Lights up and down – light color changes. During the following section LOIS and THE MAN roll over and over on top of one another making loud – oooowor! – animal noises at one another. Included between the mock roaring are:*)

MAN I'll get you.

LOIS My husband. My lover. Cock. I want to feel you inside of me. Kill me. Harder. Harder. Eat. Eat. Help. No. Oh, God! I feel it! I am yours . . . your lover.

(*Then together.*)

LOIS		MAN	
No.		Yes.	
Yes.		No.	
No.		Yes.	
Real, real.		Yes.	
No.		Yes.	

No.   No.

Yes, yes.

LOIS (*more desperate*) Real, real! (*Choking and coughing.*) I am no
longer acting!

MAN (*suddenly – abruptly*) We must stop. Go back.

(*Pause. They are both breathing very heavily. They look at one
another with combined feelings of anger and guilt.*)

LOIS (*still in the trance of "game play" – crawling, moving toward
the man*) You love me. I have everything anyone can . . . or
could want. I can buy you with dirty, filthy, sexy money. I
have sex appeal, breasts, legs . . . that act as a vise . . . that pull
you in . . . that lock you in . . . me . . . forever! Don't pull
away from me. I couldn't stand it. (*Kissing his shoes, grabbing his
knees as if to pull him on top of her.*) Come. Here! I will get you.
Son of a bitch! (LOIS *reaches into her pocket. Pulls out gun. Fires
it.*) Dead. Dead. You are dead. Ha. Ha . . . (MAN *falls onto floor.
Lights down to dim.*) That will teach you . . . teach you . . . to
try to get close to me. You see this. (LOIS *fires gun at herself.*) O
. . . .ver. M–m–m.

(*Pause.* MAN *gets up. Fixes a hard stare onto* LOIS. *Picks up gun.*)

MAN (*shaking her*) Wake up. Game . . . hallucinations . . . here
is your gun.

LOIS (*half up*) Yes . . . gun . . . from the prop room. Prop gun.
Ha. Ha. Yes.

MAN You're drooling. Here. (*Hands her a handkerchief. She wipes
her face. They stare at one another.*) Get back up. (*Pause.*) Afraid?
. . .

LOIS Yes. Yes . . . afraid.

MAN . . . that you will cross over to the other side? Go insane?

LOIS (*composed, getting up*) Sometimes I wish I could. Sometimes
I yearn only to die . . . to free myself of my body . . . of this
body. It is not going mad that tortures me . . . it is the fear
that I shall never go mad . . . that I shall remain the same . . .
what we call sane . . . or conscious . . . conscious of this . . .

what we call . . . existence. Sane! And you, I suppose, are my torturer leading me toward a greater sanity . . . or insanity . . . but that is a contradiction. Isn't it? I'm in the middle . . . I want to die . . . and yet . . . more than anything I want to live – forever – to never grow old and decay. Why don't you admit that about yourself . . . that you might feel the same way!

MAN (*calmly*) I never said anything different from that. I am no exception. (*Slight pause.*) Your time is almost up. I will see you again . . . (*Picks up a pad, looking at it.*) Yes. We've changed it . . . have it marked down here for Monday. Please try to be on time . . . punctual. Punctuality.

LOIS (*dazed – unwilling or unable to leave right then although she starts toward the exit*) But what has happened?

MAN You want me to sum it up? Stick on some kind of label?

LOIS No. I just wish the confusion . . . the anxiety . . . could be alleviated.

MAN It won't. It doesn't. It gets worse. My own . . . now . . . is worse than it ever has been. With each step into knowing there is another horrifying-accompanying step into not-knowing . . . into the nothing. That is as it is, I am afraid. You have been suffering under the well-known delusion that there would be – somewhere – a "cure" for existence . . . some fixed determinable point. There is none. We all suffer the same painful sickness . . . the knowledge of the awareness of . . . our own death . . . that we must . . . each and every one of us . . . leave all of this . . . cease to exist . . . disappear. Your idea of theoretical health is merely having it collapse under the weight of just this very realization. Your entire super-structure, verbalizations, words, your inauthentic apotheosis into stardom is beginning to crumble . . . falling . . . down . . . as if you had been pushed out of a window from a high place.

LOIS What will become of me . . . of the self that I destroyed . . . the child . . . in order to become the monster image . . .

my role . . . a role I cast myself into . . . my meteoric thrust
into stardom . . . through the top of the tent! What is to
happen . . . now?

MAN (*softly like a cantata*) You are beginning to be ready . . .
to become . . . I don't know. At any rate you will not have a
return to your former illness. You will move somewhat more
freely in the world. Terminologies and categorizations will
not engulf you as they once did. This continuum . . . that
I speak of . . . this . . . learning to walk in the present will
lead you into . . . for the first time . . . a kind of . . . relating.
(*Slight pause.*) There will be a someone . . . in the world . .
. someone specific who will find you and whom you will
find. You are beginning to be ready. The trip to the moon
is completed and there is a joyful return. At first there will
be a dull ache . . . an inclination . . . a proclivity . . . a kind
of melancholy yearning for the past . . . the years of endless
turmoil, confusion, hatred, frustration. You will try to go
back but you will find that you cannot – that to go back is
to be – once again – frozen – dead – devoid of life – as on
the moon. You will fear insanity – or not going insane . . .
conscious awareness – as always – but you will not notice this
anguish . . . these two extremities. You will live. No longer
will you feel alone – although you will be aware that you
are . . . in reality . . . traveling alone toward a sudden abrupt
ending . . . a heart attack . . . a hemorrhage . . . a car crash.
Amidst the confusion, among the players and audience – you
will be with another person. Another person will be there.
You are ready to find this person whoever he may be. The
child will return to you . . . innocent . . . alive . . . violent
. . . and kicking . . . and you will be safe. You will no longer
travel without the Missing Companion. Although this will
not be seen to be a solution to the question of existence . . . it
will be a better path than the one you formerly traveled.

LOIS The physicalization? The animal?

MAN It will be forgotten. Someone will touch you differently
. . . without violence. (*Pause. They stare at one another.*) You

may go now. (LOIS *begins to leave toward the window area.*) No, not that way. (THE MAN *points to the exit.*)

LOIS (*stopping – gripped by thought and confusion*) The man who followed me here. Perhaps he is waiting . . .

MAN (*solemnly, like a holy man*) Eventually, he and all others like him will . . . disappear . . . fade into the background, birds in flight seen only from a distance through a telescope.

LOIS Then it is possible to survive for a while longer. It will be possible to live for a while longer.

Pause. There is a silence in which the two characters fix onto one another long and full – hold fixed stare – they freeze. Then the man walks to his desk area and takes out a tape-recorder, which he places in full view of the audience. He plays on the tape machine the dialogue up to " . . . has followed me . . . here . . . *" spoken at the play's beginning. The earlier exchanges should be as close as possible to this fixed tape. He listens. He does not move. He stops the tape.)*

Blackout

NOTES (in original script):

The verbalizations (monologues, terminological linguistics, etc.) should be played to represent exaggerated structures, large intellectual defense-mechanisms. These should be played against the internal thread of what-is-happening: the attempt to break through emotionally. These periods of time may be directed with theatrical impositions and physical extensions. (Exaggerated realism, mime, dance, etc.) Other time points should then be slowed down in theatrical time to complement these. There should be a play of silence-against-the-frenetic – an internal tenseness throughout. Movements, even the movement of a hand, should be established by the actor. The play is implosive with outward gesture of word and movement acting against the internalism. Sets, screens, lights, etc., may also be exaggerated in size and scope the way the protagonist might see them. We, the audience, should experience some of this subjectivity by seeing the circumstances from the internal perspective of the lead character. The direction is "the dream of psychic revelation." As in "the dream" things seem sometimes more real than they do in our awake or waking reality. Therefore, while there is a naturalistic playing in "reality," it should take certain departures onto heightened-stylistic physical and verbal levels by the actors.

STATUE

Statue was presented in 1966 as part of a new play festival at La Mama E.T.C., 122 Second Avenue. It was performed by Marilyn Roberts and Ron Link.

Ron Link as Death addresses Marilyn Roberts (back to camera) at La Mama in "Statue"

STATUE

CHARACTERS:

DEATH – *The traditional 'Everyman' image of Death as seen in medieval religious drama, a black-hooded cloak, a Halloween mask of a death-skull (dead white) – white or black gloves.*

A YOUNG MAN – *Bathing trunks of a solid dark color. Sneakers.*

SCENE:

An expanse of land in an unknown country.

DEATH *lies stretched out on the ground – a statue-face is held over the skull-masked face.*

When the lights come up DEATH *removes the statue-face, holding it in his arms tightly, close to his bosom.*

He sits up.

DEATH   I . . . (*Pause.*) dreamt . . . (*Pause. Breathes heavily in and out four times.*) I held . . . (*Pause.*) your head . . . (*Pause. Breathes heavily in and out with heavy sounds three times.*) . . . in my hands. (*Pause.*) It was . . . (*Pause.*) . . . strangely . . . (*Pause.*) . . . detached. (*Pause.*) The hands . . . (*Pause.*) . . . that held . . . (*Pause.*) . . . it . . . were . . . amputated. (*Breathes heavily two times. Calls loudly.*) Wind. Air.

(*He lays the head on the ground. Loud sound of a car skidding and then crashing. Screams. A siren wails.*)

(*The* YOUNG MAN *enters running. He stops abruptly, frightened, his breath short from the running.*)

YOUNG MAN   Pardon me. Can you direct me to town?

DEATH   What?

YOUNG MAN . . . into town . . .

DEATH (*as if invaded*) Where have you come from?

YOUNG MAN I've been running . . . for a few hours . . . I think.
I find myself . . .

DEATH . . . Lost?

YOUNG MAN Yes. (*Pause.*) I find that I don't know where I am.
Where I am going. In which direction . . . to move. I have
been running. Back on the road . . . back there . . . there was
this accident. Three cars collided. There was the sound . . .
of a radio. I think I was unconscious. A flash of bright light.
Then . . .

DEATH . . . then what?

YOUNG MAN Blackness. Then this stretch of land. I began to
run. At first out of some kind of feeling of freedom. We had
been at the ocean . . . earlier. We had been swimming. A girl
. . . another . . .

DEATH You appear to be tired. Why not sit down with me for
a few moments.

YOUNG MAN No, I must continue to run. I think I see lights
ahead. The sign of a town . . . or a city . . .

DEATH (*almost to himself*) . . . or nothing.

YOUNG MAN (*looking out toward consciousness*) What?

DEATH The appearance of things. The appearance of things!
Illusion. And then . . . only a gradual disappearing into . . .
nothingness. Only an abyss. A bounding leap that goes from
nowhere to nowhere . . . that makes no sense. Existence.
Suddenly . . . one day . . . only the traces remain. The
shadows. Only the appearance . . . and then . . .

YOUNG MAN I think I see it.

DEATH What about me? Do you see me? Do you know . . .

YOUNG MAN I don't know who you are. An old beggar. A
recluse. Some kind of wanderer. (*Pause.*) I'm going.

DEATH Where?

YOUNG MAN (*pause*) Do you have a cigarette?

DEATH (*looking about*) No. I . . .

YOUNG MAN I am off then. Off I go . . .

(*Continues to run. Hold just long enough to recognize his aloneness—his misery.*)

DEATH (*half to the audience*) As you dress I will be waiting to take you to my bosom. You will maintain only the appearance of reality for a short period of time. And then? Then you will belong to me. Like an anxious lover, I await your last breath.

End.

FEBRUARY 14 TO FEBRUARY 26

ROBERT HEIDE'S
"MOON"

(A love-play written specially for the Cino St. Valentine Centennial.)

Performances: Tuesday thru Sunday 9 and 11 P.M. also Friday and Saturday at 1 A.M.

CAFE CINO   31 Cornelia Street   For Reservation CH 3-9753

1967 poster for "Moon" at the Caffè Cino

Moon

A PLAY IN ONE ACT

Moon was first presented by Joe Cino on St. Valentine's Day, February 14, 1967 at the Caffè Cino. It was directed by the author, with lighting design by Donald L. Brooks.

SALLY	Jane Buchanan
SAM	Victor Lipari
INGRID	Jacque Lynn Colton
HAROLD	Jim Jennings
CHRISTOPHER	John Gilman

A return engagement opened on January 10, 1968, at the Caffè Cino. It was again directed by the author, with lighting design by John P. Dodd and film sequence by Bill Stern.

SALLY	Linda Eskenas
SAM	Robert Frink
INGRID	Lucy Silvay
HAROLD	Jim Jennings
CHRISTOPHER	John Gilman

Left – First cast of "Moon" at the Caffè Cino in 1967: from left, Jim Jennings, Jaque Lynn Colton, Victor Lipari, Jane Buchanan

Right – John Gilman as Christopher and Robert Frink as Sam in "Moon" at the Caffè Cino

Left – Linda Eskenas passes a joint to Robert Frink in "Moon" at the Caffè Cino

Right – Lucy Silvay as Ingrid and Robert Frink as Sam in "Moon" at the Caffè Cino. Photos by James D. Gossage.

MOON

"Each day is grey and dreary,
But the night is bright and cheery."
           from "When the Moon Comes Over the Mountain"
                     sung by Kate Smith

ENVIRONMENT:

*The set should be a maximum of simplicity and symmetry meant only
to "represent" symbolically an apartment in the Village.*

The room and the objects in it are of a dark bilious color.

*In contrast, blazing white light like the high-power-intensity lighting
that might be used inside a microscope.*

*On the wall: a square of multicolored plastic with two transistor knobs
representing dials used in the play to turn sound on and off.*

*The usual areas and objects: windows (fourth wall), shelves, tables,
seating arrangements, kitchen facilities – a range, coffee pot, cups, etc. –
the outer hallway and door into the apartment.*

CHARACTERS:

SALLY – *A young woman in a loose-fitted black sweater and skirt. An
un-made-up appearance. Ballet slippers.*

SAM – *A young man. A turtleneck sweater. Baggy pants. Sandals or
slippers. He does not bother combing his hair.*

INGRID – *A girl dressed in the latest and most exaggerated of the
newest fashions with emphasis on breasts, legs, and shoulders. Flat
shoes. She enters and leaves wearing a black fur coat. Her dress is silver.
She carries a large handbag filled with pill boxes, makeup, poppers,*

anything imaginable.

HAROLD — *A tall young man. Dungarees. A leather jacket. Heavy workman's shoes that are coated with mud.*

CHRISTOPHER — *The young man upstairs. White pants. White shirt. A clean, scrubbed appearance. A look of innocence.*

The characters, with the exception of CHRISTOPHER *and* INGRID, *wear black.*

THE OPENING:

SAM *is reclining on the daybed, back to audience.*

SALLY *sits close by on a low stool.*

SALLY *breathes heavily, twitching and playing restlessly with her hands.*

She stares full force at SAM *as if she expected some movement on his part. She makes a quiet, gurgling sound in an attempt to attract attention.*

SAM *remains tight-faced, his head buried deeply into an open book. It is not discernible whether or not he is actually reading. He seems tense, withdrawn.*

Abruptly, SALLY *jumps up as though she were about to let out a scream.*

She paces wildly like a confined beast.

Her body seems to heave as if she felt trapped in it.

Quickly, she switches the phonograph on. Over the speaker system we hear "2,000 Light Years from Home," the Rolling Stones.

SALLY *dances wildly attempting to distract* SAM. *She soon becomes caught in a free-form dance. Perhaps she is rehearsing for a dance class.*

The record begins to repeat.

About one-quarter of the way through the second playing, SAM *rushes up and shuts off the machine with forceful intent and anger, as if he might begin to let loose a rage at any given moment.*

SAM (*loud, nervous*) There are times I'd like some . . . silence . . . around here . . . peace of mind . . . quiet!

(*Pause.*)

SALLY (*pacing back and forth*) I . . ha . . ha . . feel nervous . . .
fidgety myself. There's somehow a tenseness . . a heaviness
in the air. I don't know. I mean . . . (*Slight pause.*) . . I'm not
sure what . . Oh nothing . . I guess I'm just a little on edge . .
(*She sits down.*)

(*Pause.*)

SAM (*sitting*) What happened last night . . to us? I don't seem . .
I'm not able to remember . . anything.

SALLY (*getting up, confronting him*) You became violent . . . you
had consumed a great deal of liquor . . it was strange . . . I
mean — I had never known you to become so violent before.
You came at me and . . .

SAM Let's not talk about it. Let's go into something else . . .
some other subject . . . . . . something less . . strenuous.

SALLY (*moving further into him*) Maybe you're feeling guilty . . .

SAM I don't want to talk about it . . whatever it is . . you want
to go into it . . I don't! That's final . . whatever it is — I say!

SALLY Whatever what is? (*Pause.*) Look! Will you just talk to
me? Talk! (*Pause.*) Well, I can't take it!

SAM Take what?

SALLY Your silence. Your withdrawals. Your . . non-
communication. I'm fed up.

(*Pause.*)

SAM I'm sick . . I feel sick. I have a hangover. My head is bad.
All day I . . oh, what's the . .

SALLY Does that mean we can't talk . . say anything? (*Pause.*)
Maybe you're rather be alone. Have your withdrawal . . alone.
It feels stuffy in here. Hot. Close. I can't breathe.

(*Beginning to go out. Moves frenetically.*)

SAM (*gets up, pulls her down, slaps her*) Sit down! Relax your
complicated little anxieties. Have some coffee. Later we
will discuss whatever it is that needs discussing between

. . ourselves . . . between us. For now, let us discuss only everyday things. My mind . . . (*Slight pause.*) . . . . Later I will be . . prepared to face . . to look at the ugliness . . the abstractions . . . the truth of things. Here, smoke a cigarette.

(SALLY *puts a cigarette to her mouth and lights it nervously. Quickly, she extinguishes it.*)

SALLY (*getting up, moving downstage*) Today is not such a good day for me. I feel . . nervous . . ha . . ha. Sometimes I don't know what is happening to me either . . . . what is the matter with me. Something stirs up inside of me . . like some blind instinct I can't control . . . inside of me. I feel I could burst open . . explode. I get to feeling desperate. I want to run somewhere . . away . . I just don't know . . where . . out to the store . . to a movie.

SAM (*behind her*) Just try to remain calm . . try . . (*Slight pause.*)

SALLY (*more composed*) Let's begin again . . . a new conversation . . not relating to yesterday at all . . uh . . tell me . . . I mean . . let us forget those few moments of anxiety we just had . . begin again. Calmly. Can we? Can we begin again calmly? Yes. (*Pause. She puts her head into* SAM's *lap as she sits on the floor.*) What kind of day . . . tell . . what it was like . . earlier . . . what you did . . . what went on?

SAM (*reserved*) Just a day. The usual happenings. Statistical reports. Office rituals. Making additions and additions and pushing buttons . . then . .

(*Pause.*)

SALLY What?

SAM (*half to himself*) Oh, nothing . . . I was thinking about things not really adding up . . . anywhere . . in my head . . I mean . . my life.

SALLY (*jumping up*) Is that some personal inference to me? Are you meaning to infer . . . ?

SAM (*in a rage, grabbing her*) Look, will you shut up before I break your arm? Shut up, I said!

(*A pause.*)

(*A transition.*)

SALLY Did you see today's paper? Did you see the paper . . read the news today?

SAM I don't feel like looking at it . . . my head and all. I had two Bromo-Seltzers. What an idiotic party! Stupid people! "Hello, and what do you do with your life, young man? How are you justifying your existence?" Blah! Social events! (*A slight pause. He moves onto the floor.*) Anything in it?

SALLY What?

SAM . . in the paper . . anything in it . . . today's paper . . of interest . . that I should know . . be informed about?

SALLY (*circling around him*) Only the usual everyday chaos . . . problems. Someone shot five people . . in Texas . . I think it was. A young man. Eighteen. In a beauty parlor it was. Five women. He said he did it for the publicity, to get his name in the paper. He wanted to be a celebrity . . become recognized . . . I guess. Something about high food prices having something to do with the high cost of war or . . . something. Some paintings . . old masterpieces . . . were stolen.

(*Slight pause. She gets onto the floor with* SAM. *The lights go down.*)

The moon. There was a feature article on the moon. (*Laughing to herself.*) It's strange . . . funny . . I mean.

SAM What's funny?

SALLY (*playful*) I mean . . I was just thinking . . you can't really talk about the moon the same old way anymore like people used to in Shakespeare's plays and all. You can't say . . . with poetic emphasis . . "O Moon!" like in *Romeo and Juliet* or (*singing now, somewhat flatly*) "It's only a paper moon . . hanging over a cardboard sea" or (*more throaty, matronly, like Kate Smith*) "When the moon comes over the mountain" . . I'm really crazy about Kate Smith, aren't you? (*Low.*) Moo . . Moooooooooon. (*Dramatically, staring forward.*) "The cow jumped over the moon . . hey diddle . . diddle . . the cat

and his fiddle" . . . or something. The whole idea struck
me as just "funny" . . somehow . . I guess . . ridiculous.
Moon. Blah! I mean there it is . . really just there . . if yah
wanna look at it. No longer some romantic 1920s singsong
abstraction . . . something to aspire to . . to look at from a
great distance through a telescope. Wait. Here's a picture.
I'll show you. (*Goes to handbag and brings out a newspaper – sits
back down.*) Here. (*Pointing.*) I mean doesn't it look odd and
bumpy and all? See . . here! Right here is this diagram . . the
first moon city. Moon city. They plan to build it . . to live
there . . a whole lot of people . . . on the moon – eventually
. . soon . . in the not too distant future. And later, Mars . . .
Venus. Whole communities under a huge air-conditioned-
oxygenized plastic bubble! It's kinduv fantastic . . . I think .
. I mean living up there in space and all . . . I mean not that
we're not in space too . . right here . . already, now . . I mean
. . well . . people . . . the idea of it . . real people . . you and I
maybe . . and everybody . . living on the moon. It would be
like being a real pioneer . . up there. The first experimental
community . . . mmmm.

(*Bursting her dream bubble, he gets up. Brighter light.*)

SAM So when do we make reservations?

SALLY Huh?

SAM (*going back to his novel*) Reservations . . . numbskull. Plans?
Don't we have to make plane or rocket reservations . . or
something?

SALLY (*deflated, sad, bewildered by her own enthusiasms*) Yeah . . .
yes . . I guess so. (*Pause. Angrily.*) Probably it won't happen for
some time though . . . even . . in our own lifetime, I mean. A
moon community. Maybe it will.

SAM (*taking over the room like an actor*) Probably it will turn out
to be just another Levittown, U.S.A . . . . if "we" get there
first, before the Reds . . . if that matters anymore . . the
U.S.L.B.J. . . . with shopping centers, five and ten cent stores,
Grand Unions, bowling alleys . . . superhighways, movie

houses . . . . (*slightly deflated*) . . . beauty parlors.

(*Pause. There is a prolonged silence in which the two characters do not utter a sound. Finally* SAM *brings things back to some notion of reality.*)

My book . . . the book I was reading . . . did you see it?

SALLY (*looking*) What? Oh. Book. Uh . . no . . let me see . . .

SAM (*looking around the room*) I don't know where it is. (*Finds it.*) Ah, here it is!

(*He sits down, begins to read.*)

(*Pause.*)

SALLY Can we hear the radio?

SAM No! I'd rather it remain off, if you don't mind. I'd rather listen to just . . . silence.

SALLY Okay. Okay. Don't yell! (*Slight pause. Nervous.*) Would you like some coffee?

SAM If you're gonna make some . . . if you're having some . .

SALLY (*in kitchen area*) Is the book good?

SAM What?

SALLY (*looking for a confrontation*) Damn you. Will you listen! I said – is the book you are reading any good?

SAM It's okay.

SALLY (*angry*) Well, why are you reading it if it's just okay? Haven't you any better way to live out your existence?

SAM How?

SALLY Mmmm. I don't know. You said once you wanted to paint a picture or something.

SAM (*ignoring her last statement*) No. I mean it's good . . . I guess. (*Slight pause.*) Anyhow, I know how it ends.

SALLY (*curious*) How?

SAM (*perturbed*) How?

SALLY (*demanding*) How?

SAM (*scratching his head*) Mmmmm. Well . . . . you really wanna hear? Well . . . this couple have been making it, see. I mean both of them are married . . . I mean each to someone else like; but they are having this affair see . . with one another, that is. Get it?

SALLY Yeah. Dope!

SAM So they are driving back from this weekend on the French Riviera, St. Tropez, I think. It's French . . the book . . . I mean it takes place, see, in France. Well, the whole book is about how they can't . . either one of them . . have an affair . . even . . anymore.

SALLY What?

SAM Anyhow, they are suffering from a kind of modern metaphysical boredom . . and all . . living in an increasingly mechanized and alienated world. They feel alienated from one another . . alienated even in themselves . . see . . each individual self. They can't get together . . . . yet they can't really be apart either. He . . the man, is married to this famous chanteuse named Cleo who is never at home 'cause she has this . . her career . . and so he feels, existentially speaking, that he is in her eyes – like an object, like an old table or chair – very Sartrean – I mean, they talk a lot about life being one big nothing and all . . . in the book . . . (*Slight pause.*) . . or was it Heidegger.

SALLY (*under her breath*) – Heidegger.

SAM See, he, the main character, is a philosophy student. So, anyhow, he doesn't feel related to this wife who is so obsessed . . uptight . . having this "overneed" for her career. She sings these very sorrowful songs . . .

(SALLY *jumps up making a screeching sound. Looks stage front. Looks into the fourth-wall mirror.*)

. . . and, when she's not doing that, she is looking in the mirror – checking out her image and all. Well, she doesn't like sex either . .

SALLY (*loudly*) Who? Who?!

SAM Cleo . . even though she's supposed to be some sex image to her fans. They write her dirty suggestive letters which she, in turn, answers. (*Sally mimics letter-writing.*) See. It makes Henri . . . that's our hero's name . . feel disgusted . . even though he never brings the subject forth . . out into the open. So Henri takes up with Françoise . . . see. She's married . . kinduv . . to this uncle of hers who's this novelist . . older. Anyhow, he knows about the affair. In fact, he encourages it. See, he's bored too . . with everything.

SALLY (*worried*) Then what happens?

SAM (*running amok*) Well, it gets complicated 'cause everywhere they go . . well . . it gets more and more frenetic . . the tension . . the plot . . hysterical . . . and Françoise thinks she is pregnant by some oriental houseboy too.

(*He grabs* SALLY. *They play out the "game" of the novel fully. They mimic driving a car together.*)

Well . . . being bored and all she drives off on this highway into this Mack truck . . (SALLY *screams.*) . . in a red Porsche – sort of like James Dean. It ends with a double funeral where Chloe sings "Chanson d'Morte" . . "The Song of Death" . . .

(*Lights down. We hear the voice of Cleo singing in French over the loudspeaker with full orchestra. This goes on for one full minute.*)

(*Lights up.*)

. . but everyone is bored even there too. I mean, what does death mean if you're really hip and all. Anyhow, to make a long story short . . Cleo meets the uncle . . at the funeral, which the uncle paid for . . heh . . heh . . and they grab hands . . .

(SALLY *and* SAM *grab hands. Hollywood music ensues loudly. They act out a Hollywood ending.*)

. . touch one another. They feel . . . well . . through the death of Françoise and Henri they have a reawakening . . a kinduv catharsis into . . being able to "really" feel and all. You know, like maybe things are not so bad after all? So anyway, they go off and make it or something. I mean it ends on a kinduv positive note . . y'know . .

(Music off.)

. . but not too positive . . he he . . he. Hey, are you listening?

SALLY I thought you said you just read the end?

SAM *(in a fury)* Yeah, I did . . but I read this review of it in the *Village Voice*. I mean, they gave the whole story and all. That's what made me wanna read it. They said it was . . . well . . subtle in its exploration of character relationship . . that's what made me wanna read it. I mean . . *(Intense. Angry.)* . . people feel alienated. They don't know how to get together. Oh, Christ . . . I don't know! Don't ask me questions about what I'm reading. I lost my goddamn place!

SALLY *(dreamy)* Maybe they'll make a movie out of it.

SAM Yeah . . they are already with Jean Seberg and Marcello . . no . . it's not him . . somebody like him . . Belmondo . . . no. It's . . what the hell is his name? Trig . . Trig . . . . . Trigonet . . Jean-Louis Trigonet . . I wish I had a name like that. Yeah.

(Movie soundtrack music pours forth. The lighting goes kaleidoscopic.)

Brigitte Bardot will be Cleo and maybe Charles Boyer for the uncle. Ha ha. A super-technicolor, panavistic . . spectacle . . in pornovision!

(On the word "pornovision" SAM and SALLY roll around on the floor together in mock copulation. They breathe heavily, remaining on the floor. They make sounds, then separate, exhausted, still on the floor.)

SALLY *(entering movieland)* Jean-Louis Trigonet. How do you spell that? Wasn't he in "The Sleeping Car Murder"? Didn't we see that at the Eighth Street . . or was it the Garrick?

SAM T-r-i-n-t-i-g-n-a-n-t. Did we see that? Did we see that one?

SALLY Yeah . . . I remember . . you fell asleep in it.

SAM Oh, was it good?

SALLY Okay . . . I guess . . . . it's not my type of thing.

SAM Who got murdered?

SALLY Murdered?

SAM Yeah. "Sleeping Car Murder." Murder mystery. Who got murdered?

SALLY Six people . . I think . . two homosexual lovers plot the whole thing to get this lottery check from this actress . . Simone Signoret. She is in love with one of them . . not knowing he's gay . . or knowing . . and thinking she can change his direction . . I don't remember which. Ha.

SAM (*moving restlessly*) Oh, yeah . . and one of them works for the cops or something . . as a detective . . . . and he's working to try to solve the case!

SALLY Then . . you weren't sleeping?

SAM Well, partly.

SALLY (*running after him, tickling him*) How does it end? I'll *murder* you, you ass! How does it end? Tell me.

SAM (*rolling onto the floor*) Stop it! Cut it out! Stop!

SALLY (*straddling him*) They don't make it. They're gonna live happily ever after on some South Sea island in a rose-covered cottage on Simone Signoret's money . . but they don't make it . . they get caught and they don't make it. Ha! Ha!

SAM (*half sarcasm, half humor, getting up*) Tough! Nobody makes it, bitch.

SALLY (*serious now, angry*) They don't? Why not?

SAM (*flying into fantasy*) 'Cause I say so and I'm the President and I have the power and I'm gonna blow up the whole world anyway. Blow it up. (*Throwing imaginary hand grenades.*) Boom. BOOM! Booom.

SALLY (*confronting*) You're a paranoid schizophrenic living in Greenwich Village with delusions of grandeur and an inclination toward anticipating disaster out of every situation. Ha. How's that for a penny analysis?

SAM (*furious*) I could be Jesus Christ and you wouldn't know the difference.

SALLY (*in a full-fledged argument*) He was another paranoid too.

SAM Says who?

SALLY (*moving in circles around* SAM) Albert Schweitzer, baby . .
in this book I read – "A Psychiatric Study of Jesus." He said
there is a lot of evidence to support that old J.C. may have
been another psychotic with another Christ complex out to
save the whole world just like you . . or maybe destroy it.

SAM (*throwing his arms around her as if they were about to ascend
into space*): Boom. Boom. Boom. Then we could go live . . .
pioneer on the old green cheese moon.

SALLY (*breaking off, sitting*) Ah, who cares. I'm sick of the whole
world anyhow. Why pretend anything else?

(*Pause.*)

SAM You sure you read that book correctly?

SALLY Whadahyamean?

SAM I mean you're always reading things into things. Your
imagination. Your fantasy projection transferences. (*No reply.
Pause.*) How about lighting a joint?

(*Goes to kitchen, where he gets joint.*)

SALLY (*after him in the kitchen*) Go ahead! You light it!
Transcend existence. Catatonize yourself. What do I care?

SAM (*grabbing her, pulls her down*) What!?

SALLY Go ahead! Break my arm too.

SAM Nobody's breaking your arm. (*Slight pause.* SALLY *waves her
arm at* SAM *in jest and anger.*) Let's sit down and keep quiet . . .
shut up . . for a while.

SALLY (*a last stand*) You'd like to avoid all communications
with me . . . just blow pot all day long . . reach Nirvana or
something . . who knows what or where you want to get to?
The moon. Dreams. Movies. I'm sick of it all. It's all just "*lies*"
anyway. (*Hysterical.*) Lies! (*Screaming.*) Lies!

SAM . . . Now, calm down. You're having one of your free-
floating anxiety attacks again. Just calm down, sweets . . love
. . . valentine.

SALLY (*biting*) At least it's not free-floating paranoia or simple schizophrenia or some swimming-in-a-sea-of-ambiguity . . like you.

SAM Your terminology is really flying. You sound like some coffee-klatch in the dorm after Psych I . . at NYU. The girl who's always waving her hand in the last row, who knows all the answers but none of the . . . Now, just calm yourself. Here. (*Hands her a joint.*) Light it. (*She does.*) It's not the answer – I know – any more than LSD, STP, or anything else . . . or going to the moon, but it does manage to keep me calm . . sometimes.

(*He sits.*)

My nerves. My body is still depressed from all that rotten alcohol we drank last night. Put on some music . . . on the machine. Indian.

(*Gets onto the floor in yoga position.*)

I want to meditate . . concentrate . . groove . . with something . . spiritual.

SALLY (*standing over him*) Do I have to meditate?

(*She puts on Indian raga music. They sit, eyes closed, attempting meditation. After a moment*)

I can't concentrate on anything today. Somehow . . I . .

SAM Shut up! Meditate . . or just keep your trap shut! I can't talk anymore!

(*They remain silent, listening to the music, passing a joint back and forth to one another.*)

(*After a long moment, INGRID and HAROLD are heard by the audience moving down the corridor outside the apartment. They are pushing and shoving one another, physically close to violence.*)

INGRID (*berating, loudly, trumpeting*) What kind of people don't put their names on the bell . . I ask you?! (*She passes back and forth looking at various doorways.*) I think what they told us was 4-R . . that means rear! These stairs are killing me. Maybe we should go back down . . go have a drink somewhere by

ourselves. Oh, wait. Here. (*Looking.*) There's nothing more
embarrassing than knocking on the wrong door. (*She pulls out
a nose popper and begins sniffing, trying to get higher.*) That man
was naked and I think he was having sex in there . . with a
boy, too. Sex has a very decisive, odoriferous smell I tell you.
Don't you have anything to say? (*Moving close.*) I suppose you
would like to have joined in or something, into the sexual act,
but yet you can't raise it up when it comes to me.

(INGRID *reaches into her handbag. She pulls out a pillbox and begins
gulping pills. She offers one to* HAROLD. *He refuses.*)

Now try to compose yourself. (*Slight pause.*) Act natural.
Try not to indicate . . to show . . that we are having marital
difficulties. It's not in good taste to wear your problems
out in the open for public consumption, as it were . . this
being a social situation. Now try to remember these simple
rules . . Oh . . ha . . ha . . Here we are. Hello. Hello. (*Loud.
Demanding.*) Anybody home? Hello. Shhh. Shh.

SALLY (*disrupted*): Who's that?

SAM (*trance-like*): What? . . Shhhh . . Quiet! I'm thinking . . .

(SALLY, *realizing a presence, gets up and turns off the music. Puts on
ballet slippers.*)

INGRID (*a false cheerfulness*) Uh . . . . Hi − You . . . uh . . .
left your door open. Can we come in? (*Examining the place
suspiciously.*) You shouldn't leave your door open . . you know,
with all the murders, rapes, and robberies going on . . . in the
city . . uh . . heh . . . mmmm.

(*An awkward silent heavy tension takes over the room. The two
couples stalk one another.*)

SALLY (*polite, pulling herself together, breaking the freeze*) Oh . . .
. well . . come in . . . sit down . . wherever you can . . there's
not much room. Let me have your coat.

INGRID Yes. (*Removes her coat and scarf.* SALLY *disposes of it quickly.
Goes to* HAROLD.) Harold, your jacket!

HAROLD (*staring downward, a tight lip*) I prefer to keep it on . .

thank you.

INGRID A cold. Harold is afraid of catching a cold, aren't you, Harold? (*No answer. A false merriment.*) I said to Harold . . I bet you people forgot about having us over . . . . . . er . . the party . . last night? Remember? Ha . . ha . . Well, we almost didn't come. (*An awkward pause.*) We had your address . . . your phone number. We were gonna call . . . first. We tried. Didn't we, honey? Didn't we try?

HAROLD (*dull, not listening*) Yeah.

INGRID (*anxious, somewhat terrified*) You've had your phone disconnected. I said to Harold . . . I bet you forgot. It was just a casual, meaningless suggestion on your part. Just drop by. And here we are . . Heh . . mmm. (*Slight pause. To* SAM.) Harold would rather have his face in the TV or be screwing nuts and bolts into his machines. It was my decision to venture out. (*Cornering* SALLY.) You can still renege . . . shoo us off . . . . if you want to be alone. Tee . . hee.

SALLY (*trying to place her guests in her mind*) Oh . . uh . . no . . uh . . we don't mind. We were just . . sitting . . listening to some music . . weren't we? Why . . uh . . don't you sit . . . ?

INGRID I'll just sit down . . . . (*Accidentally falling.*) . . . . Ooooooooooooooo!

HAROLD (*half to himself*) The clumsy never succeed.

INGRID (*getting up, menacing*) What did you say?

HAROLD I said . . "The clumsy never succeed" . . . just an old saying from my mother.

INGRID (*angry, staring long and hard*) Your mother! She certainly didn't teach *you* anything . . about success . . in the *real* world.

(HAROLD *moves toward her with violent intent. Abruptly, she switches her attitude to the coquette, realizing she is with "others."*)

What an interesting and cute apartment you have. Ha ha. Very bizarre. Very interesting. I'm sure our turning up is a complete surprise . . I said to Harold . . it was a casual suggestion . . on your part. (*Desperate.*) Lots of people write

their names and addresses on little pieces of paper and
hand them to people they meet . . at parties . . never really
expecting . . acknowledgement . . or a visitation.

SALLY It doesn't matter. We were very drunk. Part of the
evening is a complete blur . . . in both of our minds. Yes?

(HAROLD *walks blindly into* SALLY. *She stares full force at him, then
breaks it off.*)

Something happened which we don't remem . . ber.

(*This last statement is followed by a long, dead silence in which
the four characters stare blankly, bewilderedly at one another. An
uncomfortable tension takes over the room.*

INGRID (*gazing at* HAROLD *and* SALLY): Er . . . . . ah.

SALLY (*snapping her fingers nervously*) We . . uh . . were having
some coffee. (*Pause.*) Would anybody like some coffee . . or
something?

HAROLD (*following her*) Yeah.

INGRID (*nervous – trying to make conversation*) Harold doesn't
say much . . really . . in company. (*Cornering, advancing toward*
SALLY *in kitchen.*) We were just married . . . a year it is. We're
just beginning to get used to one another . . . understand
our position in relationship to one another as to who has the
upper hand and all that stuff. He's a little shy . . . awkward . . .
ha . . ha . . in a social situation.

(*Slight pause. Leaves kitchen. Sits next to* SAM *on sofa.*)

What time did you people leave last night's festivities?

SALLY (*moving away from* HAROLD's *steady advances*) Time? What
. . time? I'm not sure . .

INGRID (*angry, sarcastic*) We left early. Harold got sick . . mixing
the drinks. Didn't you, Harold? Didn't you get sick last night?

HAROLD (*with controlled violence, a smirk across his face*) Yeah.

INGRID That's why we left early. I mean as opposed to staying
on and on. Harold feels . . . . that it's better to leave before
things . . . people . . become decadent as they very often do at
parties. He wouldn't like it . . (*She moves closer to* SAM, *putting*

her arm around his neck seductively.) I mean . . . if somebody
tried to screw . . . I mean . . rape me . . . made advances or
anything. (*More excited.*) Harold is capable . . . I mean Harold
might . . it is within his capacity to murder someone. Didn't
you say you might murder someone, Harold . . if someone . .
I mean . . made advances on me . . on my person . . at a party
. . or someplace?

HAROLD Yeah.

INGRID (*going into her purse*) I carry this tear-gas gun. My Aunt
Emma gave it to me . . She sent it through the mail all the
way from Kansas . . that's where I'm from . . mmm. You
never know about men . . . she says . . in New York City. (*She
gets up and pulls out gun, pointing it bluntly at* SAM.) Yah wanna
see it?

HAROLD (*grabbing her – they wrestle for the gun*) Gimme! . . . that!

INGRID Harold! You're hurting me. It might go off. Harold!

HAROLD (*twisting her arm, throwing her down*) Sit down!

INGRID My arm!

SALLY (*ignoring the situation, trying to remain cool*) I think coffee is
ready.

SAM (*quietly*) You people like music?

INGRID (*going up to* HAROLD) We should apologize.

HAROLD (*breaking from her*) I'll do my own apologizing if there's
any to be done. (*To the rest of the room.*) What my wife, Ingrid,
is trying to communicate to you all is that I have . . a kind of
. . violent personality . . an uncontrollable temper. When I get
worked up . . . .

(*Pause. He sits down. Lights go dim.*)

You see, I was a Marine . . in the Marines. (*Slight pause.*) Of
course . . even as a kid . . . well . . I'm not sure what it is.
(*Slight pause.*) Back in Texas where I come from . . . a man was
murdered . . . I mean to say that I don't conceal any longer
this nightmare truth. I loved him . . I guess. He was my
buddy . . in the Marines and after. We went everywhere . .

together. Well, one night . . . we shared a double bed . . I . .
(*Slight pause*,) He was asleep. I was fooling . . kidding around.
I put a pillow over his face. He had asthma or something
. . respiration trouble. Anyway, in the fooling around . . .
he stopped breathing. I took the pillow off his face. His eyes
were open . . staring . . at me. Later there was an inquisition,
you see. I was set free. It was decided that what he had had
was a heart attack. Somehow, in me . . . I knew that . .

INGRID (*jumping up abruptly*) Oh . . . Stop it! Stop telling
everyone you meet that morbid and ludicrous story. You
don't know . . you can't be absolutely certain that it wasn't
an accident. You said that he had a heart condition . . or
something. Why continue to implicate yourself any further.
This wallowing in guilt.

HAROLD (*still "in" the story, moves up*) There is . . . there was . .
an intention . . . somewhere . . in me. There must have been.
I don't understand.

INGRID (*quickly, going at him like an attorney that is onto a victim*)
We understand! It is obvious . . . psychologically obvious . .
a clear deduction that you were in love with this man . .
that because of convention . . this love . . . you could not
consummate it. It turned then into hatred. You hated yourself
and him for remaining unfulfilled . . repressed.

HAROLD (*loud*) Shut up!

INGRID (*moving in tightly*) Why lie! You can't express . . the truth.
So you choose me with all my convenient sexual fears to share
your guilt . . to continue to support your image of manhood . . .
punishing me for what was done to you by your family. I'm tired
of playing the role of mother-substitute. I'm . . . .

HAROLD Shut up, I say . . . you bitch!

(*He grabs her throat, pulls her to her knees, and begins to strangle her
with intent to kill. We hear* INGRID *make a gurgling sound.* SAM *and
SALLY watch frozen in terror.*)

SAM This will have to stop!

(SAM *pulls* HAROLD *off of* INGRID, *bodily forcing him to yield his grip*

They are on the verge of a fistfight.)

You will both have to leave . . . just *leave!*

INGRID *(still on the floor)* I'm sorry. Please. Let us stay. Just for a moment. Till we pull ourselves together.

(An awkward silence follows. INGRID *stays on the floor for a long while. Finally she gets up. Goes to kitchen. Gets a drink. Sits back on sofa.)*

Harold has vivid fantasies. He goes to an analyst three times a week. These stories . . he . . prefabricates them to bring attention to himself. There is no basis in truth to what has been said.

*(*SAM *moves to the phonograph.)*

SAM *(nervous)*: Do . . uh . . you like music? I'll put on a record.

SALLY Not now.

INGRID *(sitting nervously, humiliated)* Yes . . play it . . anything.

(They listen through a three-minute record – Dave Clark 5, "Do You Love Me?" During the record the lights go up. INGRID *swallows about seven different pills.* HAROLD *and* SALLY *stare at one another.* HAROLD *is attracted.* SALLY *is strangely drawn to his look.* SAM *begins to do a shaking rock and roll dance. Each character is caught in his own private world, lost, lonely, bewildered. At the end of the record,* SALLY *puts on her coat and hat.)*

SALLY *(quickly)* Er . . ah . . ha . . ha. Would . . uh . . you all excuse me for a moment? I think there is something I forgot to get at the store.

(She leaves.)

INGRID *(desperate)* Where is she going?

SAM *(half-dazed)* She said to the store. She sometimes leaves abruptly.

INGRID Her leaving seemed peculiar just then.

*(*INGRID *looks at* HAROLD. *He is on the sofa lying down, legs outstretched, reading* SAM's *book.* INGRID *gets onto the floor herself. She heaves convulsively, making sounds. She has taken too many*

drugs. The room spins in her head. She gets half up after a long moment.)

I don't know. I'm not sure why . . we came here. Harold . . we must go . . home . . now. (*Getting her things.*) I feel a sudden panic seizing hold of me here. (*Going up to* SAM.) I am sorry. Perhaps we will see you again . . sometime. Harold. Leave one of our cards. (*They put on their things and proceed to leave.*) You invited us from the party. (*She menaces* SAM *a final time.*) I said to Harold earlier that you had probably forgotten. Goodbye. Come along, Harold.

(SAM *waves half-heartedly with his hand, his back turned to the audience. There is a long moment in which he walks about the room examining its various sections. He goes to the phonograph: but does not play it. He walks to fourth-wall window area staring straight down. We hear traffic sounds. Finally he lies down, exhausted.*)

(*Enter slowly –* CHRISTOPHER *– in white pants and a sweater. He carries a loaf of bread in a pan.*)

CHRISTOPHER Er . . . ah . . . hello.

(*No reply.* SAM *is asleep. Finally, startled by a strange presence,* SAM *jolts up, confronting* CHRISTOPHER.)

We . . . my friend and I . . . we made some bread . . upstairs. We just moved in. We had nothing to do today . . so we made . . . we made some bread. (*Slight pause.*) There is a funny smell in here. Well, I'll just leave it then. (*Begins to leave.*)

SAM (*puzzled*) No. Wait.

CHRISTOPHER Yes?

SAM (*goes to him*) Did you want something?

CHRISTOPHER (*quietly*) No.

SAM You moved in . . . upstairs . . . in the vacant rooms?

CHRISTOPHER Yes.

SAM What is your name?

CHRISTOPHER Christopher. My friend is Joe. He's asleep.

SAM Oh. (*Pause.*) Would you like some wine . . or coffee?

CHRISTOPHER (*hesitant*) No. I must get back. I'm a painter . .
see. I want to sort of get to bed early so I can get up . . . .
in the morning . . to get the light. The skylight . . . . the
light here . . . . upstairs . . is the reason we took the space
. . it being on the top floor. I need it for my painting. The
daylight. Well, as I said . . I wanted to bring you down
one of the loaves . . . we made two . . . see who was living
underneath . . . introduce myself . . . . So . . .

SAM What do you paint?

CHRISTOPHER (*moving about the room, intense*) Circles mostly. Just
circles. You'll come up and see them sometime. I'm kinduv
obsessed with circles, see. They are meant . . I guess . . to
represent . . ha . . ha . . the earth, sun, moon, and all the other
planets in the heavens, the solar system. I use many brilliant
colors, electric colors, red, green . . yellow . . . they hurt your
eyes if you look at them too long. (*Pause.*) Well . . we heard
the music. We thought you might like some. We'll see you
again . . . . come back down . . maybe . . tomorrow you'll
meet my friend.

(*Exit* CHRISTOPHER. *There is a moment in which* SAM *stares at the
bread. He picks it up, putting it in the breadbox.*)

(*Enter* SALLY.)

SAM (*after a moment, softly*) Where did you go?

SALLY I don't know . . I just had to leave . . get out . . get some
air. I brought back some milk. (*Puts paper bag she is carrying
down.*)

SAM They've gone.

SALLY Yes, I see.

SAM I don't remember ever having met them. Do you? . . . at
that party?

Sally: No . . I . . (*Pause.*) I don't want to talk about them . . .
now.

SAM What is it you want to do?

SALLY I don't know.

SAM What were you thinking about . . what were you doing .
. what happened to you while you were out? Tell me. Talk to
me. Philosophize . . . anything. I feel . . . .

SALLY (*entering the game*) Oh . . not much happened . . really.
I walked around the same block two . . three . . times. I
thought . . if only there were someplace to go . . to . . to run
away to. I thought . . I would like to leave this city . . go back
to St. Louis where I came from – all the time knowing . .
inside . . I could never go back there anymore. Backwards. I
said to myself . . there is nowhere to go . . nowhere left for
you to run to. I passed by the newsstand . . on the square. The
headline on the evening paper glared up at me saying . . "A
Man Walks on the Moon." (*She laughs.*) It struck me as being
funny somehow. Then I ran back here . . right then . . right
away. That's all.

SAM (*lightly, in a matter-of-fact manner*) One day . . I suppose . .
as you said earlier tonight . . . there will be this community
. . . a community of men who will be living on the moon in a
plastic bubble . . but it will not seem either strange or funny at
all . . to anyone who will just . . be . . there – in that situation.
And things will not be that much different from what they
are . . right here . . right now. The truth is, none of us will
really ever know anything about the deeper, darker mysteries
of existence. We will never know . . never . . never really be
certain about what it is we really are searching for in this life
anyway . . . in this world. The endless questions . . thoughts
. . that well up deep down inside of us. As of now . . at this
point in time and space we remain uncertain . . except for
having reached the moon – maybe. Hallelujah!

SALLY (*holding him – a determined, firm attitude*) But if we could
be certain . . maybe . . someday . . of something more . .
than just the beating of our hearts. Listen! (*She puts her hand
to her breast.*) Boom. Boom. Boom. One day they will just
stop pounding . . but for now . . . they just go on . . and on.
Boom. Boom. Boom.

TOGETHER Boom.

Boom.

Boom.

Boom.

Blackout.

JOE CINO INVOCATION

Joe Cino Invocation featuring H. M. Koutoukas was performed on October 31, 1969, at the Elgin Theater as part of a festival of plays.

Joe Cino

John Gilman with H. M. "Harry" Koutoukas

JOE CINO INVOCATION
OCTOBER 31, 1969

A MONOLOGUE TO BE READ BY WHOEVER IS PLAYING JOE CINO

The past is already past and yet weighs heavily everywhere upon us. The psychic now is everywhere and forever and nowhere. 1970 is the new beginning . . . of evolution. Prior to this what had been called evolution has been in reality – involution. Let us begin. Let us bow our heads in non-prayer. Let us look inside to the source – deep. Inner.

(*A pause.*)

A moment of silence please.

Saint Cino, the little Saint of the Theatre – Merry Christmas flying by beyond Eden, beyond Oz, never-never-land Cornelia Street. In death we salute your life. As in life you saluted – bargained with a shadowy death, Saint Cino!

Saint Cino naming names:

Jon Torrey

Joseph Cino

Michael Smith

Harry

Harry

H. M. Koutoukas

Ronnie Link

Dick Barr

Charles Lubier
Bob Costa
John Gruen
Edward Albee
Jeff Weiss
Johnny
Johnny Dodd
Freddie
Freddie Herko
Al
Al Carmines
Ellen
Ellen Stewart
Lise-Beth-Talbot
Storey Talbot
Storey-Lise-Beth
Jacque Colton
Linda Eskenas
Lanford
Lanford Wilson
Marshall Mason
Neil Flanagan
Bob Patrick
Robert O'Connor
Kenny Burgess
Shirley Stoller
Robert Dahdah
Bernadette Peters
Mary Boylan
John Gilman

James Jennngs
Victor Lipari
Marie-Claire Charba
Billy Hoffman
Sam Shepard
Robert Heide
Bob Heide
Warren Finnerty
Helen
Helen Hanft
Tom Eyen
Charles Stanley
Ondine
David Starkweather
Lee Paton
Donald Brooks
Don Kvares
Hope Stansbury
Magie Dominic
Tiny Tim
Kate Smith
Mabel Mercer
Maria Callas
Russ Columbo
Bill Haislip
Lucy Silvay
Doric Wilson
Bob Brown
Josef Bush

[*Harry — add other "special" names at your discretion.*]

End – God Bless the crystal madness – realist - call upon St.
Cino the saint of those who were not commercial

Here, have a coffee – cappu-cino with colored sprinkles –
whipped cream – ham on rye with pimento – and cheese –
bring me in an all-blond Nazi play – forget the confrontation
bit – don't let them get in through the door – find your
actoring talent at Rikers; they are the best. Get that black
bitch off the fucking door – she's giving me dark looks – do
whatever you're gonna do and leave me out of it. Get your
ass over here with a play . . . your opening date will be
February 14th – and I will die shortly afterward on – after
Easter. The Easter be-in-Central Park. Asbury Park – on
the Tilt-a-Whirl – Harry – *Life Magazine* is photographing
"The Bed" but I'll believe it when it happens. Go over to
Ellen's. She wants the whole bit! Keep those freaks away.
It's Christmas, St.Valentine, Hallowe'en, Happy Blessed
New Year. Go to the A&P and get two pounds of American
cheese - three boxes of Ritz Crackers – Wesson Oil – Yes!
Magic Time – Ladies and Gentlemen . . . . Saint Cino –
little Saint – I will see you again in . . .

(*Pause.*)

1971 – That's your release date after you . . . leave me alone!
Do your own thing. Do it by yourself. Alone – what you
have to do you kukaya bitch – and get it on stage. They want
to close us up again. Turn it lower, lower. Josie's freaking out
upstairs again. The music's too much for her. I love you; but
I must go. Do your work and shut up. Joe. Joe. Stop sending
nasty notes to Michael – he really loves you – I think. He
will not forget . . . Saint Jude – Saint of the Impossible. Hey
Jude! Hey Cino! Saint Cino – Saint of the Magic Crystal
Cobra Cult – the impossible . . Magic Time. Do you believe
in magic?

(*Into the audience.*)

Do you believe in MAGIC?

(*Repeat.*)

Do you believe in Magic?

Caricature of John Gilman shooting the Mongols — cover image by Peter Bramley Cloud Studio from "New American Plays, Vol. 4," edited by William M. Hoffman

ROBERT HEIDE, a fellow playwright friend of mine since the legendary days of the Caffe Cino, is a poet of the silences between words in human conversation. Funny and bone-chilling, his plays can make you laugh and feel intensely uncomfortable within a brief stretch of time. In *Moon* a hippie Greenwich Village couple banter and argue until relief comes with a visit from the young man upstairs bearing homemade bread. We don't know why the loaf of bread is significant, except somehow we in the audience are moved to tears. In *The Bed* two men wrestle with their anxieties, fear, and anger and also try to manipulate each other to get out of a bed they cannot bear to leave. As our own lives become more and more alienated by the digital age that we have become increasingly confined to, it is worthwhile to look at a prophet of our human isolation: Robert Heide.

— William M. Hoffman, editor, teacher, Caffe Cino playwright, author of the Broadway play "As Is" and the opera "Ghosts of Versailles" with composer John Corigliano

AT WAR WITH
THE MONGOLS

A TRAGIC FARCE IN ONE ACT

At War with the Mongols was first presented on July 30, 1970, by Eric Krebs, Jeanne Ford, and Philip Cohen at Brecht West, 61 Albany Street, New Brunswick, New Jersey. It was directed by the author with the following cast:

MEG	Linda Eskenas
MICK	John Gilman

Lighting and sound design were by Philip Cohen, set design by F. P. Cuneo.

Following this engagement the play opened with the same cast on August 14, 1970, at the Cubiculo in New York City.

On December 7, 1970, a third production was offered at the Old Reliable Theatre Tavern in the East Village (on a double bill with a new version of Robert Heide's *The Bed* directed by Neil Flanagan). It was directed by the author with the following cast:

MEG	Francine Middleton
MICK	John Gilman

Cesar Geraldo

*John Gilman and Linda Eskenas in "At War with the
Mongols"—originally entitled "Mongol Invasion of U. S.
Mainland"—in New Brunswick, New Jersey*

At War with the Mongols

for Linda Eskenas and John Gilmant

CHARACTERS:

MEG – *A girl with long straight hair and angry features wearing a red turtleneck pullover, dungarees, bare feet.*

MICK – *A ravaged young man wearing a red, white, and blue T-shirt, navy bells, bare feet.*

A NOTE CONCERNING DIRECTION:

Direction should examine the darker aspects of the situation, inner and outer; but should also focus on humor levels that go *against* the essential despair of the existential predicament. Example: soldiers in a muddy foxhole finding and making jokes as the enemy closes in. Some of these feelings can be discovered in and through examining anger-games; some through Laurel and Hardy yin-and-yang slapstick. The awareness of absurdity is the key to the humanity of the protagonists.

> *"Disillusionment in living is the finding out nobody agrees with you not those that are and were fighting with you. Disillusionment in living is the finding out nobody agrees with you not those that are fighting for you. Complete disillusionment is when you realize that no one can for they can't change. The amount they agree is important to you until the amount they do not agree with you is completely realized by you. Then you say you will write for yourself and strangers, you will be for yourself and strangers and this then makes an old man or an old woman of you.*

*"This is then one thing, another thing is the perfect joy of finding some
one, any one really liking something you are liking, making, doing, being.
This is another thing and a very pleasant thing, sometimes not a pleasant
thing at all. That depends on many things, on some thing.*

from "The Making of Americans" by Gertrude Stein

SCENE:

*A room in an abandoned house by the sea. There is a squared-off area
which represents – The Room. A bare stage floor. The floor is made up
of weathered boardwalk lumber. This wood is also used intermittently
on the wall areas and nailed closed over one large (stage center) window
area. Fishnet covers the top of the stage, creating an artificial ceiling.
Dark musty colors pervade.*

*The wall perimeters of the set are lined and covered with odd debris
picked up on the beach, from garbage dumps: found objects such as
smashed car doors, a 1940s auto grill, rubber tires, used and battered
restaurant signs, old rusted Coca-Cola, Mission Orange, and cigarette
signs, a wooden radio, bookshelves filled with magazines and yellowed
newspapers, a Shirley Temple poster, a kewpie doll head, a child's
midget auto, bits of broken mirror, and empty boxes. A built-in closed-
door wall cabinet containing small-size soda bottles, potato chips, hard
candy, and sugar cubes.*

Ancient Oriental percussion music ensues for three minutes.

*The actors walk onto a dimly lit stage during this musical interlude
and immediately sit in deep-staring straightforward meditation postures
assuming the attitude of Angry Buddha. They maintain this angry
stillness.*

*Another record played full volume follows – Murray Head,
"Superstar." (Other choices for this spot might be "Reflections of My
Life" by the Marmalade, "Communications Breakdown" by Led
Zeppelin, or any contemporary "new" record in a similar style and
with a similar immediate-type message and effect.) Following is "You're
Welcome" by the Beach Boys. During the "Welcome" sequence mood
lights come up.*

PROLOGUE

Sound of machine-gun fire. Sound of thunder accompanied by a blaze of white light.

MEG (*direct – almost frightened – calling out*) Thunder.

(*The storm sounds are followed by the rushing in and out sounds of waves, which begin loudly, subsiding slowly into the background.*)

Waves . . . the soothing waves.

(*Moving toward* MICK.)

In. Out. In and out.

MICK (*half to himself*) Yes.

(*There is the distant cry of a gull mingled with the disappearing sound of the sea. Lights up slowly. Underneath, the in and out sound of breathing on the speaker system.*)

MEG (*as if in reverie, half-crazed*) This room in this house by the sea seems to be reminiscent somehow of a place . . . known to me a very long time ago . . . perhaps in a former life . . . perhaps it was a dream. I recall . . . I can't quite recollect the situation or the incident I am conjuring up – herewith – from the deep subconscious regions of my . . . (Looking at MICK.) . . . of what is left of . . . my mind. (*Breathing sound off, lights slightly up. Mocking.*) Am I awake then? (*A baby's cry is heard in the distance.*) Yes. Am I beginning to think once again? Yes. (*She moves her arms like a marionette – walks in a circle and lands downstage center.*) But what does anything have to do any longer . . . at this point with "thinking" mechanisms . . . thought movement . . . the mind? (*Staring angrily straight into the audience.*) I am trying . . . making the attempt . . . desperately . . . to become clear about this situation . . . to pull myself . . . my head . . . together . . . to save myself from the whirling undertow of a hundred million unfulfilled dreams – and from a world gone amok!

(*Slight pause. Lights up.*)

MICK (*telling* MEG, *then the audience*) In my life . . . I once had
. . . I remember having had . . . aspirations . . . made plans
even . . . toward becoming . . . (*The sound of an* IBM *machine.*)
a systems-analyst expert for a large American firm processing
and entering factual data all day long . . . into a computer . . .
a machine that would forever . . . on a daily basis, that is . . .
feed back – the answers.

(*Sound off. Light dim almost to blackout then up quickly.*)

SCENE 1

MEG (*arguing, confronting*) Answers.

MICK (*in deep anxiety and paranoia*) Now all that is done with –
and, it seems – there remain – only questions.

MEG (*biting sarcasm*) Questions!

MICK (*furiously, pacing*) The unanswerable ones . . . and they
won't . . . in any sense . . . at this . . . juncture-of-the-game –
stick!

MEG (*vicious, confronting him*) Has it become hopeless . . .
impossible then – going on – as we are?

MICK (*staring her down, hands on hips*) It would appear that way
– right now – if we can maintain any longer any trust in the
way-things-appear . . .

SCENE 2

*The loud sound of exploding bombs accompanied by orange or red bomb
light followed by the repetitive sound of machine-gun fire in the distance
which develops in volume increasing in pitch to surround the audience.*
MEG *and* MICK *duck immediately to the floor on all fours, hands over
ears.*

MEG (*excited, angry*) . . . the fuck is that for Christ-sake?

MICK (*darting around the room – nervously*) Gunfire. Bombs . . .

exploding – not too far from right here – I'd guess. The
Mongols. The battle . . . the war . . . rages on . . . becoming
somewhat closer all the time . . . encroaching upon our lives
. . . our very existence . . . our hideaway . . . our privacy – I
would guess. Haven't heard any reports since the goddam
radio went out. Last I heard several hundred thousand were
laying siege on Chicago like locusts.

MEG (*controlled pause*) I had almost managed to forget about the
Mongolians for a bit – about why we came here in the first
place. Christ! It is an annoyance to say the least. I mean, what
do they want!? They've destroyed – bombed-out, burned
four of our major cities in two weeks – our capital – tortured,
brutally killed nice American women, their milk-fed fat
babies . . . Christ, why don't they stop it! Where's it going to
end already?

(*Machine-gun and bomb fire off. Quick light change – sunshine-
bright.*)

MICK (*going to cabinet*) I'd hoped this place would be a safe
outpost . . . a resting place for us . . . we'd be able to endure
. . . for a while.

MEG (*in thought, nervous*) Maybe . . . if . . . what are you doing
now, idiot?

MICK (*near cabinet*) Our supplies seem to be dwindling –
petering out.

MEG (*anxious*) What's left?

MICK (*into cabinet*) Let's see. (*Almost spoken to himself – matter-
of-fact.*) A few bags of potato chips . . . a jar of assorted hard
candy . . . and several bottles of Coca-Cola. Oh, wait. One is
Hire's Root Beer. That's it.

MEG (*with voracious glee*) It's not altogether . . . completely . . .
hopeless then . . . (*Slight pause. Madly coy – mocking the idea –
swimming with it.*) Will we be able to obtain . . . catch fish . . .
or something . . . from the ocean?

MICK (*blank*) This morning . . . at dawn . . . when I was out
. . . on the beach – I found a great many – dead . . . covered

with a thick, black, oily substance . . . Pollution, I would
think. (*Moves toward* MEG.) Certainly inedible, indigestible
– poisonous! Some hard-shell crabs – tiny little ones – deep
under the sand – we can always count on a few of those.

MEG (*near the edge, still making light of it*) This is the last point
then . . . the last stopover . . . before . . . prior to . . .

MICK . . . prior to?

MEG (*giggling*) Total madness . . . de-civilization. (*Sound of
clucking chickens.*) A return . . . a crawling backwards . . . a
regression to the animal . . . geek . . . and then vegetable state.
(*Almost happy, sardonic.*) Then . . . emptiness.

(*At this point* MEG *begins to make a crowing sound like a chicken and
moves about with barnyard abandon.*)

MICK (*sitting, meditating on it*) – condition – the "condition" of
being vegetable.

MEG Condition. Yes. (*She mimics a moronic posture with facial
twitches.*) Being without instinct, impulse . . . thought.
(*Barnyard sounds off. Slight pause.*) I can't quite fathom . . . you
know . . . digest . . . the whole proposition . . . I tell you . . .
This outcast situation we find ourselves to be in. Help me!
Help me! Somebody! (*Slight pause. Deflated.*) I think I'm going
to be sick. Illness . . . overtaking me. Would you excuse me?

(MEG *moves to an upstage corner – as the lights dim – back to
the audience. She makes a loud heaving sound. This sound is
accompanied by spastic electronic sounds or music.* MEG *returns to
front downstage-center. A slight pause as* MEG *looks forward in
contemplation of the situation at hand.*)

(*Lights dim. Sound off.*)

SCENE 3

Lights up.

MICK (*cool*) How was it?

MEG (*blank – downstage*) What? How was what?

MICK The illness . . . being sick? How was it?

MEG (*vicious – irritated*) It has passed . . . a lucky thing we don't have any children along with us – on this trip!

MICK (*taking personal offense*) What?

MEG A child. I said it's lucky we didn't make the mistake of bringing a child – into the world – the way things are now and all.

MICK (*attempting optimism*) It isn't too bad. Things could be worse. I mean . . . we're still alive and . . .

MEG (*vacant*) It would be a lot of trouble. Wash! Wash! Ma! Ma!

MICK Yes, it would be that. It would be a lot of bother – an extra stomach to feed . . . to fill up . . . especially during a Chineeze-American war.

MEG (*dreamy, half in sexual excitation*) Will the soldiers . . . the beady-eyed yellow men . . . the Mongols . . . will they kill us right off if . . . when . . . they discover us . . . here? Will they use torturous methods – cut our faces open with soda bottles?

MICK (*gleeful – into the game*) It's hard to say what they'll decide to do. (*Abrupt switch.*) Let's not focus on the supposed outcome of events-eventually-to-happen. Let's try to set our minds . . . our thoughts on things more constructive. (*Raising his finger, belaboring it like a schoolteacher.*) Positivism. Yes, that will be it. In a crisis – nearing Doomsday – we must become positivistic.

MEG Why?

MICK It's possible we may be going on for some time as we are in this isolated . . . somewhat isolated . . . spot.

MEG (*furious at this point, pounding imaginary windows*) Dilapidated.
I would call it dilapidation . . . unlivable . . . this place. Our
windows are boarded up. I can't stand it. Our windows are
boarded up. Oooooo . . . God. Mmmmmmmm.

MICK (*cool anger*) We manage to go on . . . living . . .

MEG (*in the throes of near-madness*) . . . from moment to moment
. . . oddly enough.

(*Pause.*)

MICK (*going to cabinet*) Here, take this.

(*Hands* MEG *a sugar cube. She melts it in her mouth.*)

MEG Mmmm – – Uh. No. Okay.

(*She is in meditation position.*)

MICK It's next to last. Mine is our last.

(*He swallows. He sits.*)

MEG (*childlike – jumping up and into fantasy*) Perhaps . . . maybe
. . . I could sing a song . . . like we were in London –
underground – during the blitz. World War II. I understand
people would sing during disasters . . . blackouts there.
(*Singing at the audience.*) "We'll meet again – Don't know
where – Don't know when – But I know we'll meet again
some sunny day." (*Excited.*) They would all be together in the
tubes, see . . .

MICK (*in a huff, grabbing her*) Stop romanticizing! It grates . . .
you're grating on my nerves. Let's not . . . please . . . reduce
our level of thinking to singsong entertainment! We must
begin to make a new plan! We must make provisions! Escape!

MEG Look! I've been trying to hold up the best I can . . . and if
you think it's easy . . . under the circumstances with . . . you
. . . and if . . .

MICK (*loud*) You've been holding up. That's a joke. I've been
holding you up, you mean . . . supporting you through this
. . . situation. Ooooo!

MEG (*at a loss*) Will you be quiet! (*Quickly kneeling and bowing
Indian-style.*) We could try prayer again . . . to get us the hell

out of here.

MICK We've done that too many times. It hasn't helped. I'm sick of you and your silly suggestions!

MEG (*slow, in a fury*) I've been trying to meditate on the positivistic aspects . . . the idea of death . . . dying in a positive sense . . . since I have come to the conclusion . . . the realization . . . that we might be killed . . . kaput . . . bumped off . . . at any time . . . by the Mongol invaders.

MICK (*trying to maintain an Existential position*) Well, we still manage to be going on . . . right now . . . for the time being, that is.

MEG So it would seem. Yeah.

(*Sound of gunfire. Full light blackout. Sound off.*)

SCENE 4

Lights up. MEG *and* MICK *are lying on the floor.*

MEG (*jumping up quickly, as if waking from a nightmare*) What day is it? What day is today?

MICK (*in a fog*) I don't know. What does it matter?

MEG (*agitated*) I just thought I'd ask — for the sake of conversation, ass.

MICK (*argumentative*) Running out of time . . . and talk . . . that's what day it is.

MEG (*hopeful — trying to go beyond herself, her limitations*) If we could start again . . . anew . . . begin at the beginning . . . discover when things went asunder . . . in our lives.

MICK (*not wanting to join in*) You're drifting again . . . not being clear-headed. Stick to the point at hand, freako!

MEG (*in a trance — like a child at play*) Begin again like a new wave breaking — coming to shore — back again, then coming to shore. Listen. The sea . . . (*The sound of waves breaking.*) . . . in and out . . . in and . . . It becomes quite soothing. Listen.

MICK (*stubborn*) . . . nothing. I hear nothing.

(*The sound of the waves grows louder. Lights fluctuate with the sound.* MICK *becomes almost sexually excited. Orgasmic.*)

Yes. I can hear . . . it . . . is . . . yes. It is . . . soothing. Yes. Yes. You're right.

(*They both stare straight forward in trance-like meditation. Pause. Lights dim to blackout. Sound off.*)

SCENE 5

Lights up.

MICK (*moving a step backward during lights up*) Where were we?

MEG (*still half in sexual feeling*) Makes me feel . . . becoming . . . giddy . . . stupid . . . dizzy. (*Spins around in a daze.*) The incessant motion . . . on and on . . . (*She begins laughing, pushing toward ego-transcendence.*) Oh, God. I'm going up . . . getting there.

MICK (*rolling on floor as if in agony, as if on a bad trip*) Mad. Uh. We must be going mad . . . stir-crazy . . . flipping out . . . going over . . . uh . . . to the other side . . . finally. I feel it. My head . . . ugh . . .

(*Sound of machine gun fire in the distance.*)

MEG (*swooping about in a large circle like an animal stalking its prey*) There isn't much sanity these days anyhow . . . much you can count on . . . to be sure about . . . our resistance . . . our inner resources seem to be breaking down . . . here . . . minute by minute . . . day by day. We're going under! I can see it! Slowly. Not much we can count on except that those goddam Mongols have invaded the land and we are bound to be wiped out . . . before long – by Chinamen!

(*On "Chinamen" we hear Chinese speaking, singing, and music.*)

MICK (*trying to interject a positive note*) Perhaps we'll be taken as hostages – not killed at all – permitted to fit in somewhere –

someplace in the new order – the new scheme of things!

MEG (*controlled, mocking, venomous anger, almost hysterical doing-her-own-thing*) That isn't likely. Probably we'll be captured and shot – or thrown bodily out of a helicopter. To fall – down, down, down. Wheeeee. Or maybe fed to fire-spitting green dragons. In the final analysis maybe death would be preferable to some continuum under a reign of the terrible Mongols. We don't have – we don't speak the same language – "lingo" – as they do, after all. Fung. Sung. Loo. Goo. Mai. Pai. Pen.

MICK (*in a quandary*) What language?

(*Lights change.*)

MEG (*yelling*) Mongolian!! (*The sound of Chinamen speaking all at once accompanied by Chinese music and singing. Almost screaming.*) They won't understand a word we are saying! As we beg them for mercy it will sound like gibberish . . . GIBBERISH!

(*Sound off. The lights fluctuate up and down, covering the color spectrum.*)

MICK Won't they bring an interpreter when they come to gobble us up?

(*Chinese music continues.*)

MEG (*freaking out – going further into it*) Our minds . . . our thoughts . . . our language . . . our bodies have been banned . . . overthrown . . . have been found by the bloody Mongol warlords to be of no use in the new system. The last propaganda sheet I read said that . . . Agnew said that! Nitwit! Where is your head?

MICK What?

MEG (*with precise movement – almost to the audience*) I can't quite piece it together . . . except that things . . . you know, things – as we have known them to be up until now – the entire hysterical . . . historical picture – Western Civilization. Remember that one?! and – uh – (*singing*) "East of the sun and west of the moon, we'll build a cottage for two, dear" – the American Way . . . has become – obsolete – and that the lives

we . . . you and I and everybody . . . have been leading have
become useless . . . are no longer serving any real, definitive,
or actual purpose. For the greater good of mankind – the
world at large. The Mongolian takeover. Mankind! Mankind!
Yes. Revolution! Society . . . we are in need of a complete
change and so fate has put it and us into the hands of the all-
powerful Mongols.

(*Music off. Lights up.*)

MICK (*disgusted, trying to put it into a real perspective*) The
Mongols! What can they bring to bear on things that will
change anything? Really. Ridiculous. I can't believe it.

MEG (*uncontrolled anger – spewing it out*) The West is falling into
the hands of the East, I tell you!

MICK (*going along with it – he playfully falls to the ground as if shot*)
What can we do?

MEG (*more furious*) Nothing. We can do nothing but wait to die
at the hands of the Mongols. We're finished.

(*Mixed bag of Chinamen conversing and Chinese music over sound
system.*)

(*The next two speeches are spoken simultaneously.*)

MEG (*tripping out*) Finished . . . We're finished . . . It's all over
. . . See yah! . . . Bye! Bye! . . . So long . . . Sugar? . . . No
sugar . . . No. Yes . . . Tee. Hee . . . Blahb.

MICK (*simultaneously – grabbing her, in a rush*) Hey. Maybe there
are no Mongols. Maybe we're speeding, tripping, imagining
this whole Mongol – invasion – the cubes we took earlier
. . . did I give you some sugar? Huh? Yeah. A mind vacation
– yeah, that's it. A trip – no enemies. No Mongols. Ha ha.
Fong. Hong. Ho. Kah!

(*The loud sound of machine-gun fire. Red and orange bomb, lighting
up and down.*)

MEG Duck!

(*The sound of gunfire. They hit the floor quickly.*)

MICK (*screaming*) We're just imagining it, I tell you.

MEG (*hysterical*) No. It's true, I tell you. It's happening. The
Mongols are really coming closer – closer – nearer. Oh,
God! (*Gunfire and bombs fade out slowly. Bright white and green
light.*) If I could bite off my goddam tongue – wake out of
this nightmare – become a giant bird – escape this place –
fly into the sky – away – forever. My breath. Catch. (*On the
sound system we hear "in" and "out" breathing sounds.*) O I must
catch my breath. Breathe . . . in . . . out . . . in . . . out . . .
Yes . . . Breathe. Run . . . this way . . . and that . . . breath.
I'm developing gills . . . in my neck. A pounding in my head
. . . (*A throbbing sound, like a heartbeat.*) . . . as if I'm about to
hemorrhage . . . (*Lights up.*) Explode!

(*A loud sound like a gunshot.* MEG *whimpers in anguish. Blackout
on "Explode."*)

SCENE 6

Lights up. MEG *and* MICK *are lying down but jump up nervously
almost immediately. An abrupt mood switch.*

MEG What time is it?

MICK (*conversational, matter-of-fact, yet confused*) I don't know. We
haven't kept a clock for some time, you know. At any rate it is
difficult to wait. Isn't it?

MEG (*a lost, spaced-out feeling*) Wait?

MICK (*moving about*) For whatever is to come . . . I mean . . .
whatever the next phase is. On this journey. (*Angrier.*) It is
difficult to wait in anticipation of what will come.

MEG (*vague, cynical*) What will come? Another phase?

MICK I don't know . . . for sure . . . probably just nothing.
Maybe we'll remain stuck here forever . . . gravitated to earth.

MEG Nothing? (*Pause,*) What about the approaching – ongoing
enemy – the Mongols – our ultimate demise at their hands –
our pleas for mercy? What . . . about . . . that? Huh?

(*The distant sound of gunfire. Pause. Sound off.*)

MICK (*logical – the sound of bottles smashing or rocks thrown through windows accompanies this speech*) The problem is . . . it would seem . . . in our freaked-out togetherness . . . in our situation here . . . in the sense of one thing or one person in juxtaposition to another – you and I – it would seem to me – offhand – that we are at what might be called an interim point. Indecisive. Take this dilapidated room, this place . . . we're in . . .

MEG (*blank, childlike*) Room?

MICK (*continuing*)   . . . a non-point between two fixed points. The problem is to discover exactly where the two fixed points are in time and space – which is us – which is impossible. Ha!

(*Sound of bottles off.*)

MEG (*turning it into an argument*) It would seem that way, dearie. It would seem we're not getting any closer to . . . anywhere, that possibly – we've wandered onto – taken the wrong path – with one another – lost our way – or something like that – (*Moves off by herself.*) Maybe taken the wrong up or the wrong down.

MICK Stranded in this room – this place – not having any real or tangible effect on things – on the material world-outside – (*Moves toward* MEG. *Gunfire in the distance. Blend of Chinese voices.*) . . . a world inhabited by ever-approaching Mongol warriors! (*Now sitting – into himself.*) . . . and we the dreamers . . . the two of us . . . alone-forever-together in the Universe . . . but I can't be certain . . . of that.

(*Gunfire off. Lights up.*)

MEG (*thinking it out – laughing in childlike discovery*) Hey. Wait. Ding. Wow. Idea. I got an idea. Hey, I've got an idea. The Mongols . . . the Mongols . . . they may not really exist except in our heads. We just . . . made them up . . . invented them . . . out of some necessity . . . an enemy . . . to fill the void in our own tangled and thwarted relationship . . . to rationalize for our own anger, guilt, and multitudinous hostilities. Wow. Man, I'm telling you. Where is my mind?

MICK (*his head into his lap*) Huh.

MEG Never having learned to feel anything at all in this life of ours, we've become outcasts to ourselves . . . to one another. (*Gunfire sounds. Moving off into herself.*) For thousands of years waiting . . . waiting for a Mongol takeover! (*Sound off.*) Maybe if we sat down and tried . . . really hard . . . concentrated together . . . we might be able to begin to banish this so-called Mongoloid enemy . . . meet one another halfway maybe? It would be an attempt. Shall we try?

MICK Okay. I guess . . .

(*Lights dim. They sit facing one another in meditation. A long pause.*)

Epilogue

The sound of waves. Lights up.

MICK How are you? How are you doing?

MEG I'm here. See. Touch. Hee. Hee.

(*She clutches* MICK's *arms with her hands.*)

MICK Yes.

MEG (*gets up*) Some Coke? Or chips?

MICK Mmm-m-m-m-m-m-mmm. (MEG *hands* MICK *two Coke bottles and chips in a transparent glass bowl. They eat, savoring every bite, and drink from the bottles. Lights up – to reality-white. Slow exaggerated time-play as if in a* TV *commercial.*) Mmm-m-m-m-m-m-mmm!! Good!

(TV *music ensues – heavy violin version of "Park Avenue Fantasy" from "Some Like It Hot" or suitable Hollywood music.*)

MEG (*eating*) You like 'em? Mm-m-mm.

MICK Mmm-m-m-mmm. Hungry. Coca-Cola hits the spot. Yes.

MEG (*rapturous*) It's the real thing. Coke is the real thing.

MICK (*really believing it*) And chips. I love potato chips made in the good old USA. Wise. Treat. Lay's. Can't eat just one. Ha. Ha.

MEG I like their good crisp and salty flavor. M-m-m-mmm. I love snack-time in the fun-time pleasure-filled USA. Ha. Ha.

(*Lush music off.*)

MICK Mmm-m-m-m-mmm.

(*Lights flash. Short gunfire sounds in the distance. Sound off.*)

MEG What was that? Bastards.

MICK What? I didn't hear nothing.

(*Pause. Lights up.*)

MEG What are you thinking?

mick I am thinking it is good to get out of your head sometimes for a while . . .

MEG Yes.

(*There is a sound-light sequence in which MEG and MICK sit staring benevolently at one another. During this interlude the lighting turns bright pink as if they were transported into a space bubble. Over the sound system we hear the following dialogue from "The Wizard of Oz."*)

SCARECROW Look, here's someone who can help you.

DOROTHY Oh, will you help me? Can you help me?

GLINDA THE GOOD You don't need to be helped any longer. You've always had the power to go back to Kansas.

DOROTHY I have?

SCARECROW But why didn't you tell her before?

GLINDA Because she wouldn't have believed me. She had to learn it for herself.

TIN MAN What have you learned, Dorothy?

DOROTHY Well, I think that it wasn't enough just to want to see Uncle Henry and Aunty Em; and it's that if I ever go looking for my heart's desire again, I won't look any further than my own backyard because if it isn't there, I never really lost it to begin with. Is that right?

GLINDA That's all it is. Are you ready now?

DOROTHY Yes. Say goodbye, Toto. Yes. I'm ready now.

(*The sound of waves follows immediately, beginning softly and growing in volume toward the end. Lights up.*)

MICK And you? What are you feeling now . . . inside?

MEG (*intense – stepping forward slowly, moving arms upward – like a bird; gaze steady*) I feel . . .

I feel . . .

I feel . . .

I feel . . . I feel like I'm gonna live forever and ever . . . and ever.

Sound of waves loud, then off, blending with the lights fading. End with Chinese percussion and film clip or slide image of Buddhist monk burning.

Blackout.

SPLIT LEVEL

A PLAY FOR TWO CHARACTERS IN ONE ACT

Split Level was first presented (on a double bill with Heide's *Moon*) on January 13, 1972, by Alfred Brooks and Maxine Munt, in conjunction with the Colorado Council on the Arts and Humanities, at The Changing Scene, 1527½ Champa Street, Denver, Colorado. It was directed by the author with the following cast:

AXEL	John W. Conway
VIOLA	Ginger Valone

Split Level opened in New York in May 1972 at Bastiano's Studio on Cooper Square on a triple bill with plays by Tom Eyen and Christopher Mathewson. It was directed by Ron Link with the following cast:

AXEL	Edward Bell
VIOLA	Leslie Chain

*The three plays in Ron Link's Playwrights Workshop
Club production "3 by 3" at Bastiano's Studio for
the Arts included "Singer in a Big Band" by Tom
Eyen, "Split Level" by Robert Heide, and "Molly's
O" by Christopher Mathewson*

Split Level

CHARACTERS:

AXEL — *A bulky, overtly virile male figure, khaki or brown jacket, plaid shirt, overalls, hunting boots.*

VIOLA — *She is wearing a shoulder-padded coat over a plain dress and high-heeled shoes. Her hair is teased into a permanent surprise-swirl bouffant. Makeup is heavy into the 1950s pixie style, a garish attempt to look dewy and soft.*

THE TIME:

Late afternoon of a winter day.

THE SET:

The tower room of a vacated public building. A musty picture of George Washington hangs off center on one wall. A long wood conference table and stacked chairs to one side indicate that this might have formerly been a meeting room of some kind. An overhead clock that has stopped working hangs just over an oblong window, which is open. Cardboard boxes with commercial advertisements cover part of one wall. An eerie blue-green light filters into the dark, almost bare room.

The man, AXEL, sits on the floor and stares pensively out the window. By his side but concealed from view, perhaps resting on a lower beam just under floor level and beneath the window area, is a high-power rifle.

VIOLA, his wife, paces the floor and clutches at her throat. She is in deep thought and anxiety. After a long silent mounting tension between the two parties she speaks, beginning almost to herself.

VIOLA The things I've wanted . . . . . yearned for . . . dreamt of
. . . in this life . . . . that I never thought could be actualized
. . . how stupid I was . . . . (*Abrupt mood switch.*) What time do
you have? Your watch!

AXEL Uh . . . . . three to four . . how longuv we bin here?

VIOLA How long'll it be before they begin?

AXEL (*short*) Not long, Quit your stupid fidgeting . . . . .
playing with yourself.

VIOLA (*angry*) I'm not playin' with myself, you damn pig . . . . .
uh . . . . it's nervousness . . . all this time just sittin' and just
waitin'. Seems my whole life is been just waitin', for what? I
don't know. I wish I could figure . . . . . this room is cold!

AXEL You shouldn't have come . . . . . . along . . . . on this one.

VIOLA (*muttering*) . . . . on this one . . . . (*Mood switch, almost
apologetic.*) . . . . I wanted . . . . but I wanted to be . . . felt it
was my duty as a loving and normal wife . . . . bein' here
with you my completely normal and loving husband. Yes, I
understood those vows . . . . before . . . . not too long . . . and
our dream will become fulfilled . . . . . a reality.

AXEL What dream?

VIOLA What we'd talked about so often.

AXEL I can't remember. I can't think any.

VIOLA You are a thick skullhead.

AXEL I'm trying to concentrate . . . . . keep my wits
. . . . . together . . . . (*Music in the distance.*) Ya hear music? The
parade. I think it's about to begin.

VIOLA (*distracted from thought*) Oh. (*Pause.*) We have a splendid
view. (*Looks out window.*) Yes. Splendid. Mmmmm. (*Pause.*)
Wanna cigarette? Lucky Strike?

AXEL Not . . . . now. (*She lights her cigarette.*) You don't smoke.
Give me that. (*Takes cigarette out of her mouth roughly. Squashes it
in his hand. Puts it in his pocket.*) Where'd jah get those? (*Grabs
pack.*)

VIOLA The . . . uh . . . . corner . . . . grocer . . . I . .

AXEL Want to leave traces . . . behind?

VIOLA I guess I wasn't thinking. I wanted to pacify my nerves.

AXEL You've stopped smoking . . . . gave it up. You want a
hole in your neck like your Uncle Willie? Cancer?

VIOLA I was feeling anxious. Oh, well. Tomorrow will be
different . . . . a new beginning for us . . . . the end of an
old and tired road . . . . and ten thousand dollars is not a bad
sum . . . . tax free . . . . despite the recession. It's more than
we've had our paws on . . . . for one hour's . . . one day's . .
. . work. When I think of how we've struggled . . . suffered.
You working in a factory . . . . as a bartender. This is our big
chance to be like . . . . the others . . . yes . . take our proper
place in a proper community.

AXEL What community, Viola?

VIOLA Someplace far away . . . . some nice suburban
community . . . . with one house securely planted next to the
other . . . . one not too different from the other . . . wall-to-
wall carpeting . . . . olive green . . . and . . . and . . . yellow
walls . . . not too bright . . . two bedrooms . . . . then . . . .

AXEL . . . then . . . what?

VIOLA Organdy . . . . white . . . curtains with some kind of
floral pattern. You'll see . . . .

AXEL What? See what?

VIOLA (sentimental and on the verge of tears) How happy we'll be!

AXEL Uh. Huh.

VIOLA (now vicious, manipulative) We've never had the
opportunity up till now. This minute! Ha. Ha.

AXEL (beaming) I hear the music . . . . . growing . . . . louder.

VIOLA Yes.

AXEL It won't be long. I love the sound of an American
marching band.

VIOLA I love America . . . yes. It won't be long.

AXEL Remember you must continue to act in the normal
manner. You'll express some shock . . . but at a minimum
. . . . please.

VIOLA What . .

AXEL Your reaction.

VIOLA Oh, yes.

AXEL Not to . . . to . . . overreact to . . . . . the situation . . .
the news. Afterward . . . which won't be long . . . we will
pick our boy up at Granny's just as if we'd heard nothing . . . .
had come from the shopping center, the Food-O-Mat, with,
well, our usual products . . . . Pepsi, Ready-Whip, frozen
turkey pot pie, Wonder Bread, Scott toilet tissues, Hunts
Tomato Catsup, Hostess cream-filled Twinkies, pickled pigs'
feet and pork butt with sauerkraut, Aunt Jemima Buckwheat
Pancake Mix – and Vermont Maid syrup for breakfast. Some
Oreo cookies for the kid. Lays potato chips, Fritos – and
Cheese Doodles that we gobble up in front of the TV. Ha. Ha.
I'm getting hungry just thinkin' . .

VIOLA Thinking . . . . what?

AXEL (*proud*) That we are Americans through and through.
After all it is for America . . . . the American way of life . . . .
the . . . uh . . . . family . . . . and all it stands for . . . the . . .
uh . . . . church . . . . that I am doing this . . . er . . . ah . .

VIOLA This courageous act. It is . . . . will *be* a cour-a-geous act.

AXEL Yes. Courageous . . . . . stupendous. Remember when I
wrote you from the front? All those chinks 'n' Japs I knocked
off. Huh? (*Grabs her.*) You think I dunno what it's all about?
Huh?

VIOLA Stop hurting! You're pinching. Let go of me.

AXEL (*more intense*) You think I want a pack of degenerate
. . . commie queers running things . . . . phony liberals . . .
infiltrating our country – and our youth – being fucked up
by gibberish. Eastern Chinese bullshit. Indian swamis. How
I hate and despise those races . . . the yellow jackets . . . the

Indians. Tryin' to get our youth to stop thinkin' . . . to
meditate . . . . ha. Ha. You see . . . . this . . (*Picks up rifle.*) . .
this here rifle. Power . . . . with which to wipe 'em out. The
only thing they understand.

VIOLA (*nervous*) Not now. Don't point. Not yet.

AXEL You watch.

VIOLA What?

AXEL You came here, bitch. Yah wanted excitement. Now you
watch. Here. (*Hands her his field glasses.*)

VIOLA (*looking*) Yes. Yes. I see them. What jackasses . . . fools.
What do they know about anything . . . . so rich . . . and
smug. So condescending to the likes of us.

AXEL (*focusing with gun*) I never liked this job . . . . much . . . .
but somebody's got to pull the trigger. There! . . . . .

VIOLA (*desperate*) He's waving at the crowd. The crowd is
cheering. Yes. Now. That's it!

(*A gun shot. A red light. An orange light. A white light. Loud music.
Then abruptly into silence.*)

AXEL (*still*) What now?

VIOLA (*crazed*) People . . . crowds . . . running amok . . . . in
different directions. *You* . . . . you finished him! His miserable
existence . . .

AXEL Yes, I know.

VIOLA (*grimacing*) His face is a bloody mess. (*Pause.*) I love you,
Axel.

AXEL We'd better get a move on. Get yourself up. You're
sweating. Put on some makeup.

VIOLA Yes . . . . my lipstick. Raspberry Red. Ha. (*She pulls
herself together, opens compact, puts on lipstick.*) How does that
look? And my hair?

AXEL (*impatient*) Let's go.

VIOLA Not until you tell me one thing?

AXEL What?

VIOLA That you are happy. (*Pause.*) Well? (*Pause.*) You won't
regret a thing. You'll see . . . . our dream . . . . our dreams
will come true. We'll have that house we talked of . . . . .
split level . . . with a two-car garage. The children will love
us . . . . and we will love them. Isn't that right? They'll go to
Sunday School, never look dirty or think bad thoughts about
our great land . . . our way of life . . . . and . .

AXEL Quit blabbering. You sound like a TV ad.

VIOLA I'm not moving until you say it.

AXEL (*irritated*) Say what?

VIOLA You know.

AXEL Oh, Christ, we're not babies!

VIOLA Say it.

AXEL (*childlike*) Then can we go? Okay. You know I love you,
wifey-poo.

VIOLA And I love you too. We are . . . ha . . ha . . . . we have
normal love . . . you and me. We are normal, aren't we? We
know where we want to get and we are getting there. Aren't
we? Aren't we getting there?

AXEL Yes.

*They look at one another still not quite certain if they understand what
the other person is thinking or saying.*

Blackout.

INTERIM PLAY

INTERIM PLAY

CHARACTERS: AZ

                     BIV   *Three adults*

                     CID

The three characters may be interpreted by any of the following combinations: male-male-female, or female-female-male, or female-female-female, or male-male-male.

An expressionistic set. No more than three colors should be used for set and costumes. Perhaps the furniture should be slightly larger in dimension than it would be in "everyday" life. The main emphasis would be a large door, three chairs, and a table.

AZ *and* CID *are seated.* BIV *stands near the door, which is closed.*

AZ So this is it then. You really intend to go this time.

BIV I've said all I have to say. I've had it. *This is the end.*

CID (*eyes downward*) What's going on inside that head of yours?

BIV I don't know. Does it matter?

AZ Well, there's the door. I could care less at this point. What about your things?

BIV I'll get them . . . . later.

AZ Why not . . . now?

BIV (*muted anger growing toward rage*) I . . . don't . . . want . . . to . . . take . . . the time . . . now . . . to do . . . that.

AZ (*more hostile*) Well . . . if you go out that door this time . . .

don't come back. I'm warning you. I'm tired of these outbursts
. . . arguments . . . over . . . seemingly . . . nothing . . . of
playing this scene over and over . . . and over . . .

CID (*more rational*) What is it? Where do you intend to go? This
persistent indulgence. Think about your behavior patterns for
a change, where they are taking you. To what? Abandonment
of all value systems. Do you want to just abandon . . . everything
. . . lose yourself? Drift?

BIV No.

CID What then?

BIV I don't know. Games. Dull-ache-repetition. Old hostilities . . .
unresolved solutions. I'm losing . . losing . . the ability . . . to act
. . . out . . . my life . . . in this situation. Something like that.

AZ Oh . . . . something like that!

BIV *Some thing like that.*

AZ Well, then go. Just go. Get out. You're making me ill, nervous.

BIV Maybe I won't . . . go!

AZ What?

BIV I might decide to stay . . . a while longer . . . figure things
out . . . myself . . . for myself . . . I don't know.

AZ Oh.

BIV Is that all right?

AZ Be my guest. Do whatever you like. I have other things to
think about.

(AZ *picks up a book, pretends to read, puffs on a cigarette.*)

(*A pause.*)

BIV (*motionless – head bowed, eyes open, hand trembling slightly*) I'll
just stand here for a moment then . . . and . . . and . . . think
. . . if . . . you don't mind . . . I'll just . . . . .

End

MOTHER SUCK

A MONOLOGUE

Mother Suck was presented on April 15, 1975, by Ron Link as part of a benefit at Art D'Lugoff's Village Gate. It was directed by Ron Link with Helen Hanft in the title role.

Helen Hanft and Robert Heide

MOTHER SUCK

CHARACTER:

MOTHER SUCK — *A nice old lady who wears a print dress with a cream lace collar, brown woolen stockings, red-cross sensible shoes, tight marcelled curls; carrying a wrinkled brown paper shopping bag, a small overnight bag, a handbag. A dried-up red rose is attached to her dress.*

SCENE: *Ostensibly a bus terminal waiting room.*

TIME: *Present.*

She approaches us timidly but with aggressive intent. She speaks in nervous crescendos bordering on hysteria. Winks, twitches, and squints accompany a rigid posture. Her sentences sometimes come at us as questions. A girlish grin not far away from a giggle.

MOTHER SUCK Hello. I just got in here on one of them Greyhound buses. I never been to New York before . . . to such a big place. Oh! Once when my husband Herbert was alive; but that was a many years ago. Yes. Mmmm. Here.

(Goes into shopping bag.)

Would you care for an orange? Go ahead. Take it. Here, I have a couple.

(Tosses them to select members of audience.)

I couldn't eat any travelin'. Got bus-sick. I did. Sick! Mmmm. Uh. I'm from Doylestown, Pennsylvania(?). I'm meeting my son Leland. Oh. His bus don't get in from Baltimore for more than two hours. I got here early to be sure I wouldn't miss him. So I got two hours to kill. I'm wearin' this half-dead rose . . .

Uh. Would you like a piece of cake? Go ahead! Eat it!
(*Anxious.*)

Eat it! It's good cake! My son Leland likes cake. Maybe
your friend might want a taste. I made it myself just like any
American mother would. Yes. You may be wonderin' what
I'm doin' here talking to you all – a nice, white Protestant
lady like me. Mm. You see, it's about my son Leland. There
are things that I just don't understand. There are things I
guess I'll never understand, being a Christian woman. Well,
not that anything's wrong with Leland! He was always such a
nice boy, always good to his mother. I fed him well . . "Eat!
Eat!" I would say – and he had thoughts of goin' into the
ministry with my pushing him a little . . he being a little slow.
Hmmm. Well he *was* more shy, more sensitive, you might say,
than most other kids; preferred to play with dolls and nice
things, not toy tanks, guns, and soldiers like the other boys.
I think it was them Hollywood pictures thet led him astray
though – all those evenings he spent at the movies . . . It was
there that he met thet . . . . you know . . . became friendly
. . . heh . . heh . . . with that mean old man down the street,
the one that used to throw stones at all the kids when they
hollered by his house . . . always walking this collie dog too
. . . you know . . . the one nobody in the neighborhood ever
talked to. Schmid his name was, I think. He worked in one
of them used car lots downtown too. Well, you know . . .
he and Leland hit it off real swell somehow . . . this man
that everybody says was so mean. They even drove down to
Flahridah together on a vacation, the two of 'em. Yeah. In a
red convertible thet had no top. It always puzzled my mind
the way they became . . . so friendly. I mean Leland never
liked people much neither. He always kept mostly to himself
– and his mother. I'd hear this man whisper somethin' in
Leland's ear and then the two of them would burst out in this
"wild" laughter(?)! I said to Leland it wasn't polite to laugh
like thet. What would the neighbors think! After a while
Leland began to stay away more and more nights too. His

studies began to fall off and he never went to church or choir
practice no more. Always laughing this "wicked" laugh!!
I says to Leland, "Stop laughing! It ain't nice for a good
Christian to make those sounds – and furthermore, where
are you going so late nights?" He never answers. I guess . . . .
heh . . . heh . . . you might say I lost my hold on him. Then,
well . . . he has this nervous breakdown(?). It started with
his lip twitchin'(?). His father used to do thet. I says, "Stop
it! Your father used to do thet!" Then worse came to worse
and he starts in seein' one of them psychiatrist persons like
I seen on the TV at my friend's house. Well, once this man
calls me up and says, "I want you to come to my office."
Leland didn't even tell me he was seein' anyone like thet! I
would've put a stop to it had I known! So, anyway, I went
right down there and paid a call on this psychiatrist man.
He looked odd let me tell you! He had a big round face and
thick glasses. He asked me these embarassin' questions – like
was Leland breast-fed and stuff like thet. Then he mentioned
something about Leland and this girl named Falashia!(?) So
afterwards – I was waitin' for Leland to come home. And I
says, "Why didn't you tell me about this here new girlfriend
of yours named Falashia?" Well, I tell you upon hearin'
her name mentioned he hauls off and smacks me so hard.
I nearly went unconscious. My lip bled! I bit my lip. So as
I was laying there, half stunned, he runs upstairs, packs a
suitcase, and runs out slamming the door so hard my beautiful
Victorian stained-glass panel was smashed to smithers. I got
up screaming, "Leland, Leland! Where are you going? Come
back!" Well, that was the last I heard of 'em for some time.
Then I got this here postal card from him all the way from
San Francisco. You wannah see it?

(*Scrambles in shopping bag. Finds it.*)

It's a picture of Leland wearing a long blonde wig from this
nightclub, where he is now the featured attraction. It says,
"Mom. I'm a comedian now and a big hit in the show business."

(*Puts card away.*)

That was the last I heard from Leland for two years. Then I got this letter . . .

(*Goes back into shopping bag.*)

. . . just a week ago from this hospital called "John Hopkins" in Baltimore, Maryland. It says, "The operation on your son Leland was a success." I says to my friend, "I didn't even know my poor boy was sick."

(*Slight pause. Almost in tears.*)

A mother suffers to bring a child into the world and . . .

(*Quick mood shift.*)

So then I get this call. It is Leland! He says he's okay, only I says, "Leland, you don't sound like yourself. Your voice is pitched higher and why haven't you called me sooner?" So anyhow, here I am in this sinful city to meet my long lost son Leland. "You might not recognize me, Mom," he says. "I, me . . I won't recognize you, my own son?" I said. Ha! Ha! I'm wearin' this here rose at his suggestion and he'll be wearin' one too so we'll be sure . . . absolutely sure . . . we recognize one another . . mmmm.

(*Pause.*)

I'm getting on in years . . . getting old . . . tired. My! I was planning on puttin' myself in one of them old folks homes, you know, but now I figure I'd better spend my remaining years . . . sell my propertee in Doylestown . . . move in with Leland, cook for him, take care of him so's he won't get sick no more and I won't be so all alone either. Heh. He's soon gonna have a screen test too, he tells me. Some movie being made called "Queen of Outer Space" or "Planet X" . . . or someplace. "Outer Space"!? That don't sound like a Christian idea to me! Phew! I'm outta breath talkin' to all you strangers! Well, I gotta go meet my son now – God be with you people. Heh. Heh. And if any of you have a mother like me – be kind! A mother needs the love of her children. Bye.

Exit – laughing to herself.

American Hamburger

A Gastro-Metaphysical Farce

American Hamburger was presented by Crystal Field and George Bartenieff on November 24, 1976, at Theater for the New City (Jane Street) as part of Village Writers on the Village: a Bicentennial Celebration. It was directed by Robert Dahdah with the following cast:

Village Tourist	Baruk Levi
George Washington	Robert Frink
Maxwell Bodenheim	Lawrence Sellars

Baruk Levi as the Village Tourist, Robert Frink as George Washington, and Lawrence Sellars as Maxwell Bodenheim in "American Hamburger"

AMERICAN HAMBURGER

CHARACTERS:

VILLAGE TOURIST

GEORGE WASHINGTON

MAXWELL BODENHEIM

SCENE: *A park in Greenwich Village near McDonald's.*

VILLAGE TOURIST I don't live that far away from the Village
. . . I'm from Jersey . . . just across the river . . . a little factory
town called Kearny. Not much happens there . . . there's a
sameness, a repetition. I teach school . . . history . . . but my
main concern . . . my obsessions . . . are mostly erotic . . . I
come here on my Indian motorcycle to cruise . . . look for
a sexual encounter. As a child I had sexual fantasies about
George Washington . . . I guess I thought he was a perfect
father figure . . . other than that . . . I love the costume freaks
in the Village. One night I thought I saw Martha Washington
or was it Betsy Ross on roller skates carrying a wand like
Glinda the Good . . . from Oz.

MAXWELL BODENHEIM The old Village in the twenties was a
tough, exciting place to be . . . we commingled . . . in those
days with thugs, sneak thieves, pimps, gamblers, voluptuous
whores . . . waterfront sailors . . . in fact . . . later in my more
dissolute forgetful years . . . my own life was taken by a tight-
ass sexual sailor – longshoreman, he actually was, although
legend persists that it was a group of sailors that killed myself

and my wife that night. At some point I guess one ought to
go with the legend . . . it must have been perpetuated for
good reason . . . well . . . it was after a bar-to-bar drinking
binge . . . murdered . . . you see . . . I too liked to lurk about,
to "cruise," as you call it . . . feelings of hopelessness . . .
despondency would overtake me . . . you see . . . and . . .
the phantom of night would move into my very being . . .
overtake me . . .

GEORGE WASHINGTON I camped around here . . . myself . . .
Greenwich Village . . . I think it was called Green Village
then . . . my headquarters were around King and Vandam
below Houston . . . during the Revolution . . . of course
as legend has it for me . . . I slept around a good deal.
Everywhere you go . . . a sign is posted "George Washington
Slept Here." Indeed. I couldn't have slept in all those places.
Could I?

BODENHEIM Maxwell Bodenheim is my name, General . . .
who would fail to know you . . . General Washington . . . I
am honored. I represent the old Village Bohemia that is with
us no more . . . things come and go . . . change quickly . . . it
is strange to have the sense of having been here before . . . is
it not? To appear and then disappear . . . like a retrogressive
photographic image. Death . . . to have been through that
ultimate orgasmic experience . . . but that reality is past –
beyond . . . why look at it . . . as if staring into a maze of
mirror-infinity.

WASHINGTON What is this, some sort of trick poetry? This is
unbelievable . . . sir . . . that I should find myself at a common
meeting ground with the likes of you . . . what does this
mean? I have always been regarded as a pinnacle of virtue . . .
a soldier who fought in the name of – *truth*. Even in the order
of things past I deserve better than this.

TOURIST I run into more costume freaks! Why, on Christopher
Street I saw the Statue of Liberty with green hair and green
skin . . .

BODENHEIM Each of us has his own truth to deal with . . . his

own inclinations . . anyone can meet anyone in the Village.
Also this man could be an imposter, a costume freak as you
called him, in a powdered wig, and I a bag-of-tricks poet . . .

WASHINGTON You would certainly have been regarded as
riffraff in my day . . . your kind . . . certainly would not be
welcome in discreet polite . . society . . . formality never bred
contempt.

TOURIST I travel around America a lot . . . during my school
vacations . . . it's funny . . . all of the towns . . . are beginning
to look the same . . . McDonald's . . . Arthur Treacher's Fish
and Chips . . . Tico Taco . . . are mushrooming everywhere.
My thing is raunchy stainless steel 1950s diners with pink
mirrors . . . it's hard to escape the fast-food ethic, polysorbate
80, sturbestrome Colonel Saunders's chicken injected with
female hormones . . . boy! I do like Nathan's hotdogs though
. . . but eating there is like eating in a pig trough . . . everyone
just gobbling it up . . . do you remember the Battle of the
Stonewall?

WASHINGTON No.

TOURIST . . . on Christopher Street. Sexual liberation. That's
what it was all about. Now the Stonewall is a bagel restaurant.
Can you believe it?

WASHINGTON Things change. Yes. I hear there is even a
hamburger chain called Minutemen . .

TOURIST Yes, in New Jersey, and Roy Rogers, Pat Boone
– and Johnny Carson – have hamburger stands turning up
everywhere.

BODENHEIM I liked to hang out at a place . . . in my day . . .
called the Hell Hole . . . over on the corner . . southeast . . on
Sixth Avenue and Fourth Street. Actually it was called The
Golden Swan – a sign with a golden swan hung out front . . .
but we who frequented it knew it as a true hell inferno.

WASHINGTON Rubbish.

BODENHEIM We would drop a nickel into a player piano that
would pound out garish melodies, "Brazen Agonies" I would

call those tunes . . . usually Irish ditties like − "My Wild
Irish Rose" − "the sweetest flower that grows" . . . awful.
The walls . . covered with photos of boxers . . . all Irish . . .
and race horses. The place was mostly all us men but painted
whores came in through the family entrance. I wrote poetry
there. The stench of beer mixed with the odor of alcoholic
piss and tobacco was foul. Ha ha. I can still smell it.

WASHINGTON Sir, you disgust me . . . your language.

TOURIST Nobody takes the Bohemia of the 1920s too
seriously nowadays. The idea they had of avant garde seems
juvenile − unenlightened − by today's standards . . . as an
off-off playgoer . . .

BODENHEIM Oh, we had nudity . . . in the "Ziegfeld Follies,"
but no serious artist paid much attention to it. It was words
that moved us then. Words.

WASHINGTON Your words wouldn't move a sow . . . I hate
Bohemians.

BODENHEIM I heard your true skin color − that you cover with
white powder and dry French rouge − is a sallow yellow and
that your complexion is pitted with worm holes.

WASHINGTON Why bring up that?

BODENHEIM . . . that your teeth are wooden. You Puritan.

TOURIST Yes. I read that in a historical biography . . . it is true
. . . but I would never teach that to my students at Kearny
High School or they might never take George Washington or
this country seriously again . . .

WASHINGTON Slander . . . I will not abide these insults.

BODENHEIM We all know that men of your time and your
position . . . fornicated . . . with their slaves.

TOURIST To me the battle of the Stonewall is the most important
battle fought in this country. Hundreds of screaming queens
having it out with the police − wam! "We want to be liberated.
Down with oppressive straight pigs. Yeah!" Now it's just a
memory like a forgotten dream. All bills for sexual freedom

wind up in politicians' wastepaper baskets . . . no bronze plaque
even on the building itself . . . saying . . "Here was fought the
Battle of Stonewall."

WASHINGTON Stonewall?

TOURIST. A memory. Things change so fast.

BODENHEIM It is all memory when you are dead.

WASHINGTON (*aside*) Like dry rouge on a pitted cheek. Made
up as if by a mortician. Covering up the underlying truth.
What is lacking inside.

BODENHEIM Like one of the whores from the Hell Hole.

WASHINGTON I beg your pardon.

TOURIST We're all just tourists in this country. We think we
know it and we don't. We don't even know ourselves . . . in
America.

BODENHEIM Confusion was everywhere . . . still . . . we did
have a good time of it . . . in our confused state . . . at the
Hell Hole. We always *yearned* for something better. Eugene
O'Neill was one of the drunks I befriended there. He
respected me – as an artist. He was a dark lugubrious Black
Irishman with a gift for gab. He would sit for hours talking
to a cutthroat gang called the Hudson Dusters . . . hijackers,
thieves whom everyone else was terrified of. Not him. One
thing we were not – in the old Village – was pansies. Some
of us may have been queer, but we were tough.

TOURIST There are the legions – of leather and denim today on
the street.

BODENHEIM Conformists. Yearning for conformity within
nonconformity.

WASHINGTON What is happening to the land I knew?

BODENHEIM We thought nothing of sitting elbow to elbow –
artists and writers – with killers and scum – the worst enticed
us, brought out the best in our imagination.

WASHINGTON No wonder you were killed by a sailor. A piteous
victim.

BODENHEIM I became a Village character . . . a viable personality . . . my outward identity loomed much larger than my work. Now I belong mostly to folklore . . . the old Bohemia . . . a memory. What difference does it make?

WASHINGTON I never thought of taking up pen. I was always content to be just myself – what are those men doing over there in the park? Smoking . . .

TOURIST Oh . . . black beauties, speed and grass. They sell it . . . drugs . . . to passersby . . . mood-changers.

OFFSTAGE VOICES Black beauties, loose joints, uppers, downers, get your mood-changers here.

WASHINGTON Oh yes, we would smoke on certain occasions – Ben Franklin, myself, and the others. It wasn't uncommon.

BODENHEIM And didn't you die of a sexual disease, Mr. Washington?

WASHINGTON Don't say it . . .

BODENHEIM Of a venereal complication . . .

WASHINGTON No . . . don't mention it . . .

TOURIST History does have the last word, they say. The force of history can be pretty tremendous at times. Truth does emerge . . . somehow . . . it comes out of nowhere . . . sweeps us up . . . into change . .

BODENHEIM Sometimes things change for the worse . . . like peace or hopeful prosperity interrupted by gunshot fire into . . .

TOURIST Like hamburger and chicken restaurants cropping up everywhere . . . money. The almighty fucking dollar. Yeah.

WASHINGTON America is changing and change is good . . is progress . . when it comes.

TOURIST It changes but it all looks the same . . . just one giant hamburger.

WASHINGTON Just one hot dog . . .

BODENHEIM . . . in America . . . things covering up . . to conspire . . to evade . . .

WASHINGTON I remember crossing the river into Trenton. With my troops.

TOURIST There are a great many eat-in diners in Trenton now. McDonald's has a strong hold there.

WASHINGTON Is he a general, this McDonald?

TOURIST McDonald's is a capitalist organization that sells hamburgers to millions of hungry Americans . . . they can't get enough to fill their fat faces.

WASHINGTON So it's all hamburger then?

TOURIST All hamburger. Hamburger is spreading everywhere – it is our favorite.

WASHINGTON America always had good taste.

BODENHEIM Yum. Yum. Let's all go to McDonald's and get ours.

WASHINGTON A good idea.

TOURIST The fast food ethic is contagious. I'm getting hungry. Boy. I'd even choose a hamburger over sex anytime. And sex is . . . was . . . one of my favorite obsessions. Mmmmm.

BODENHEIM Me too. Yumm.

WASHINGTON I prefer peanuts.

TOURIST You can get a peanut burger in certain places . . . like the South.

WASHINGTON Tell me. How is it that you have joined us . . young man . . since we are . . well . . sort of . . . you might say . . free-floating spirits.

TOURIST Oh, yeah . . . well . . . I forgot to mention to you guys . . . that . . . see . . . well. The other night . . . I had had . . . well a couple of drinks as well as . . . ha ha . . . a couple of tranquilizers . . Librium . . I'm . . ah . . . kind of a nervous type . . . teaching school and all . . . and my father . . . he hated my guts . . . but that was beside the point. I lived with my folks in Jersey . . . he despised my being gay . . he saw me once in the garage . . . I was only nine . . with my friend Arnold . . . he beat the shit outa me . . . so what about it . . .

Anyhow it was after doing my usual Friday evening rounds, Hotel Keller Bar, Peter Rabbit, Boots and Saddles, I took a walk down by the docks near the trucks . . . a lot was going on down there, it seemed . . . I felt kind of way out there . . . see . . . music was blaring from the bars. Anyhow I was between two stationary trucks . . . I don't know what it was that I was looking for . . . see . . . anyhow . . . I wasn't too drunk to notice several young guys . . teenagers . . . in the dark . . . they looked like kids from my American history class – one had a knife – I went toward them . . . I said "Stop!" "Help!" But no one came . . . I didn't even feel the jab of the knife. I was scared. Why is this happening to me, I asked, and . . . and . . . well . . . so what I'm trying to say is, I've experienced the death trip myself. It's sort of new to me, all this. It's only been a couple of days. Quite a heavy . . . next day . . . Saturday or Sunday . . . I was dragged out of the river . . . must have been dumped there. Funny, I don't feel any different than when I was alive . . . it's confusing . . . not being sure if you're alive . . . or dead.

BODENHEIM Many people are alive in life and act as if they are dead so what's the difference. At least we know we have passed on. Hamburger to hamburger. Is it so intolerable really? I spent my earthly existence pondering the metaphysics of the other world . . . death . . to no end. I might have dropped the whole question in favor of my fervor for . . . lustful ambiguity. Well, we should examine this hamburger situation.

TOURIST I sure could use a Big Mac. I sure could. I know that would give me a sense of the "real" somehow.

BODENHEIM We'll head toward the building near where the old Hell Hole used to be. (*To* WASHINGTON.) Are you with us, General?

WASHINGTON How can I avoid it? It seems to be inevitable.

TOURIST Having kicked over we still need the Big Hamburger.

WASHINGTON Strange. The last word is "hamburger."

A giant hamburger appears in the sky (photo-projection). Two golden arches on either side. Organ music ("You Deserve a Break Today"). Characters looking beatific as if preparing to enter the golden gates of heaven.

End.

Ron Lieberman designed the poster for the New York Theater Strategy production of "Suburban Tremens" and "Increased Occupancy" at the Westbeth Theater Center

SUBURBAN TREMENS

A PLAY

Suburban Tremens was first presented (with the curtain-raiser *Increased Occupancy*) by New York Theater Strategy, founded by Irene Fornés and Julie Bovasso, at Westbeth Theater Center on April 6, 1978. It was directed by the author with set design by Theo Barnes, lights by Larry Steckman, and sound by Sheila Paige.

FREDA STONE	Regina David
ANGEL DUST	Paul Lieber
JILL STONE	Carolyn Olga Cruse
JACK STONE	Tony Teslicko
MR. FEDDER/MR. STONE	Mark Simon
TV ANNOUNCER (VOICE)	Sturgis Warner
TV REPAIRMAN	Lawrence Sellars

Tony Teslicko, Mark Simon, Carolyn Olga Kruse, and Regina David in "Suburban Tremens"

Lawrence Sellars as the TV repairman comforts Regina David. Photos by Timothy Bissell.

Regina David and Paul Lieber as Angel Dust

Suburban Tremens

CHARACTERS:

FREDA STONE — *A fantasy suburban housewife. Her hair is frost-tinted and teased and spray-frozen into a permanent surprise-swirl bouffant style that sits on her head like an oversized wig. She wears a stretch-pants outfit made of some synthetic fabric like orlon or dacron. Makeup is dewy and overdone as if she were working behind a cosmetic counter at a drugstore. Her image is a beautician's exaggerated idea of how-to-look in the suburbs as if she already existed in an artificial stage setting — i.e., her home environment.*

Out of despair, boredom, and a defensive anger FREDA *has determined to try to cover these feelings with what seems at times to be aggressively happy attitudes — like the women depicted in television commercials acting almost as if she thought life ought to mirror a situation family comedy series with one bad pun following the other interrupted by instant canned laughter. It is a futile attempt to substitute attitudes for emotion.*

JILL STONE — *The daughter. A teenager, she wears little makeup; her long stringy hair is parted in the middle. A loose-fitting sweater, dungarees, and sneakers. Often she smiles vacantly, staring into space. At other times her moods swing from passivity into blind violent rages.*

JACK STONE — *The son. He is in his mid-twenties. He wears a work shirt, jeans, and military boots in a careless manner.*

MR. FEDDER — *A part-time gas station attendant. A disheveled, forgotten look, unshaven, unkempt hair. In his middle years. He wears a one-piece gas-station uniform, a wool jacket, heavy shoes, and a hunter's cap.*

ANGEL — *A growing-older lifeguard and former rock singer with a still-*

youthful appearance. Street-wise, slick, but with a touch of innocence commingled with perversity as if he were holding onto a dark secret he wanted to let go of but somehow could not. He is dressed in the Asbury Park punk style, a leather jacket, a leather wrist brace, black dungarees, and cowboy boots. His movements are light, swift, then suddenly still like a cat.

MR. STONE *— The father. The man in the cellar. He wears an animal head-mask, preferably that of a pig or boar. If a head-cover is not employed it would be essential for the actor to devise a makeup to give the impression of a disproportionate face that has become dehumanized through abuse and lack of concern.*

TV REPAIRMAN *— A white jumpsuit and little white hat. In this outfit he might also appear to be a mental-hospital intern.*

Note: The actor playing MR. FEDDER *may double as* MR. STONE.

SCENE:

The living room, first-floor bedroom, dining area, kitchen, and patio of a suburban split-level dream house in a planned New Jersey community built on a fake canal not far from Atlantic City and situated on a newly paved street called Bestview Place which has several road signs posted on it reading Dead End, Children at Play, and No Horn Honking. The interior of these rooms has the neat starched effect of a model room in the furnishings floor of a department store, as if no one ever lived in them; prominent are antique furniture reproductions of Colonial times, a pseudo-painting of George Washington in a military outfit, pictures of country scenes, barns, fall foliage and dramatic winter sunsets, overstuffed chairs, eagles fiercely clutching American flags, a massive TV *set in an early-American-style cabinet dominates the living room (this should be more symbolic than literal in that it is mainly the light emanating from it that is the key element), a collection of wooden decoy ducks, a small bar which contains vast amounts of gallon and half-gallon bottles of various kinds of name-brand whiskies, displaying also a lineup of metal beer-advertisement trays and rare beer cans. The patio features a charcoal grill and an empty swimming pool not yet completed. A garage filled with debris, cases of empty beer bottles, and a Japanese motorcycle. The bedroom area of the son is equipped with stereo and has large posters of athletes like Arnold Schwartzenegger or Mark Spitz on the walls.*

TV cameras are present as if some of the action were taking place as a television drama within a television drama. A door marked Cellar Area – Keep Out – Man at Work. Whenever the TV is on or a commercial is spoken over the loudspeaker, a strange blue-white light covers the playing area from the TV set, which faces into the living area.

Silence may also be employed onto an open vista as if through a picture window visualizing some of the scenes the characters talk about.

A non-literal set should indicate in its design some of these impressions of suburban life, e.g., houses that look alike, TV antennas, the essence of repetition in America.

Prologue

Death on the Installment Plan

Spoken almost as a chanting chorus – FREDA STONE, *her daughter and son,* MR. FEDDER, *and* ANGEL *are in black coats and hats. Organ music.*

FREDA (*resigned*) He seemed to be finally at rest . . . in peace at last.

JILL (*tearful, angry*) He seemed content . . . but he didn't quite look . . . exactly . . . like himself.

FREDA He was made up to look almost alive . . . more . . . real . . in a sense . . than he had ever looked . . in fact.

JACK Undertakers do a remarkable job.

FREDA His worldly labors . . . his strife . . . are at an end.

MR. FEDDER Perhaps he will find it . . . what he had been looking for . . . in the next life.

ANGEL It was a lovely funeral . . . but the stench of flowers was overpowering, don't you think? . . . I'd never seen so many chrysanthemums, hyacinth, tuberoses.

FREDA You father had many business associates . . . but none of
them showed up. They all hated his guts. He never cared for
flowers.

JILL (*sobbing*) I never knew him. None of us really knew him.

FREDA (*to* MR. FEDDER) He preferred his life . . . in the cellar
and he lived in the cellar of his mind . . . the subconscious.
He never really knew who he was. But . . . he was a good
provider . . . and he left us . . . the dearly beloved . . . myself
. . . and my two babies . . . well provided for. He was insured
up the ass . . . worth more dead than alive. That's the way the
insurance man at Metropolitan Life expressed it.

MR. FEDDER It was a beautiful event . . .

FREDA Paid for . . . in advance.

ANGEL I liked the part about ashes to ashes . . . dust to dust . . .
and the minister . . . he sounded almost like a TV announcer
. . . so well-modulated . . . so sincerely objective.

FREDA The funeral director advertises his business on television
. . . (*Slight pause.*) I need a drink. I can't breathe. I'm not sure I
can make it. Air. Air.

JILL I am hungry . . .

MR. FEDDER We should all eat . . . and drink.

FREDA Life is tough. What can you do? I've shed all my tears
. . . before.

Blackout

Scene I

*Post-Christmas – mother and daughter, early evening just after supper.
In blackout over the sound system we hear the last cut from "Elvis in
Concert," "Special Message from Elvis's Father – Vernon Presley"
followed by tape-recorded television commercial.*

ANNOUNCER (*loud, aggressive voice*) Friends, now is the time
to buy into New Jersey's Atlantic Meadow Estates just a
short distance away from America's new gambling mecca

vacation paradise – Atlantic City – where you can turn your hard-earned cash into a fortune with sunshine and pleasure. New suburban developments are now being offered to the public for the first time in what used to be mosquito-infested swamplands, now reclaimed landfills. You can live near the casinos, right next door to fun and excitement. Buy now while you still can to insure a plot on which to build your new suburban home. Call Atlantic Meadow Estates now! SU 7-3200. I repeat, SU 7-3200. Don't miss your chance for the good life! That's Atlantic Meadow Estates, a new life in the dream community of tomorrow, Atlantic Meadow Estates!

Lights up. FREDA *is carefully lacquering her nails. A small tray filled with an assortment of nail-cosmetics is on the coffee table.* FREDA *is seated on the couch and* JILL, *next to her, is peeling a lime for the bar. These activities underscore the opening segment.*

FREDA (*dreamily*) We are lucky . . . the way we live . . . in this planned community . . . self-sufficient unto ourselves . . . a tight little family unit. We don't need anybody. Our way of life is what is known as . . . in the real estates brochures . . . a *new concept* in . . *living.* No unsightly old trees . . . easy garbage disposal. Everything new. We had done it . . . all . . . for ourselves . . . feelings of emptiness at times, yes . . . oh, did I say that? But why complain when you think of all those poor oppressed persons . . . minorities . . . is that what they are called? . . taking dope, black beauties, speed, cocaine – in Harlem and Greenwich Village ghettos . . . robbing banks . . . mugging innocent passersby . . . begging for "strange change" on the streets. Ugly? I have seen it happening . . the coming attractions on television . . . close enough for me. Thank God we have electrical alarm systems installed . . . upright policemen who display American flag patches on shiny black leather jackets. Americanism. Protection! Yes, we do have . . we need . . . *protection!* All we can get . . . to live a life free of crime. (*Directly to daughter.*) You don't know how lucky you are having been watched over all your young life to . . . never

be exposed to . . . well, we shouldn't even think of things like
that . . . not here . . .

JILL (*flatly, jumps up*) You mean . . . rape . . . murder . . . assault . . .

FREDA Don't say it . . . don't even say those things . . . the
image of that happening to you . . . my little . . (*Begins
crying.*) Oh, if you knew what your mother has been through
worrying . . . constantly planning . . .

JILL What are you talking about, Mother? My future . . . what
will happen . . . what will happen, do you think?

FREDA Nothing. Never mind. We won't discuss it. Consider
the subject . . . closed for the present. (*Slight pause.*) Uh . . .
honey . . . yah . . look . . so pretty . . but why don'tcha smile
. . . as if you were in a beauty contest? Little Miss America.
Ha ha. Remember? You didn't win . . . but you smiled real
cute at the judges. The other little girl – the number one prize
winner – didn't look half as good as you did. Remember? I set
your hair in those corkscrew curls . . . golden curls . . . . like
Shirley Temple? You were only five then . . . I was so happy
then. You almost won, remember . . . second prize? Go get
your mother the picture . . in the drawer . . .

JILL Leave me alone . . . will you! Jesus Christ.

FREDA Don't curse. Don't you curse at me, young lady! (*Takes
cosmetic tray off of table, putting it on a shelf stage right.*) Your hair
. . . your hair needs to be set . . . . It's become so straggly,
straight, and limp . . . and far too long. It should be cut . . .
and restyled. You want to be beautiful, don't you? (*Seated
again.*) To get ahead in the world? To find love . . . instead of
looking like a dragged-out left-over burnt-out 1960s hippie
. . . like one of those stupid flower children that turned into
Charles Manson killers. Remember on TV? Linda Kasabian . .
Susan Kreniwinkle and . . . and . . . Squeaky Fromme who
tried to shoot President Ford? Now those girls came from
nice homes. What has happened to the America I knew . . .
as a girl . . . in South Amboy? It is all . . . incomprehensible.
Seventeen. Would you believe it? What has happened to

me . . my life? My hands have aged, my face, my legs are beginning to show varicose veins . . . (*Sobbing.*) Time has played a dirty trick on me . . (JILL *starts to leave.*) Where are you going, young lady?

JILL Out.

FREDA (*jumping up – confronting*) Out? Out where?

JILL (*putting on a sweater*) Just for a drive.

FREDA Where? Where for a drive? Where do you go on these incessant drives of yours?

JILL Around . . .

FREDA Around where? Where is there to go in this area . . . a young girl alone . . . in a car . . . you could be shot by a Son of Sam sniper who hates pretty young girls.

JILL The highways and byways. That's all. Sometimes I . . . stop at a Burger King or an Arthur Treacher's Fish and Chips. It's perfectly safe. I can take care of myself.

FREDA (*angrily*) Sit down. (JILL *sits.*) Where is your father?

JILL I don't know . . . he must be down in the cellar as usual. Where else would he go . . . in this house . . . for a little peace?

FREDA What do you think he's doing down there? What do you think he does . . .

JILL I don't know. He repairs things. He fixes . . . (*Pause. They stare at one another.*) Is that all? (*She gets up to leave.*)

FREDA (*pacing like a trapped animal*) My nerves . . . are on edge . . . today. Doesn't that mean anything to you? Poor me . . . get me . . would you pour me a little drink . . . a bourbon . . . on ice . . . no, it must be too early in the day for that. What time is it?

JILL (*absently*) What time?

FREDA (*hysterical*) I said what time is it? Where is your Sleeping Beauty watch? That you got for Christmas?

JILL I don't know.

FREDA (*sly, manipulative – a quick mood shift*) Well . . . make it a
Bloody Mary . . . I'm glad the holidays are over . . . we had a
lovely . . . (*Pause.*) Didn't we? Wasn't it a lovely Christmas?
Didn't you like your presents . . . brightly wrapped . . . under
the tree . . .

JILL (*depressed*) I wanted a real tree . . . this year . . .

FREDA (*hurt*) Honey . . . it was real . . . real enough. Plastic
with pine odor essence included. We can't have needles
dropping all over the house . . . dropping onto the rug . . and
if it's a real one, then you are obliged to water it . . .

JILL (*blank*) Oh.

FREDA It's common sense. No one wants to be bothered with a
real tree these days. Don't you see what I mean?

JILL Yeah. I guess so.

FREDA Dirt. It only makes for a dirty house. Now . . . what did
your mother ask you to do? A drink . . . get me a . .

JILL The doctor said . . .

FREDA (*angry*) I don't care what the goddamned doctor said . . .

JILL (*like a nurse*) Have you been taking your stellazyne? Your
nitro-glycerine pills . . . your lithium . . . as prescribed?

FREDA You're trying to remind me of my breakdown . . that
I suffered a nervous breakdown . . . of my irregular heart
palpitations. Well, I guess I've made it through one more
Christmas . . . another year. That is something. You don't
think I know what's waiting ahead? Think life is some picnic?
Work . . . your poor bastard of a father has done nothing but
work all his miserable life. (*An undertone of mockery, almost as a
joke.*) Why, sometimes I wonder how or why he even bothers
. . . one and a half hours each way every day on a commuter
train . . . into the city . . . wearing a suit, tie, hat . . . carrying
an attaché case filled with papers and then . . .

JILL Then?

FREDA (*suddenly reverting to convention*) Why . . . home again . . .
then suppertime with the family . . . what else . . . is there?

JILL (*under her breath, a sullen anger*) And into the cellar . . . to get drunk . . . to drown himself in . . . to forget . . .

FREDA Huh? (*Pause.*) Why how can you say that about your own father? He has a right to . . .

JILL To what?

FREDA (*looking downward*) . . . kill himself if he wishes. It is every man's right to do as he pleases, particularly if he is still able to sustain . . . work. If it is his wish to die then he has a perfect right. We have no power to pull him out. Haven't we tried? Haven't I? Where did it get me? Overbrook State Hospital Psychiatric Ward. Should I fall to pieces over what he's doing to himself?

JILL You are a nasty . . . b . . .

FREDA (*letting her hostility flow*) Go ahead and say it, you little slut . . . a nasty bitch. Call me whatever you like. Just wait till you marry . . . settle down. What do you know about things . . . life . . . the world . . the meaning of an American dollar? Why that man down the street . . . Zuckerman . . . is that his name? They live in a house almost identical to ours. (*Near tears.*) His wife had one breast removed in surgery . . . and now . . . the other one has to come off too . . . that is the price of success. I can't understand it, can you? Can *you* understand it? He's chair-president of Federal Savings and Loan Stock Association . . . a member of the American Legion and a lot of other important clubs including the Bayshore Golf and Tennis Club. They have a Cadillac Coupe de Ville. Now, how do you think that man feels? Miserable – and the anxiety the women suffer . . . no one comprehends . . . while men conduct business . . . ascend to grandiose positions of power and money . . we sit in the background . . . ladies in waiting. (*Calling out as if for help from the beyond.*) Waiting for what? A moment's relief from the intensity of boredom . . . somewhere . . where? (*Forlorn.*) . . . a leisure village old age community . . . fenced in with barbed wire . . . a death camp for senior citizens . . . or a nursing home that is actually an asylum run by the Italians . . . the burial plot . . . the coffin . . . the

funeral . . . all paid for . . . the quick-pay-as-you-go death
installment plan . . . that's what's ahead for us. And you think
I don't know it?! Now what's on TV? Turn it on but not too
loud . . . my nerves. I want to look at it . . . but not hear it . . .

(Obediently JILL *turns on the* TV. *An intense ghostly glow from the*
TV *screen bathes the entire stage with blue-white light.)*

. . . and get me my drink instead of just standing there staring
like a bug-eyed alien from *(pause)* . . Remember that weird
movie "The Day the Earth Stood Still"? I saw it at a drive-
in movie back when . . . well . . . Now move. Is that Merv
Griffin? Is that Zsa Zsa Gabor again? Or her sister? They
both look alike, faces pulled tight and bleached-out hair. Oh
. . . I've thought of having a face . . . my face uplifted . . .
but what for? (JILL *hands her a drink.*) Your father doesn't care.
Where the hell is he, did you say?

JILL   I said in the cellar.

FREDA   In the cellar . . where else? He's been so morose all day.
Today. Lots of suicides are committed just after Christmas
and New Year's. Post-holiday depression. Do you think he's
working? He should be here with us in front of the TV with
his beloved family. He is living in the cellar of his mind, The
subconscious. Ha. Ha. That's a joke. Not a good one. But a
joke nevertheless. The joke's on me. Ha ha.

(Pause.)

(Light dim.)

Two years ago your father almost electrocuted himself in that
basement . . . snipping live wires. He was fixing a duck-decoy
lamp down there. Remember? In the basement . . . Do you
remember that? No, of course not. For a young girl . . . your
memory . . . is going. Ha ha. You're turning into a mental
cripple. Yes. Your father was legally dead for three minutes
. . . but he . . . revived. He's never been the same since.

(Jumps up.)

This drink is too sweet. What did you put in it? There's a
maraschino cherry in it . . . I can't abide maraschino cherries.

(*Goes to bar, mixing herself a double bourbon on the rocks.*)

They contain Red Dye No. 2, which causes loss of vision . . . blindness . . or is it uteral cancer? Did you know that? Which is it? Food additives . . . I read about it in the *Times* magazine supplement. We've all become overprocessed . . or something like that. And where is your brother? I wanted to talk to you about him.

(*Slowly* JILL *leaves without her mother noticing.*)

Lately . . . since he dropped out of high school . . . he has not been what you would call normal . . . in his behavioral patterns and . . . well . . . since I'm always the last to know what's going on around here . . . I . . . where is she? Where's that girl gone? Drifted off? Drift . . ed away . . . leaving me . . . again.

(FREDA *stands facing front.*)

(*Fade.*)

SCENE II

A short time later. Lights up.

JACK Mother, this is Mr. Fedder . . . from down the street . . . he just started work with me at the Sunoco station . . He's going to help . . . look at . . try to get the motorcycle . . working.

FREDA (*anxious*) You're not intending to ride that goddamn motorcycle . . . again . . you broke one leg . . . and your arm was in a cast . . . for months.

JACK (*sullen, embarrassed*) Well I . . . thought . . it should be fixed . . . in working order.

FREDA (*to* MR. FEDDER) He should be learning to be an executive . . a business manager . . going to an accredited business school like the one that advertises on the TV. That's where the money is supposed to be, isn't it. The "big money"

.. business finances. Instead he wastes his time working in a
gas station .. where does that get you?

JACK Mother ... I .. please ... let's not ... I like cars. I enjoy
getting into engines.

FREDA (*to* MR. FEDDER, *perversely curious in an off-handed manner*)
You look very oddly familiar ... was it the Golf and
Tennis Club? In the bar? Your name is Fedder ... and not
Zuckerman. You are not Mr. Zuckerman, are you?

JACK (*blank*) He has a house identical to ours ... just on the
other side of the canal.

FREDA (*startled*) Identical?

MR. FEDDER (*looking up and down and around*) Well ... it is
painted a turquoise blue but otherwise it is .. yes ... I would
say it was almost exactly the same ... with one exception ...
one major differentiation ..

FREDA (*demanding*) What? What is the difference? (*No reply.*)
Oh. Across the way ... yes. You live on the canal ... we are
lucky to live near a waterway which leads to Barnegat Bay
and into the Atlantic Ocean. Do you own a boat?

JACK (*absent-mindedly*) He's a mechanic ... of sorts. Isn't that
right? A mechanic? (MR. FEDDER *nods.*) Anyhow you might
remember the very night President Nixon resigned from
office a woman drove a Buick station wagon into the canal
... they ... the police ... they fished .. it .. out. Well, that
lady was unfortunately Mr. Fedder's wife ... she was the
vice-president of the Republican Women Voters Club in this
county and .. she felt ... what was it?

MR. FEDDER (*shy, polite, embarrassment*) It was in the local paper
... the *Asbury Park Press* ... did you see it? They wrote about
Nixon ... uh ... my wife ... it wasn't on the front page ..
sort of a backpage news anecdote.

JACK (*an empty sadness*) So he is by himself ... he has children
somewhere ... in California. They moved away. Too cold here.

MR. FEDDER (*as if he had a memory block, a temporary amnesia*) Yes, that's right . . . living near the desert. One of them works in TV . . . . for a TV station in communications systems . . I believe.

FREDA (*nervous*) I missed the TV weather . . . is it cold out? I said, is it cold . . . what would the weather be like . . . outside?

MR. FEDDER It is damp. It was raining . . . but it stopped.

FREDA (*disturbed, as if she might have said the wrong thing*) Oh . . . then it is not cold.

JACK A thin coat of ice has formed . . . over the canal. Just yesterday there were waves. It was choppy. Today it's . . .

FREDA (*sudden*) It is cold. (*Pause.*) You must feel terrible.

MR. FEDDER (*startled, a forgotten look*) What? About what?

FREDA Your wife? I mean . . .

MR. FEDDER (*piecing things together as if what happened was a dream not quite remembered*) It seems like it was some kind of an impulsive . . . action on her part. Hard to understand these things. She had a propensity for strange moods. They would take her over . . I never quite knew what she was thinking . . . what was inside . . . in her mind. Quiet. Maybe she was certifiably insane. A manic depressive, for all I know. I really can't say. I'm not qualified in that area, you see . . . I don't know . . . the police asked me a lot of questions as to her disposition at that time . . . but I would not say . . . I would not call it an interrogation. They seemed sympathetic . . though I don't know why. They never knew her . . . or me. It's over and done with. I really don't mind doing without. (*To* JACK.) Where is this motorcycle of yours?

JACK In the garage . . .

(*Pause. Enter* JILL.)

FREDA Oh . . . this is my own sweet little girl named Jill . . . this is – what are you doing?

(JILL *goes to kitchen area, switches on radio.*)

I swear she is sometimes out of . . . control . . . beyond parental control. What can you do with them? Send them to the Youth Guidance Center? She doesn't respond . . .

(*Over the radio we hear Elvis Presley:*)

Are you lonesome tonight?

Do you miss me tonight?

Are you sorry we drifted apart?

(JILL *switches the station.*)

But I can't help falling

in love with you . . .

FREDA (*angry*) Turn it down!

JILL (*childlike – dancing around the room*) Elvis is on every single
station . . . Mama . . .

FREDA (*attempting to use charm to cover anxiety*) Now that he's
dead . . . people . . the public . . love him more. People love
you more . . . they honor you . . . when you are dead. But
at least he *did* something with his life . . . in order to be
commemorated . . . immortalized on TV and radio . . . forever
. . in the minds of . .

JILL (*near tears*) It doesn't make sense. None of it makes any
sense at all . . .why die just to make other people feel good
about you?

FREDA (*near hysteria*) It does. It *does* make sense . . . perfect
sense. What else is there? To have a good life and then . . . to
be well thought of . . . by others. (*Close to tears.*) Turn it off.
Turn that goddamn thing . . . off. We have a guest here. I
. . . no one can hear themselves think. It's too loud . . you're
turning me into a bag of raw frazzled nerves. You know my
condition.

(*Angrily* JILL *goes into the kitchen area, pulls out the plug, and hurls
the radio out the window. A loud crash is heard with the sound of
glass breaking.*) . . . what is that? What was that? (FREDA *rushes
toward* JILL.) What is happening? Have you gone berserk?
What have you done? (*She grabs* JILL.) Thrown the radio out
of the window? Where is your father when I need him? In
the cellar. Do you think money for appliances grows on trees?

You've got to be stopped. (JILL *picks up a kitchen knife – heading toward her mother.*) Give me that. Are you? . . . Help. Help. (FREDA *faints.* JILL *looks at the knife and puts it down.*)

JACK (*flustered*) What's happened . . . what?

JILL (*dully*) She's fainted. Maybe she's dead. I don't know. I blacked out . . . I got so angry that . . .

JACK (*angrily*) You stupid little bitch.

JILL (*pleading for recognition*) It's not my fault. She's the one that drives me . . . is her heart beating?

JACK (*dully*) Yeah . . . it's still beating . . .

MR. FEDDER Should we get a doctor . . . call the hospital?

JACK No . . .

MR. FEDDER Your father . . . where is he?

JACK In the cellar.

MR. FEDDER Should I go get him?

JACK No. If he didn't hear it . . . better to leave him out of it. He'd only make things worse. Let's move her onto the couch. (*They lift her onto the couch.*) There. She seems comfortable now. (*Pause.*)

MR. FEDDER (*staring at her*) . . . maybe if we slapped her face.

JACK No . . . she's coming to. It's not uncommon . . . these attacks. It's mostly . . . anxiety. Acute anxiety, according to the doctor.

FREDA (*groaning, coming to*) Oh. Where am I? Oh . . . uh . . . get me a drink . . . a tranquilizer. Where are my pills?

(JACK *sits with* FREDA. MR. FEDDER *and* JILL *stare blankly at one another.* JILL *smiles, almost with a hint of seductiveness – a banal sense of victory mixed with futility.*)

MR. FEDDER (*moving toward* JILL, *cornering her*) I was going to take a drive, maybe take in a movie . . . a drive-in . . . the Bayside Drive-In.

JILL (*seductive in an absent-minded manner*) Isn't it cold . . . for that . . . for a drive-in?

MR. FEDDER (*like a father offering candy to a child*) They attach
heaters into the car . . . along with speakers.

JILL Oh . . .

MR. FEDDER You seem nervous . . . upset . . . you're ashen . . .
maybe you'd like to come along . . . for the drive . . . or . . an
ice cream soda . . or . .

JILL What's playing?

MR. FEDDER (*laughing*) Something about outer space – meeting
people from . . . the beyond . . . life on other planets.

JILL I'll get my coat . . .

(JILL *exits.*)

FREDA (*recovering herself and swallowing pills*) Yes . . . I did
read about your wife . . . I'm sorry to say . . . in the local
newspaper. I remember they said she was wearing a mauve
outfit . . . one of my favorite colors . . I wore a mauve gown
at my high school prom . . . that's why I remembered it. It was
a hot August day, wasn't it?

MR. FEDDER (*sentimental*) Yes. She went under . . . and . . . well
. . . that was it. Naturally there was a rescue operation . . an
attempt at resuscitation . . to no avail . . . It was regarded
as . . . an accident. The car was insured. I got an instant
replacement. It's hard to go anywhere without wheels.

JACK (*disturbed*) Mr. Fedder may not want to talk about it. It's
depressing . . . I mean, why go into it?

FREDA (*going further into self-pity*) You must feel lonely. Alone.
Would you care for a cocktail . . a bone-dry martini . . . or
maybe you would prefer a cup of coffee, though all we have
is instant. Instant coffee with Pream. Powdered milk. The
combination tastes like . . . instant death . . . it nauseates me
. . but it is cheaper . . . easier . . in the long run.

MR. FEDDER What?

FREDA Instant products. Coffee. Want some? I'd have to heat
water and mix it.

MR. FEDDER No . . . I'd rather not, thank you.

FREDA (*moving in almost face-to-face*) I never did trust Nixon . . . did you?

(*Enter* JILL *in coat and scarf.*)

Where are you going?

JILL For a drive . . . with . . .

MR. FEDDER (*smiling*) I asked her if she would like to accompany me . . . for a drive or if we can find a movie . . . that is, with your kind permission.

FREDA (*flattered*) Why of course. Her father never takes her anywhere . . . (*To* JACK.) Where is your father?

JACK In the cellar. Isn't he?

FREDA (*almost to herself*) Oh. Well . . . I've become so accustomed to my own company . . you see . . . (*To* JILL.) Didn't you have your craft pottery class . . . tonight?

JILL (*trying to play "sweet little girl"*) That was supposed to be yesterday but the instructor had the flu virus or something.

FREDA Well then . . . don't be too late . . . Oh . . . Mr. Fedder . . . don't you keep a dog . . . a large dog . . . a collie? Didn't I see you walking with a . . . large . . .

MR. FEDDER (*a nasty undertone*) A mixed breed . . . she's a mixed . . . a mongrel bitch, actually.

FREDA (*accusatory*) I thought I saw you . . . once . . . across the way with a somewhat large animal.

MR. FEDDER She is rather large . . . she eats a great deal. I got her after my wife went . . . for companionship.

FREDA (*bitter*) You need a dog . . . around here . . . for protection. We have no dog. Dogs can be a pest . . . in a house though.

MR. FEDDER (*unable to restrain his own anger and resentments*) Yes. They consume almost as much as we humans. And sometimes they are vicious and have been known to bite . . . to attack even those who own them . . . in anger . . when they don't get their way. Well, I think we will be off then . . . if it's alright to go . . .

(*Exit* FEDDER *and* JILL, *who is giggling like a child.*)

FREDA (*goes to the bar and mixes a drink*) I'm worried about your sister. Something is happening . . . going wrong . . . with her.

JACK What?

FREDA (*obsessive like a detective probing a case*) She has taken to going out for long automobile rides . . . in the car . . . by herself . . . I think she picks up . . . men . . . on the highways. She ignores young men in her own age bracket. She seems to have become uninterested . . . in her studies. I'm sure that craft pottery class was tonight and not yesterday. She could be killed . . . raped . . . murdered . . . like you hear about on TV. Last week she said she was staying overnight at her girlfriend's . . . Edna. Then I ran into Edna's mother at Food Town. She said she hadn't been there . . . at all . . . that night.

JACK Did you confront her with this information?

FREDA No. I've been waiting . . .

JACK (*righteous, overconcern*) Waiting for what? What about . . ?

FREDA Your father doesn't know . . it would kill him if he knew his daughter was . . .

JACK What . . . ?

FREDA I think she must have gone to a motel . . . with a man. That's my guess . . I found . . . in her purse . . matches . . . from the Water-Bed Motel on Route 35 in Lakehurst . . you know, near the Army base? Fort Dix. (*Slight pause.*) Your sister is turning into a little whore . . . right before our very eyes. Something must be done. But what? Maybe she was with a soldier.

(*Sound of a motorcycle stopping and doorbell ringing in rapid succession.*)

Who's that?

JACK The doorbell.

(*Lights dim.*)

FREDA Maybe we shouldn't answer. My hair's a mess. Where are my slippers? See who it is.

(JACK *goes to door. At the same moment* ANGEL *enters the entrance hall area.*)

ANGEL (*in a confused state*) . . . uh . . . it . . . must've been open.

JACK . . . what . . . ?

ANGEL . . . I just dropped by . . . see . .

JACK Oh . . . Haven't I seen you with your bike . . . at the garage . . . the Sunoco station . . ?

ANGEL Yeah. Maybe. I might have . . though I'm not sure. Where is it?

JACK Highway 33 near the circle just beyond Jeannie's Diner.

FREDA (*in the bar area pretending at "being busy"*) Who is it?

JACK Wait a minute – goddamn it! (*To* ANGEL.) What do you want? I mean, is there something . . . someone . . . you wanted to . . ?

ANGEL Can I put my bag down? My guitar . . .

JACK No law against that. But what is it . . . you . . .

ANGEL I have this address . . . (*Pulls out a piece of paper.*) . . . see. This is the address I writ down.

JACK Yeah?

ANGEL Well, she said to come over.

JACK Who? Oh . . . must've been my sister.

ANGEL Yeah . . . that could be it. (*Showing a piece of paper.*) Is that her name?

JACK Yeah. That's it. (FREDA *moves toward* ANGEL.)

ANGEL (*to* FREDA) You must be the mother.

FREDA (*tense*) M-m-m-mm. What did you say . . . ?

ANGEL We first met . . . uh . . your daughter and I . . at Mr. Pizza . . . I was having a Neapolitan slice with a Coke . . you know, just across from the Marina Mall Cinema II in the shopping plaza . . . Mr. Pizza. It's a chain. There are a great number of them . . in this area . . .

FREDA (*rigid*) Yes . . . I understand . .

ANGEL She said I should look her up. Stop . . by . . that is . . .
if I was in the neighborhood. I have her name written down
see.

JACK You want to take off your jacket?

FREDA (*quick*) His jacket?

ANGEL Oh . . . no . . well, not right this minute . . . the Marina
Shopping Center . . . you know it?

FREDA Yes. What was she doing there?

ANGEL What? (*He sits down, making himself at home.*)

JACK Would you want a drink . . or?

ANGEL No . . . no thanks. I'm attempting to lay off . . booze.
At least the hard stuff . . well . . . maybe if it's not too much
trouble. I could be persuaded.

FREDA (*continuing to confront*) I said what was she doing . . there
. . . when you met?

ANGEL Oh . . . shopping . . I guess. She had just bought a
bathing suit.

FREDA In the winter? Maybe she's thinking of going to Florida
. . A bathing suit? Did she pick you up?

ANGEL What?

FREDA (*angry*) I said did the little slut pick you up?

JACK (*flustered*) Mother! What sort of impression . . I mean . .

FREDA Well?

ANGEL (*as if joking*) We did cruise around on my bike into the
Pinelands . . . the woods . . . then I just took her back . . .

FREDA Back where? To the shopping mall?

ANGEL Yes . . .

FREDA And what did you do . . . in the woods?

ANGEL Oh . . . I forget . . . we had a couple of beers, I think,
and . . .

FREDA . . . and . . .

ANGEL I can be very accommodating to the situation. That's

not what you are asking . . . is it, madam?

FREDA I see. I see. Yes. It all comes together.

ANGEL (*moving in*) My name is Angel. Yeah. That's a nickname.
I'm . . uh . . . well . . . sort of strung out for a place to crash.
I've been kicked out of a room . . you . . . uh . . . don't know
of a place, do you? Your daughter said . . . maybe . . you don't
have an extra . . just a place I could flop. I've got a little bread
. . .

(*A pause.*)

FREDA (*as if conducting a personal interview*) What do you do?

ANGEL I beg your pardon?

FREDA . . . your occupation. What is your profession?

ANGEL . . . a little bit of . . . of . . everything. I can do . . .
well . . almost anything. You name it, I'm ready. Asbury
Park. I came to Asbury Park with a rock group . . . four of
us from upstate . . . called the Mood Changers . . actually
we were billed as Angel Dust – that was my name . . . Angel
Dust and the Mood Changers . . . I was supposed to be the
lead singer . . . like Bruce Springsteen . . . see . . . we had a
tryout. Well, eventually it split . . . we just couldn't quite get
it together see . . . one of the guys OD'd . . he's dead. So then
I was a lifeguard this last summer for a while at Point Pleasant
Beach . . . I did that in Florida too. I've bummed around
a good deal. I've worked as a mechanic sometimes . . . an
auto wrecker . . as a bartender . . . oh . . . and I did self-help
intensive training you know . . . sensitivity training. They
teach you that you can be whoever you want to be if you
want to be it. To be yourself. I think that's it. To try to find
out who you are. Get it?

JACK (*looking for attention*) Maybe you could check out my bike
. . . in the garage . . .

ANGEL (*taking his jacket off*) Yeah . . . I've been into a lot of
weird scenes too . . . see . . . but now I'm trying to play it
straight . . . well as much as possible . . you know what I
mean? To really be me . . . who I am . . I grew up mostly in

a Catholic foundling home . . . I go where I go. No parents.
At least none known to me . . . see . . an outsider . . . free
and easy . . . that's me . . . thought I'd find some security
. . . somewhere . . . something. But so far . . . no luck. Lots
of things have happened to me . . . just traveling around. I
guess you could say I've been in it mostly for the kicks. Weird
scenes.

FREDA (*repulsed, fascinated*) Like what?

ANGEL I've met all kinds of . . . freaks . . ha . . ha . .

FREDA (*suddenly flirtatious like a young girl*) You have a tattoo on
your arm . . .

ANGEL Yeah . . . about that place to stay if you could . . . just . .

FREDA Could? If we could . . . ?

ANGEL Put me up for the night. Well . . . just for tonight,
maybe, I could do some work. Anything. I'm kinduv
desperate. On my last legs . . wiped out . . . I didn't know
where to turn so I came here. Just a hunch. The paper was in
my pocket so . . . I looked it up . . .

JACK I have an extra cot . . in my room . . . and we are looking
for a man . . . at the station. Mr. Fedder is only a temporary.
Maybe you could . . .

ANGEL Fit in. I know I could fit in. I would appreciate it. I
know it's trouble . . .

FREDA (*to* JACK) What do you think of this?

ANGEL Just temporarily . . . till I get it together . . .

FREDA (*suspiciously interrogating*) You've never been to jail or
prison . . . have you?

ANGEL (*aghast*) Me?

FREDA (*swooping around the room*) Two men escaped from
Rahway State Prison Farm on Christmas Day . . . one black,
one white . . . it was on the TV news. It was while the inmates
were eating a holiday turkey dinner . . . they snuck out
through the commissary. They bound up and gagged a cook,
and two guards were held at gunpoint. The black was caught

. . . the white is still at large . . . he was in for rape . . . they say he is dangerous . . . and armed. He may be hiding out somewhere in this area, they think. That couldn't be you? Could it? Do you carry a gun?

ANGEL (*as if he were not sure of the accusation*) Uh . . . no . . . uh . . . I've never even been in . . . except once I . . . uh . . . that was only a misdemeanor . . . locked in the Tombs overnight in New York. A drunken spree. I don't even remember. I slept with bums. New York is shit.

JACK (*childish*) Would you like to look at the bike? It's Japanese-made.

ANGEL Sure . . . I can assure you I will not be any problem.

FREDA (*nursing her drink*) Where did you come from . . . originally . . . I mean?

ANGEL California. That was where I started my . . . then Florida . . . then here . . . then . . . just a continuous endless migration.

FREDA (*in a spaced-out manner*) California is a nice place . . . warm. I like the climate. The tall palm trees. I like to ride around there in an open convertible.

JACK Would you like a beer?

ANGEL (*sullen*) Okay . . .

JACK (*as if looking for approval and understanding from an older brother*) You can sleep in my room . . . if you like.

ANGEL (*absently*) It doesn't matter . . . where . . I . . don't really care . . .

FREDA (*dreamy*) Since you are a traveler . . . since you have been in a great number of places . . . you must have experienced a good deal . . . in your travels. You must have met many different kinds of people.

JACK Are you hungry?

ANGEL Yeah . . . well . .

JACK We have half a bucket of Colonel Sanders chicken with cole slaw in the Frigidaire . . . left over from dinner.

ANGEL I could go for it . . . you . . . got TV in your room?

JACK Yeah . . .

FREDA (*giggling*) You remind me of someone I knew a long
time ago . . .

ANGEL Who is that?

FREDA (*laughing*) My husband. (*Pause.*) What does your tattoo
say?

ANGEL (*a seductive attitude*) Oh . . . it says M–O–T–H–E–R –
mother. But I don't really have one . . . I just had it put on . . .
in Asbury Park . . just for fun. For the kick.

(FREDA *nods off in a semi-sleep. The lights dim.* JACK *and* ANGEL
*cross front and move into a hallway area just outside the living room
setting.*)

JACK Don't mind her. She's a little off. She's had two nervous
breakdowns. She was in Overbrook once . . a state hospital
. . on a rest cure . . . she's had electric shock treatments. It
was recommended. We had to . . I had to sign. The old man
was in no shape . . . himself . . to do it. Now all she does is
drink, take tranquilizers, watch TV, and tries to figure out what
everyone else is doing. Obsessed. The old man . . . he never
comes out of the cellar. He boozes . . . guzzles . . . down there.
He manages somehow to get to work these days but that's
about it . . . he comes upstairs when he's ready to crash . . .

ANGEL Some life.

JACK Hey! I collect hermit crabs . . live . . ever see them? And
I also have a collection of porno . . . I have a deck of playing
cards with sex scenes . . . would you like to have a look . . .

ANGEL Why not? I'm game.

JACK Every conceivable position.

ANGEL I have some poppers. We can watch TV and get high. Is
it color?

JACK Yeah.

ANGEL I love color. Yeah. I love to turn the sound off . . . listen
to music . . . and watch . . . color . . . the images . . . know

what I mean?

JACK You like disco? I have stereo earphones. Headphones.

ANGEL Yeah. Wow. I could go for it!

(ANGEL *and* JACK *enter* JACK'S *room, which is up one level behind a curtain. They sit on a cot and look at pornographic playing cards.* ANGEL *removes his shirt, settles in.*)

(*Lights dim indicating passage of time.* FREDA *wakes up and switches on the* TV.)

FREDA Has anybody seen my TV Guide? Where is that girl? Wait till she gets home. I'll murder her. Everyone leaves me . . . alone. What's on TV?

(*We hear a commercial interlude:*)

TV ANNOUNCER So when you think you're ready . . . go down to Crazy Eddie. His stereo equipment is the best in the land . . .

(*This segment ends with:*)

Crazy Eddie is insane!

(*Followed by:*)

Good evening. This is the ten o'clock news. An epidemic . . . a new concentrated strain of the pig flu has broken out in the New Jersey, New York, and Connecticut suburbs. It has been named the Suburban Pig Flu since its main impact so far has been in the suburbs. Symptoms are headaches, dizziness, and a propensity for confused thinking followed by a loss of will and a lack of motivation and, finally, chronic boredom. So far eight people have died of this disease, all in Monmouth County, New Jersey. It seemed they all attended the same dinner-dance, belonged to the same club, and lived in a similar planned housing community. Watch what you eat. There is at present no known inoculation for this new strain of the pig flu. I repeat . . . there is no inoculation at the present time for this dangerous disease. Watch for other symptoms such as spitting up blood, fatigue, and lethargy.

(*At this point the man,* MR. STONE, *with a face that is half human,*

half animal, bursts out of the door marked "Cellar" making eerie
sounds, grunting, drunken, angry cries filled with a fierce lust. He
rushes toward FREDA *and in his thrust we hear the sound effect of*
glass smashing to indicate the sound of the TV *screen breaking. The*
light in the room changes from blue-white to a low-key half light,
giving the stage a dreamlike quality with shadows that loom larger
than life as in some nightmare forest. The figure jumps on top of
FREDA, *who appears to be in a state of extreme shock.*)

FREDA (*moaning and groaning*) Oh my God. What's happened
to the TV . . . the picture tube is out . . . Help. Help. You're
drunk. Leave me alone. You smell like a pig. You disgust me.
You're soused. You're a swine. I hate you. Stop it. Stop it. Oh
. . . no . . no . . .

(MR. STONE *is snorting and moving up and down on top of* FREDA.
They are on the floor in a half light. Front door opens. A shaft of
light. It is JILL. *At the same time the bedroom area is lighted. We see*
ANGEL *and* JACK *wearing headphones. They are dancing, snorting*
poppers. We vaguely hear music that has a disco beat. They move
toward one another in slow disco action.)

JILL (*anxious but smiling*) Mother, is that you? Are you okay? Is
that Father with you?

FREDA (*gagging as if being choked*) Help.

JILL (*in a little girl's voice*) I can hardly see you. I just wanted you
to know that I'll be staying over at Mr. Fedders's tonight. We
couldn't find a movie I hadn't seen so we just drove around.
He's waiting for me. He's making some chicken matzoh
ball soup and we got some hamburgers in little boxes from
McDonalds. I saw Ronald McDonald. He was handing out
little flags . . . Mr. Fedder is so nice. I let him touch me but
only once. See you later. Don't worry.

(*Exit.*)

FREDA   Oh God. Oh God.

(*Fade.*)

Epilogue

Morning the next day.

MR. STONE, *still wearing animal head, is propped up in a smoking jacket in an overstuffed chair with a pipe stuck in his mouth. The members of the family,* FREDA, JILL, JACK, *and* ANGEL *are assembled looking blankly at him.*

TV REPAIRMAN (*staring into the bright white light of the* TV) Your picture tube is now functioning – thanks to instant TV repair – things can return . . .

FREDA (*smiling*) . . to normal family living. Thank God . . . I mean . . thank you . . doctor.

TV REPAIRMAN (*seductive*) TV Repairman – twenty-four hours a day immediate servicing. We don't want the public to be for one instant without. Our job is to fix the damage faster than . . .

FREDA (*excited*) Television does relieve tension . . . nerves . . . anxiety . . . I remembered your commercial on late-night TV. I kept the number.

TV REPAIRMAN Thank you – thank you. Sign this bill and I'll be on to my next broken set in need of repair.

FREDA Repair. Attention . . . and love . . .

(FREDA *signs. He exits.*)

What a wonderful man. So sincere and honest . . . and our parlor set is once again functioning . . . which is the main thing. Now for the second item on the family agenda.

(*This speech is drawn out accompanied by soft dinner music of the type heard in shopping malls, elevators, and suburban restaurants, melodies such as "Theme from A Summer Place," "Three Coins in the Fountain," or "A Garden in the Rain.")*

Now that you are becoming young adults there are serious truths . . . problems . . the problems we must all face . . . as

we move out of the protective childhood fantasy lands into
the traumas of the real world . . the world of mature adults.
All of us have been afflicted . . . at one time or another . . .
with some depressing disease . . . measles, chicken pox,
mumps, scarlet fever, whooping cough, cirrhosis, colitis,
dysentery, gallstones, bursitis, eczema, neuritis, neuralgia,
palsy, free-floating paranoia, headaches, dizziness . . . illness
. . . often is a condition which can go beyond . . . out of . . .
our control. Last night as your father was violently bumping
up and down on top of your mother, heaving and spitting
. . against his doctor's orders to calm down and avoid excess
excitation . . . he suffered what has been diagnosed as a major
coronary stroke and a crippling paralysis following orgasm.
He is currently unable to move. The doctors say eventually he
may recover his faculties and join us again. Don't try to talk to
him. He has nothing to say . . . and don't concern yourselves
with the future. Things will go on just as they were before.
No interruption of any great consequence has happened . .
yet. We are insured and will be provided for during this
temporary crisis. In fact, now that his illness has progressed,
he may be able to just sit and watch TV with us forever . . . till
death do us part. Sometimes, if we look on the bright side of
things, sickness, even a terminal condition, which this is not,
can actually bring some people back together again . . . closer
than ever. We can still maintain the appearance of being just
another typical American family – one that has discovered
the true secret of real happiness . . . security, and protection
– the sane condition of successful interdependent relations in
suburban living. We can not . . . we will not be disturbed by
what is going on out there.

She switches on the TV.
Sound – Elvis in Concert – "My Way."
Lights fade on family portrait tableau, all looking blankly into the TV.
"My Way" continues playing through for the curtain call.

INCREASED OCCUPANCY

A PLAY IN ONE ACT

Increased Occupancy was first presented as a curtain-raiser to *Suburban Tremens* by New York Theater Strategy at Westbeth Theater Center on April 6, 1978. It was directed by the author, with set design by Theo Barnes, lights by Larry Steckman, and sound by Sheila Paige.

WILCOX I	Paul Lieber
WILCOX II	Lawrence Sellars
MR. MONEYPENNY	Mark Simon
EXTERMINATOR	Tony Teslicko

Timothy Bissell

*From left, Mark Simon as Mr. Moneypenny, Paul
Lieber as Wilcox I, and Lawrence Sellars as Wilcox II
in "Increased Occupancy," presented as a curtain-raiser
to "Suburban Tremens"*

INCREASED OCCUPANCY

CHARACTERS:

WILCOX I — *An artist. He wears white overalls smeared with white and black paint. Work shoes. Work shirt.*

WILCOX II — *A co-artist. He wears white overalls also smeared with white and black paint. Work shoes. Work shirt.*

MR. MONEYPENNY — *A dark suit that is baggy and dirty. A cream-colored shirt. An overcoat and a red scarf.*

EXTERMINATOR — *In white jump-suit, carrying a black bag, wearing steel horn-rimmed glasses.*

SCENE:

An almost bare room painted white. A large unfinished canvas painted with large black and white broad strokes. An outer hallway area. A window frame. A door. A ladder. Paint buckets filled with brushes.

OPENING MUSIC: *"Who's Afraid of the Big Bad Wolf"*

TIME: *Mid-afternoon*

PLACE: *The City*

Intense White Light

SOUNDS (TAPED): *city traffic, horns, a police siren.*

WILCOX I *is on a ladder screwing a light bulb into a ceiling light fixture.*

WILCOX II *is hammering a plastic drop cloth over a window frame.*
WILCOX I *drops the light bulb.*

Crashing sound.

WILCOX I   God damn it. I got a shock. An electric shock.

WILCOX II   Clean it up.

WILCOX I   (*picks up dust pan and broom, sweeping the glass onto the pan and dumping it into garbage can*)   I could've been killed. Jesus.

WILCOX II   (*hammering a last nail into the window frame*)   That should do it.

WILCOX I   Won't it take oxygen out of the air?

WILCOX II   What?

WILCOX I   Besides . . . isn't it getting warm . . . I mean . . warmer . . . outside?

WILCOX II   Warmer . . . yes . . . but it is not actually . . yet . . . spring. Winters seem to be . . . becoming . . . more and more prolonged in this latter part of the twentieth century. We seem to be entering the new Ice Age. Knifelike icicles are still forming on the windowpane. Added to that we are still running out of . . . energy . . . the energy supply is drying up . . . and . . money is also . . . dwindling. Nevertheless we are in a transitional seasonal time period of winter moving into spring . . . or is it spring moving into winter? I don't know.

WILCOX I   When will it be spring?

WILCOX II   Soon.

WILCOX I   Oh.

(*Pause.*)

Should we work . . . on the painting . . . on completing the work on . . . it's been two months.

WILCOX II   Not today . . . I'm not inspired. I feel . . . . tired . . (*A loud pounding on the door. To* WILCOX I.)   Who's that?

WILCOX I (*at the door*) Who is that?

MR. MONEYPENNY (*tightly*) It's me.

WILCOX I Me. Who? What do you want? Leave us alone.

MR. MONEYPENNY You left your garbage in the hall.

WILCOX I Well?

MR. MONEYPENNY It fell . . over. Orange peels, coffee rinds, cat dung are all over the place. It is a health hazard . . . I tell you . . . and a fire department violation as well. You must transport your own garbage and debris out of the building . . . or keep it in there with you until which time you are ready to remove it. It cannot be placed in the hall where it is in jeopardy of being knocked over. There is no longer garbage collection or disposal by landlord required on these premises. Did you receive my order?

WILCOX I Er . . . . uh . . . . what . . order?

MR. MONEYPENNY The writ stating that superintendent services have been discontinued . . . revoked . . due to higher and higher building costs that are constantly passed on to me.

WILCOX I Okay . . . leave it there . . . I'll attend to it . . . later.

(*Pause.*)

MR. MONEYPENNY That's not all . . . that's not the only business that I came here for . . .

WILCOX I What . . . what else . . I'm busy.

MR. MONEYPENNY Complaints have come my way that drunk and disorderly parties have been held in these rooms . . . . by you . . . into the early hours of morning during which time other tenants are in need of sleep. Parade access is a violation.

WILCOX I What?

MR. MONEYPENNY Access by parade in a loud manner from the street to your dwelling and the entertainment of unsavory characters.

WILCOX I Oh . . .

MR. MONEYPENNY (*angry*) Degenerates . . . . even bums were

seen entering . .

WILCOX I Mr. Moneypenny . . that is character . . . .
characterological assassination . .

MR. MONEYPENNY What? What did you say?

(*No answer.*)

(*A change of attitude.*)

May I come in? I need to come in there . . .

WILCOX I What for?

MR. MONEYPENNY I need to . . . to touch your radiator.

WILCOX I Why do you want to do that?

MR. MONEYPENNY To see how warm it is. It may be too hot. I
want to see what the temperature is . . . inside . . .

WILCOX II (*touching radiator*) Cold. The radiator is cold. No heat
coming up whatsoever.

MR. MONEYPENNY . . . who . . . is that . . . in there . . . . with
you? Whose voice is that, sir?

WILCOX I It is . . . er . . . my associate. We are working on a
painting . . . an important work of art . . . together.

MR. MONEYPENNY (*hysterical*) Open this door. (*Pounding.*) Open
up. Open up.

WILCOX I This will have to be stopped. (*He opens the door.*)
Now what is it you really . . . . ?

MR. MONEYPENNY (*barging in, hostile, he directs himself at* WILCOX
II) Who are you?

WILCOX II (*befuddled*) I . . . uh . . . I . . . .

MR. MONEYPENNY You are the person I spoke to the other day
. . . two days ago . . . you opened the door just a crack and
claimed to be . . . called yourself Mr. Wilcox. Do you take me
to be a fool?

WILCOX I I am Mr. Wilcox.

MR. MONEYPENNY So it has been understood . . . until I
encountered this person here whom it has been obvious to me

. . . and to the other tenants . . . has been an occupant . . . has been living on these premises. Is that the case?

WILCOX II I am Mr. Wilcox.

MR. MONEYPENNY Now let us not play at being confusing. We all understand this game.

WILCOX I He has been staying over . . . as a houseguest . . . for a while . . . while we have been working on . .

WILCOX II Mr. Whateveryournameis. Look at that painting. Have you no regard for . . . artistic . . . realities?

MR. MONEYPENNY Now don't try to confuse me with this something you call art. Now let us talk as gentlemen. Your original lease states that you are to be the sole occupant herein. Correct?

WILCOX I I don't know.

MR. MONEYPENNY You should read it, my boy. You do still have it . . . in your possession . . . don't you?

WILCOX I (*quickly*) Oh . . . yes . . . why . . . naturally . . .

MR. MONEYPENNY This means there exists herein the condition of . . . the question of . . . increased occupancy. Do you know what that is?

WILCOX I & WILCOX II (*together*) What . . that . . . is?

MR. MONEYPENNY (*interrogating* WILCOX I) Did you know this person . . . . claimed . . . on this said occasion . . . two days before . . . . to be yourself . . . to have your very same last name?

WILCOX I (*covering*) He is my brother.

MR. MONEYPENNY A lie. A lie is easy to expose. An old saying – "Lying shows, never goes."

WILCOX I I thought it was "Cheatin' shows, never goes."

MR. MONEYPENNY What does it matter? It's the same damn thing.

WILCOX I Oh.

MR. MONEYPENNY And you told me when you rented from

me that you were the sole and only child . . . the son of two deceased parents. Were you lying then?

WILCOX I I was . . . I mean . . I am an orphan . . . alone.

MR. MONEYPENNY Then you were lying.

WILCOX I I'm not exactly sure. I think they are dead . . .

MR. MONEYPENNY You . . . *think*? What was their name?

WILCOX I Wilcox.

MR. MONEYPENNY Wilcox. Yes, that is the name on your original lease. Your last name . . . yes? (*To* WILCOX II.) And your name is . . . ? Well . . . in any case . . . the point . . . is . . . the fact is . . . you can't stay here. You must remove yourself from these premises . . . the facts are . .

WILCOX II Facts? What facts?

MR. MONEYPENNY (*pointing at* WILCOX I) The lease . . states . . . that this Mr. Wilcox whose name is affixed and signed to the lease can be the only . . . the one and only . . . and sole occupant . . . permitted to dwell herein.

WILCOX II (*building anger*) What is it . . . what is it you are trying to get at . . . to say? That I have no identity?

MR. MONEYPENNY That you are . . . a trespasser . . . sir . . . even an illegal squatter . . . here . . . and unless I were to decide to honor this nefarious situation . . . you call yourself an artist, you say? . . . by granting you an increased occupancy which would give me a rent hike but which I am not particularly predisposed to doing since you falsified . . . *your identity* . . . . to me . . . two days ago . . . who you are . . . I will choose to follow the escape clause which states . . .

WILCOX II Wait a minute. What about controls?

MR. MONEYPENNY There are no controls. This space is de-controlled . . . and if you don't watch yourselves you could both end up out on the street.

WILCOX I You mean another person cannot live . . . in this space . . . at my discretion?

MR. MONEYPENNY That would appear to be the case.

WILCOX II Are you out of your mind?

MR. MONEYPENNY I keep myself focused on the technical points . . . and you are not Mr. Wilcox.

WILCOX II And what about the heat . . . supplying this place with heat? The radiator you wanted to touch is cold. Cold!

MR. MONEYPENNY It is warm in here. Warm enough. It is not Florida . . . but . . . and oil is expensive . . . an expensive commodity. You could call an inspector in which case I will go into my cellar which I keep safely closed off from tenants and turn the heat up for the duration of the inspection . . . and then shut it off again when he leaves. I know the law and . . .

WILCOX II Who do you think you are . . . Hitler? (WILCOX II *grabs* MR. MONEYPENNY *by his coat and begins pulling tightly on his red scarf while* WILCOX I *picks up a hammer, clenching it tightly in his hand.)* I could puncture you with a screwdriver.

MR. MONEYPENNY Let me go, you fool.

WILCOX I Just playing, Mr. Moneypenny. Just a game . . . a funny game.

MR. MONEYPENNY Stop your tickling . . . (*He laughs.*) . . . stop tickling.

WILCOX II We are the law now. We are the ones who are in control. You might say we took the law into our own hands, haven't we? And whatever we say is true, isn't it? (*Choking him with his scarf.*) Isn't it?

MR. MONEYPENNY Yes.

WILCOX II And my name is Wilcox.

WILCOX I And my name is Wilcox.

MR. MONEYPENNY Yes . . . uh . . . no. (WILCOX II *is now strangling* MR. MONEYPENNY *with his own red scarf.)*

WILCOX I I think he's out. I think you've put him . . . out . . . cold.

WILCOX II I think he's just fainted. We really scared him. Don't you think we scared him? Certainly is frail for a landlord, a lord of the land.

WILCOX I He seems pale. Are you sure he's breathing?

WILCOX II (*listening to his heartbeat*) I can hear a heartbeat. His heart is . . . beating. No . . . it stopped. It just stopped. Hard to believe that I . . . .

WILCOX I You mean he's . . . . he's dead?

WILCOX II Ding. Dong. The landlord's dead.

WILCOX I What do we do now?

WILCOX II I think we should have a look at that lease. Go get it.

WILCOX I What for?

WILCOX II Never mind. Stop asking questions. Where is it?

WILCOX I It's in the sock drawer . . . underneath the drawer, I mean.

(*Pause. He goes to get it.*)

Here it is.

(*He hands* WILCOX II *a yellowed, crumpled-up lease.*)

WILCOX II (*reading it over slowly*) Oh . . . well . . . it's just what I thought. (*Pause. Reading.*) He's legally entitled to ten percent more on the rent for an increased occupancy.

WILCOX I You knew that . . . did you know that?

WILCOX II I thought it might be the case.

WILCOX I But now he's dead . . .

WILCOX II Well, maybe we'll get off without having to pay the increase now anyhow . . . see. Things have a way of working out . . . sometimes . . . for the best. (*Pause.*) Anyhow, I feel a new kind of energy. I think I'm ready to begin work on the painting . . our mutual painting.

WILCOX I On the painting?

WILCOX II Yes. Suddenly I don't feel tired anymore . . . I need a glass of water.

(*He drinks it.*)

. . Yes . . . refreshed. Calm.

WILCOX I Okay. What about him?

WILCOX II Him? We'll dump him in the hall next to the orange peels, coffee grounds, and cat shit. I don't think anyone heard him . . . coming in. Most of the other tenants are at work in offices and stores around the city. It will look like a simple mugging . . . many unsavory type people have entrance and egress to this building.

WILCOX I You mean parade access?

WILCOX II (*like a platoon sergeant issuing commands*) Get his wallet. Take out whatever money you find.

(WILCOX I *follows these instructions.*)

Keep the money. Now put his wallet back where you found it. It will appear to be a theft . . . like he was held up by a junkie . . see. Wipe off your fingerprints. Wipe off his fingerprints. Let's carry him into the hall.

(*They carry him into the hall, leaving him near the garbage.*)

WILCOX I There.

(*Closes door.*)

WILCOX II Finished. I didn't hear a thing today. Did you? I've been busy . . . painting . . . concentrated.

WILCOX I No. I didn't hear anything either.

(*Slight pause.*)

Think we should phone up the cops?

WILCOX II Let someone else discover him out there. We don't want to get involved. We can't afford an involvement. His was a natural . . . unfortunate death . . . by assault.

WILCOX I Just another Village mugging. Survival is almost becoming an impossibility . . in this city.

(*A man in a white jumpsuit appears at the door.*)

EXTERMINATOR Hello. Exterminator.

WILCOX I What is it? What do you want?

EXTERMINATOR Someone . . . a bum . . is asleep in your hallway.

WILCOX I What do you want me to do about it? Let him be.
He must be tired or he wouldn't be sleeping there, would he?
Mind your own business.

EXTERMINATOR How is your problem . . . ?

WILCOX I What . . . ?

EXTERMINATOR . . . with pests . . . the bug problem?

WILCOX I We have no . . problem. Leave us alone. We are . . .
busy. Go away.

WILCOX I *and* WILCOX II *stand in front of painting.* EXTERMINATOR
stands still at door, not moving. WILCOX I *picks up a thick house-paint
brush and paints a bold black stroke on the canvas.* WILCOX II *picks up
a similar paint brush and angrily adds a white stroke.*

SOUNDS: *Horns. Traffic. Faint music from a local bar.*

MUSIC: *"Who's Afraid of the Big Bad Wolf?" Lights dim.*

End.

SANTA CLAUS
IN AMERICA

A PLAY IN ONE ACT

Santa Claus
in America

Characters:

WALDO — *A comic in his thirties. He wears a gray shirt and gray pants.*

ANA — *A staff counselor wearing a white peasant blouse, gray slacks, and flat shoes. An attractive woman, she has mastered the martial arts though these are not employed in the play other than to suggest that she might possess inordinate strength.*

GOLDA — *A garish platinum blonde movie starlet overly made up and in a magenta satin slip of a dress. She is WALDO's ex-wife and the mother of JUNIOR. She is agitated and insecure in the sex-goddess image.*

WALDO JUNIOR — *He wears a powder blue suit. This character may be played by a young boy or by a teenager who seems somewhat retarded.*

Scene:

A white room with a large rectangular window overlooking a landscape of green grass, hills, and trees. This vista has a manicured look not unlike that of a country club golf course. The hills surround the room and a gray sky is beyond.

In the room are a sofa, two chairs, and a desk, all of which are slightly outsized. There are a series of doors, one leading to a lavatory, one to a closet, one to a bedroom-dressing room, and another (stage right) leading

*to an adjoining hallway waiting room which has a bench, a chair, and
end table, and a lamp. In this semi-darkened area are* JUNIOR, *who is
asleep, and* GOLDA, *who smokes and reads magazines. Two other doors
with glass and wire mesh panels open up onto a downstage veranda.
This room is in a cottage which connects to other identical cottages
which are a segment of Rolling Hills complex.*

*The set should indicate in an abstract way the feeling of endless rooms
and corridors in an interplay with the surrounding country, the grounds
outside.*

*Music ensues. The song we hear is "Here Comes Santa Claus"
on sleigh bells. There is a vocal of one chorus which subsides and
underscores the opening monologue, gradually fading underneath.*

ANA (*half spoken to the audience*) This is a place where you come
    . . . if you come to it at all . . . that is, an interim place . . .
    where we attempt to discover . . . to discern . . to diagnose
    . . . if we can . . . where someone's life went off . . . leaving
    them . . bereft . . . where there was no alternative but to
    come to us . . . or some other similar situation. Often those
    surrounding the ones who come . . failed to understand or
    even acknowledge what was happening when someone close
    was falling to pieces. Some move away . . . or simply give
    up. Others disappear never to make contact again. Not too
    many care to hang around when hopelessness, despondency,
    or despair set in. These conditions when manifested have
    been known to be contagious . . and there you are, stuck in
    isolation . . . alone with yourself . . . with no sense of future
    . . . not to mention a lack of connection between events past
    or present. When you find the time has come when you can
    no longer move forward and you cannot . . . look back . . you
    are then – *stagnating* – and in need of help.

WALDO (*anxious*) I feel like I'd like to get back into some of my
    old standup routines – but I'm not sure that I could remember
    the goddam stories . . . the jokes . . or the formula punch lines
    . . . I wouldn't know where to begin. Like an amnesiac I can't

seem to retain what I knew before. Some things seem clear, yet others seem distant . . . gray . . in some other dimension as if they never were . . . except in a dream. I feel as if I've entered a void without a self . . . and yet I also feel a sense of guilt like a condemned man in a prison. Is that what this place is?

ANA This is what we in the profession describe as a neutral space. If you look out there . . . outside . . . you will see beauteous rolling hills covered with green grass . . . and trees. You will note that there are included on this landscape . . . . recreational facilities provided for those who are capable of participating in planned activities . . . swimming, tennis, basket weaving, the crafts, poetry classes, drama seminars . . special discussion groups . . . though these are not available to those who display hostile attitudes or are overtly aggressive in their behavioral patterns. Do you understand my meaning?

WALDO Is this then an "institution"?

ANA It is an "institution" of sorts, but we don't like . . . exactly . . to call it that.

WALDO Is it a . . rest home . . funny farm . . . a nut house?

ANA We try to avoid labels of any kind . . . if we can help it. We try to confine ourselves to very simple terminology. It makes it easier to cope. Manic-depressive – paranoid schizophrenic – psychoneurotic – are regarded as outmoded terms here. We prefer to leave most things . . most doors . . . open to interpretation. That way we can continue to analyze these . . . problems . . difficulties . . in depth so as to eventually get to the root causes of a particular case such as yours, the anxieties, fears, terrors of the unknown.

WALDO What then?

ANA Termination in most instances . . . a release . . . back to the outside world . . . eventually all of it ending in some kind of death. But until that time we are here to comfort you. You needn't worry. Just give yourself over to us . . . for the time being.

WALDO This place I'm in has no name?

ANA We call it Rolling Hills.

WALDO Who is "we"?

ANA Staff and everyone else. That is also the way it is
advertised in the brochure . . and the better magazines. We
cater . . . usually . . . to a select clientele, ex-president's wives,
movie stars, public personalities who require some degree
of . . . discretion . . if not anonymity – protection from
curiosity-seekers.

WALDO Oh. Staff and everyone else . . . very exclusively
democratic.

ANA We also try to encourage an open situation so we have
no locked doors. People . . . including yourself . . . may
freely wander about . . . anywhere you like. We don't disdain
intrusion. In fact anyone may burst in on us . . . into our one-
to-one conversation at any moment – but we will be able to
handle that situation if it occurs.

WALDO (*vague*) We will?

ANA Yes, you are one of the "we," although I'm sure that
sometimes you think you are not . . . that you stand above the
others . . . isolated . . . as in a nightmare.

WALDO It sometimes feels that way, as if darkness were setting
in and no one is there . . . just myself . . breathing . . heart
pounding . .

ANA Are you in terror of the dark of night?

WALDO What?

ANA The dark . . an absence of light . . .

WALDO . . . like death.

ANA Does it frighten you?

(*No answer. Pause.*)

WALDO Is this an interview you are conducting – ?

ANA You could call it that . . .

WALDO . . . like a TV interview show.

ANA Have you ever been on television?

WALDO I believe I am famous . . . a well-known personage of some kind. I mean outside this place. I think I have appeared on television; but what I did in that medium is vague to me. I know I am very fond of commercials. But I don't think . .

ANA Your memory is improving. Yesterday you didn't have any recall . . . as far as your life on television is concerned.

WALDO Then you would say I had achieved some notoriety?

ANA You did . . . once.

WALDO Have I been forgotten? I could be last week's news.

ANA That is possible.

WALDO (*angrily*) I am sick of possibilities. I'd like to have some sense of the problem . . . of . . . what is transpiring . . . .

ANA You don't know?

(*Pause.*)

Are you angry . . at the world?

WALDO Angry . . . depressed . . what difference does it make?

ANA It does make a difference to us. Anger is more of an out-and-out emotional expression. Depression is turning the anger in on oneself so that it eats away . . . like a tapeworm . . . at the internal organs. It is better to bring the anger . . . rage . . . into the open . . . to battle it out. Turning anger in on yourself is one reason you are now with us . . .

WALDO (*childlike*) How is that?

ANA Do you remember how you came to be admitted?

WALDO Vaguely . . . . in a sort of hazy gray-out . . . like a blurred or jumping television screen . .

(*Pause.*)

ANA You tried to take your own life. You were found on the patio of your Hollywood Hills home . . . unconscious near your swimming pool . . . near death . . by a maid who took you to a hospital. Later you came to us. Try to visualize it . . . to *see it* . . if you can.

WALDO I'm sure it must have been an accident . .

ANA That is what the papers would have said – an accidental
    death due to a lethal combination of drugs . . . . barbiturates
    . . and booze just like any number of others in the Hollywood
    Hills.

WALDO Why just there? I thought it was happening
    everywhere. I still say . . . if it happened . . . which it did not
    . . . it would have been accidental.

ANA There are no accidents . . . except by intention . . . . but if
    you prefer you could call it that . . . an intentional accident.

WALDO I would rather talk about it at some other time. My
    nerves are unsteady today.

ANA We can let it go for now. So what is it that you would like
    to discuss or do . . . now?

WALDO Could I have a tranquilizer . . . or sedative?

ANA Later . . . for now it is better to remain conscious . . to
    keep talking. Would you like to talk about your professional
    life . . your television career.

WALDO I couldn't handle . . . I lost my grip on the role . . . the
    identity I was living out. I thought I was a funny man . . . but
    then . . .

ANA You were . . . or are . . a well-known comic . . . . known
    to us all . . but no one here is impressed with that . . . or
    with how many TV talk shows you joked your way through
    . . turning on the fast charm or the slick winking grimacing
    cuteness that you are so good at . . . masking hostility . . your
    anger. Tragedy masquerading as comedy. Reality is more
    than just the role you selected to play out . . . for a bunch of
    dummies who go along for the gag. We see into and beyond
    what you are trying so desperately to conceal.

WALDO (evasive) Have you ever seen me on TV?

ANA I caught your act.

WALDO And . . . ?

ANA It had its points but . . .

WALDO I can go along with that . . .

ANA Most of these TV shows are developed to appeal to nine-year-olds, that being the emotional age of the average viewer across the country . . according to some recent studies. Where did I read that?

WALDO Where does that leave me?

ANA You are here looking for some change, I would think. Perhaps you will go back and be able to accept all of that . . . in a limited way . . playing some Jokester God.

WALDO Aren't you playing God?

ANA I don't think so.

WALDO It does have an incredible force though . . .

ANA What?

WALDO Television. It sells products of all kinds . . . . elects presidents . . . It is important . . beyond . .

ANA . . . and you made a good deal of money in it . .

WALDO I never knew what to do with it.

ANA The money?

WALDO Yes. What to buy . . what to spend it on.

(*Pause.*)

How long have I been here?

ANA Several weeks.

WALDO When can I leave?

ANA I don't know. We could let you go now, but that would clearly be a mistake. There is some idea that there might be brain damage . . . due to the quantity of chemicals you ingested.

WALDO Do we . . . is there a television set here?

ANA It wouldn't be constructive. We try to remove all obstacles . . .

WALDO I always . . particularly liked to watch . . . . the commercials. So direct . . . so assertive . . .

ANA They are often aggressive – and hostile . . . . in their attempt to put across a product.

WALDO   In any case we haven't yet – determined what I am to
do . . . what I'm supposed to be . . . now that I am no longer
myself. I mean as I know myself.

ANA   As I told you the day before yesterday . . and the day
before that . . we are trying to look closely at what you have
done, what you are doing, and what you will be doing in
order to prepare you for your ultimate release.

WALDO   Where will I go when I get out?

ANA   That choice is up to you . . you haven't yet understood
what has happened to you . . . the past events of your life that
led you to this unfortunate place. Try to remember what you
would like to forget.

WALDO   Look . . I came from nowhere. I wanted to get
somewhere. We never had a nickel. I wanted to get out. I
don't know my parents. I think they're dead now. Everything
around me felt like a trap . . I ran away. I wanted to be
somebody. I don't know who. Now I don't remember
what I was looking for. Maybe it is better not to remember
everything . . . only what I want. I used to do my routines
on the streets . . . see. People would laugh. Crowds. That's
how it happened. I found I could captivate . . manipulate
them. I listened, watched, and studied the big ones on radio
and TV . . . Jack Benny . . . in particular . . Fred Allen . .
Johnny Carson, Red Skelton, Ben Blue, Ed Wynne, Bert
Lahr . . Baby Snooks . . . all the top comics. I learned about
deadpan . . the blank look after you give them the pitch. I
was born too late for vaudeville. Vaudeville had died. Radio
was dead. I came up through TV. I played off of my fucked-
up head. Depression. I made jokes about depression. Suicide.
I became famous for my "jump out the window" . . . "slash
your wrists" . . . "kill yourself" . . . stories. Life to me was a
joke. Death was another sick joke. Sometimes I hit hard below
the belt if it got a laugh. I didn't care. I was insatiable. Clubs.
Vegas. Money. Poverty.

(*Pause.*)

I remember being hired as Santa Claus one Christmas in a department store. All those greedy kids asking me for special favors. A recurrent dream. Yah wanna hear it? It keeps coming back to me. I am in this red suit with a fake Dynel white beard and wig – stuffed with goose-down pillows, black patent leather boots. High drag. I have even applied orange makeup – caked on and dry red rouge. See . . . so as to give me an authentic North Pole complexion . . .

ANA This is a dream?

WALDO I don't know.

ANA Is it real?

WALDO It could be . . but it was a dream . . see. I think.

ANA You're sweating . .

WALDO Could I have a Coke?

ANA A commercial break?

WALDO A Coke. Coca Cola. I know there is no cocaine around this place.

ANA Here it is. (*Hands him a bottle of Coke, which he gulps down quickly.*) It quenches the thirst just like they say.

WALDO (*building feverishly*) I have my sack – my Christmas sack filled with all kinds of junk . . . in the dream . . see. Department store gifts for everybody. There is no end to the supply. I fill and empty the bag over and over again . . . TV sets, bicycles, stereo earphones, giant portable radios, the kind you carry with you down the street . . disco roller skates, ice skates, telephone answering machines, tape decks, toasters, bun warmers, fans, lamps, appliances of all kinds, electric blankets, hair dryers . . . things to make life easier . . Mixmasters . . . and . . . and . . . bubble bath, boxes of luxury soap, cosmetics, perfume, perfumed talcum powder . . records . . . books . . . art books . . . literature . . . how to cook . . . how to run . . . how to live . . what to do . . . with your life . . your leisure time. How to work. How to think. Pans, coffee pots, games, toys, dolls, jewelry, watches, wallets, bedroom slippers, shoes, cigarettes . . cartons of them . . Smirnoff Vodka, Johnnie Walker Scotch, London Gin, sparkling Cold Duck by the case, gourmet items like goose liver paté from Denmark, caviar from Iran . . or fancy shortbread from Scotland, orange marmalade and jams, candied fruit and nuts . . . an endless amount of material goods . . exotic things. I am giving these away to ravaged crowds of people with arms outstretched as if I were a Santa Claus host on a TV game show . . . except I feel this terrible sense of anxiety. Later I remember being pursued by Pinkertons . . up a series of escalators. It was clear that I had come by these things by mistake. Maybe I had stolen them . . . in the dream . . .

ANA Excuse me. What are Pinkertons?

WALDO Men in blue uniforms with guns and sticks who guard stores against theft. They are the enemy of Santa Claus. Ha ha. They prevent you from taking the things you need out of the store.

ANA I see. Santa Claus wants to give it all away.

WALDO Something like that. I suppose you would call it some kind of progressive paranoia . . in your book . . . or crime . .

ANA There is a logic to paranoia . . . sometimes . .

WALDO Hey . . . how about a political party called the Progressive Paranoids? No . . a bad joke. Not funny. Anyway that is the end of that part of the dream. Part one.

ANA There is another part?

WALDO Yeah. Me . . as Santa Claus . . . mythological childhood gift-giving guru Kris Kringle, Father Christmas, chimney imp-fairy and sublimated pederastic devil. A fat St. Nick. A kid I recognize from somewhere has come to visit me in jail. Evidently I have been put there by these Pinkertons. I am still in my red suit and white-as-snow beard. The kid is whispering in my ear telling me about all the things that are missing in his dumb little life. Then telling me what he

wants out of it all . . . a career . . a house . . a red Porsche
convertible. The usual. As he is telling me about his needs
to overindulge himself I notice the expression on his face is
contorted and without expression like a very old mean man
. . like a Bowery beggar. The only thing I have left in my
pocket is an oversized red-and-white-striped candy cane
wrapped in cellophane, which I offer unto him. He grabs it
from me angrily, rips off the cellophane, bites off large chunks
of the big stick almost breaking his tiny teeth on the hard
sweet indigestible concoction, finally swallowing – gagging
and choking on the big pieces which are somehow caught in
his throat. I try to get the little demon to cough up the candy
– slapping him on the back – while he turns green gasping for
air. Anyway, the miserable brat drops dead . . . actually dies in
my arms – with a weird half-smile on his face. Suddenly he
looks hundreds of years old. Not like a kid at all. Splintered
pieces of the peppermint stick candy cane are all over . .
his body . . . my red suit . . and all over the floor. I try . . .
desperately . . . to clean it up . . . in a hurry . . . hiding the
evidence. Then . . .

ANA Then . . . what?

WALDO I wake up . . . that's it. My dream!

ANA What happens after the dream . . ?

WALDO More intense anxiety . . . the feeling of guilt as though
I myself had actually murdered the child with the hard candy.
Maybe the child is an extension of myself . . . or of a lost more
innocent self . . . lost a hundred years ago before I was born
. . . I say to myself . . maybe I did . .

ANA (shakes him, slaps him) You must wake out of your delirium
. . your state of dream . . .

(Pause.)

Don't you have a child? . . . well, we have brought him to see
you.

WALDO (still delirious) To . . see . . me?

ANA Yes. Today. With your ex-wife . . to see you . . a visit.

WALDO I thought they were in make-believe land . . Hollywood. Why would they come here?

ANA You do remember. The pieces of the past are beginning to fit. We thought it would aid in your recovery . . if you could see . . your own . . child . . that it would give you . . strength to go on.

WALDO Shouldn't I dress . . look more presentable? If I have visitors . . dress for the occasion?

ANA You didn't know today was a visitors day, did you?

WALDO No . . . since I have had no visitors I can remember.

ANA You may go into your bedroom – and change if you wish. Shall I have an attendant help you?

WALDO I think I can manage . . . thank you . .

ANA You feel all right . . . about seeing . . these people . .

WALDO I guess so . . since I apparently once knew them.

ANA You are sure? Is there anything you would like to say . . before . . ?

WALDO (*by rote*) Yes. I would like to become less neurotic, less dependent on others. Yes. I would like to be able to feel something . . to become independent – interdependent in a healthier way. Uh. Com . . . mu . . ni . . cate . . my neeeeds more di-rect-ly. Yes. I have been isolated for a period of time after a long and serious emotional illness. Yes. I tried to kill myself . . . booze . . . drugs . . anything I could get hold of. Yes. I wanted to die. Yes. Now it is reversed. Is that right? Did I recall my reality correctly?

ANA How long has this illness been with you?

WALDO Ever since I can remember. Is that right? Yes. It was always there but I tried to cover it up . . to run away . . from myself . . telling corny jokes . . . looking for applause, cackles . . whatever approval I could get.

ANA Your sex life . . ?

WALDO I was always like an animal . . . out of control . . only interested in self-gratification . . . filled with hate . .

ANA   . . for yourself . .

WALDO   . . and others. But now all of that has been changed. I am tired now. I need to . .

ANA   Go and prepare yourself . . rest for a few moments. I will bring in what is left of your family. Try to remain calm . . . keep your rages in check . . . your reactions at a minimum. We can discuss the effects later when they have gone.

(WALDO *goes to bedroom door. Exits. Enter* GOLDA *and* WALDO JUNIOR.) You may come in now. It was necessary to prepare him for your visit.

GOLDA (*agitated, with disinterest*) Oh. How is he doing?

ANA   He goes up and down . . . in and out . . . but there are signs of improvement. We are currently trying to exhaust the rages . . we hope to avoid electro-shock treatment . . to bring him back through a directive approach. (*Pause.*) You two were married for a time?

GOLDA   Two years.

ANA   What was it like?

GOLDA (*childlike manner*) He was an animal . . an S.O.B. It was two years of emotional hell as far as I am concerned. Violent attacks . . drunken brawls . . I still have the scars to prove it. Wanna see? But we did live in a big pink stucco dream house in the Hollywood hills. I still live there. Plenty of speed, coke, black beauties, uppers, downers, plenty to eat and drink. Cars. We had whatever we needed . . . the good life . . but . . we had Junior here who is somewhat precocious . . or is it retarded? . . for his age. He always had the best money could buy. He has his own nurse. I don't have time. Too busy with my film career . . my movies.

ANA   Yes. I have seen some of your pictures.

GOLDA   Like 'em?

ANA   Well . . .

GOLDA   Don't worry. I know women don't take to me as much as men. Anyhow, his father was never around . . and I was

making movies. We would get postcards sometimes from
Las Vegas, where he did his act – or catch him on TV. Junior
knows him mostly from TV.

ANA (*going up to* JUNIOR) He does resemble his father.

JUNIOR Fuck off.

GOLDA (*powdering her nose*) You won't get anywhere with him.
He has his own Beverly Hills shrink, you know . . and he
can't make a dent.

ANA Maybe . . then . . . seeing his father will help him too.

GOLDA I hope so. I hope this doesn't take too long. The only
reason we came here to the East Coast . . stopped off here
at all was because I am leaving Junior with my mother in
Jersey City. Ma wants to see him. I thought it would do him
some good to live with ordinary people for . . . well . . . for a
while. Of course I don't get on with her at all. She's religious
. . . a fanatic, in fact. She's what drove me to the streets of
Hollywood at age sixteen. That's where I met Waldo, and
then I had Waldo Junior here. We got married. He insisted.
Of course he didn't have to . . him being a big star and all
. . he could have bought me off like some others do . . but
he wanted his son to have his own name. I didn't care one
way or the other. It did help my career, though. I got a lot
of publicity . . into the columns through being married to
him . . see. I have him to thank for that. He didn't like me
running around with other men . . . but you know in the
film business. We had an amicable divorce . . . I'm sure you've
heard about it . . . or read . .

ANA He doesn't talk much about it.

GOLDA He doesn't mention me?

ANA Not too much . . . except in vague terms.

GOLDA The rat. Where is he?

ANA He should make an appearance soon.

GOLDA I'm into "primal scream" myself. It's the rage on the
coast. I'm trying to get in touch with myself. Would you like

me to scream?

ANA   I'm sure I could live without it.

GOLDA   What?

ANA   I said not at the moment . . perhaps some other time . .

GOLDA   I have a lot of depth . . down under . . below the surface.

ANA   I see . .

GOLDA   People don't understand that about me.

(*At this moment* JUNIOR *points a gun at* GOLDA. *He fires it.*)

Put that away, you moron! Do you want to upset everyone? It's . . . heh . . heh . . . a cap pistol. He got it from the studio prop room. He thinks it's a toy. It looks very realistic. Sometimes it scares people. Now calm down. He's like his father . . . out of control — no one can control him either. Anyhow, I'm on my way out of the country so it was convenient for us to stop by — I have to drop Junior off in Jersey. Did I say this before? I hope this visitation does him some good.

ANA   Where did you say you were going . . I mean after you drop Junior off?

GOLDA   I didn't . . but I'm on my way to Switzerland.

ANA   A skiing vacation?

GOLDA   I don't ski. There is this doctor there. I'm . . well . . . . on my way . . to get a nip and a tuck . . my face pulled up. Some people have been saying I look a little tired . . sagging . . drawn . . lately. I figured a little lift couldn't hurt. I'm feeling nervous. I think I need a valium.

ANA   We're not permitted . . .

(WALDO *enters through the bedroom-dressing room door in the full regalia of a somewhat disheveled, disintegrated Santa Claus character with painted red cheeks, a white straggly beard, a haphazard wig, and a rumpled, stained red suit with dirty white fur and a wide black studded belt. In addition he is wearing a black leather motorcycle cap, heavy black motorcycle boots covered with mud. Slung over his shoulder are chains and a large black leather jacket. He is also wearing military sunglasses. He stands perfectly still as if momentarily in a catatonic state. He stares straight ahead.*)

(*Aside.*) Oh . . he's in his suit. He wanted to dress up I bet . . for his little boy . .

GOLDA Certainly is checked out somewhere . . if you ask me . . I think I'll wait outside . . let him humor his kid . . *alone.* We have very little to say to one another . . these days . . . in any case . . especially in his condition. Jesus Christ! Besides, he's behind on his alimony-child care payments . . but I'll have my lawyer Mr. Grossman contact him about that. I know this place is not cheap either.

ANA We are expensive – but we do our best – Some say we are the best available.

GOLDA Well, I wouldn't call it a country club . . exactly. What is this Santa Claus bit anyhow? I thought you said he was improving. He looks insane . .

ANA He is working something through that is his own particular fetish. We try to understand – let him – or anybody . . act out . . whatever they want . . . as long as it does no harm to anyone else. We do not find it peculiar.

GOLDA I'll just slip out unnoticed. He seems to be in a deep trance . . like he was sleep-walking . . . in a dream . . know what I mean?

ANA I think so.

GOLDA He scares me. You think it's all right for his son to see him this way?

ANA It will be all right.

GOLDA Don't forget to see my next picture, which is due for general release soon . . across the country at select theatres.

ANA I wouldn't miss it. I do admire you . . . on screen, that is.

GOLDA It's a remake of *Blonde Bombshell*, the old Jean Harlow flick . . Junior . . you say hello to Daddy. Go over to Daddy. Listen to Mommy.

JUNIOR Is that him?

GOLDA Humor him. Mommy will wait outside.

JUNIOR What a freak!

WALDO (*in a deep Santa Claus voice*) Hi. Sonny. Is there
anything you would like for Christmas this year . . . from the
North Pole?

ANA I'll leave you two alone. I'll be nearby if you need me.

(*Exit* GOLDA *and* ANA *to hallway-waiting room. The faint sound of
jingling bells is heard.*)

WALDO (*ominous*) Would you like to sit on my lap?

JUNIOR Are you for real? Where did you get that outfit?

WALDO You wouldn't want to disappoint Santa, would you? I'll
tell you a funny story.

JUNIOR Okay. I'll try anything once. (*Moves closer.*) Would you
take me to McDonald's? I'm hungry.

WALDO I think that could be arranged later . . . Now, you
didn't know your old man was Santa Claus, did you?

JUNIOR I've heard lots of weird flaky stories about you . . .
that you took lots of drugs and lost your marbles according to
Mommy.

WALDO Ho. Ho. She said that. That's a good one Well, here's a
bag of marbles for you to play with, little boy. These actually
were given to me at Christmas time when I was a wee tot. I
think they came from a dime store – McCrory's five and dime
in downtown Newark. I kept them . . . saved them . . . just
to give to you . . . put these in your jacket pocket. And now
what is it you want to be when you grow up?

JUNIOR A lousy comic just like you. I saw your puss on TV. I
want a lot of money . . . just like you . .

WALDO You want to make people laugh? Be a clown?

JUNIOR Why not?

WALDO How are you getting along with your mother?

JUNIOR She's okay for a whore. She's always bringing lots of men home.

WALDO You learning anything at school?

JUNIOR Nah!

WALDO Yes. Well. Who ever has? Santa has a surprise-prize. Another nice gift for you. Would you like that?

JUNIOR Depends. What is it?
(WALDO *takes a large red and white peppermint candy cane wrapped in cellophane from his pocket.*)

WALDO Would you like this?

JUNIOR (*grabbing it*) *Give me that!*

WALDO Aren't you going to eat it . . . you bad little boy. It's good for you. Don't you like candy?

JUNIOR Yeah . . I'll eat it later, but first . . . I have something for you too, Daddy. A present. Ha. Ha.

(*He pulls out his cap gun.*)

I am going to shoot you – just like in the movies. Bang. Bang.

WALDO You wouldn't do that to Santa now, would you? Santa is a kind old man.

JUNIOR Oh, no. You can't fool me, Santa Claus.

JUNIOR *shoots gun at* WALDO. WALDO *pretending to be dead falls over.*
MUSIC: *"I'll Be Home for Christmas"* – *vocal chorus with orchestra* –

Blackout.

Music continues to conclusion.

MR. NOBODY

A PLAY IN ONE ACT

Mr. Nobody was presented on June 5, 1982, at Theater for the New City, 162 Second Avenue, as part of the Arts for Life Festival for Nuclear Disarmament produced by Crystal Field and George Bartenieff.. It was directed by John Albano.

MR. NOBODY   Robert Frink

MR. NOBODY

CHARACTERS:

MARLENE, THE WAITRESS — *Wears a black leotard, a black T-shirt with a skull and crossbones on it, a black mini-skirt, and a mini-apron. She is overly made up in the style of the day to emulate Audrey Hepburn: white powder, bright pink lipstick, and pointed black eyebrows to coincide with black-penciled-in doe eyes. What originally was meant to be "soft" is now "hard." She has stringy, unkempt hair and wears flat ballerina slipper-shoes.*

IVOR, THE ENCHANTED PHILOSOPHER — *Young, pale, and intense, he wears a black sweater, black corduroy pants, and a black raincoat.*

MUNDI — *A Village character who is somewhat androgynous. This character can be played either male or female, black or white.* MUNDI *is dressed in a gray sweater, black loose-fitting pants, and wears open sandals.*

MR. NOBODY — *A strange man whose entire face, neck, and head are wrapped around with white gauze or cotton leaving only slits for the nose, mouth, and eyes. He wears a 1940s felt hat, a tweed jacket, a shirt and tie, dark pants, oxford shoes, a tan raincoat, and white gloves.*

SCENE:

A MacDougal Street coffee shop, Greenwich Village, New York, in 1963. The set is a grouping of round tables, several wire ice-cream chairs, perhaps a backdrop with the following written in assemblage on it: Caffè Rienzi, Fat Black Pussy Cat Caffè, Café Figaro, Caffè Cino, Caffè Borgia, *and* Caffè Dante. *Coffee cups, napkins, ashtrays, spoons on tables.*

Faint sound of jazz music in the background.

MARLENE (*sullen*) What yah want?

MUNDI (*reading*) Nothin'.

MARLENE Yah want another cup a coffee? (*No answer.*) Once you've finished your coffee, you can't just sit here. You'll have to order another . . .

MUNDI There's hardly anybody in this joint.

MARLENE So?

MUNDI So fuck off. (*Suddenly angrier.*) Go fuck yourself!

MARLENE (*loudly*) Fuck you.

MUNDI *continues to read a paperback and* MARLENE — *sulking — leans against a wall also reading. Neither of these books should have a visible cover title.* IVOR *rushes in after a moment. He is carrying a big book — "Being and Nothingness" by Jean-Paul Sartre. He sits down at the same table as* MUNDI, *who does not look up.* IVOR *takes off his raincoat.*

Jazz music off.

Lights slightly up.

MARLENE What d'yah want?

IVOR Later.

MARLENE I see . . (*Under her breath.*) Creep! (*Continues to read.*)

IVOR (*attempting to break into* MUNDI'*s silence*) So whadja get out of it?

MUNDI Wha? . . . oh, it's you . . . you got any uppers, man? I feel really wasted . . . I feel like shit.

IVOR Want to order . . . some coffee? I got some change.

MUNDI Been begging money again?

IVOR I asked you what you wanted, blockhead. I'm makin' it okay.

MUNDI This is my second or third cup, man. It ain't getting me noplace. Shit! What is this shit?

IVOR What?

MUNDI (*defensive, angry*) My life, man! Do you know what's happenin' . . . what it's all about, huh? You sure been comin' on strong – like you know what's goin' on . . . like you have . . . some answers or somethin'.

IVOR I gave you some books to help you out. You said you wanted to read . . .

MUNDI (*sullen*) I know.

IVOR Did you look at 'em?

MUNDI I can't read that shit!

IVOR Did you try?

MUNDI I can't make no sense of it. Eggz . . . ist . . . what's it called?

IVOR Existentialism.

MUNDI Yeah . . . that beat shit. You fuckers think you can put on a black sweater . . . and lookin' pale as death . . . yah try to preach . . . change the whole face of the world or something . . .

IVOR So what part did yah read?

MUNDI Look . . . I was sitting in the roach-infested lobby of the Earle Hotel and I'm reading this fuckin' . . . what's it called?

IVOR *Being and Nothingness.* Here is my copy. (*Lays his book on the table.*)

MUNDI Yeah . . . is that that *Sarter* or is it *Kamuss*?

IVOR It's pronounced *Sartre.*

MUNDI No, the one I was readin' was Kamuss. I know it was.

IVOR Maybe it was *The Rebel.*

MUNDI So I got to this here part where he says . . . Kamuss . . .

IVOR *Camus!*

MUNDI . . . where he says it's all nothin' . . .

IVOR What? Wait a minute . . . you sure it's not this book? (*Referring to "Being and Nothingness."*)

MUNDI (*looking it over*) Nah! That ain't it! I didn't look at that

one yet. Anyhowz . . . as I was sayin' . . . what was I sayin'
. . . oh . . . I got to this part where he . . . whoever the fuck
it was . . . says we're goin' through all this shit for nothin' . . .
for nothin', man! (*Slight pause.*) Do you got any uppers?

IVOR No.

MUNDI (*almost as an aside, agitated*) I feel like killin' myself
today. (*Slight pause staring straight forward.*) So I got to this part
where Kamuss . . . or was it Sarter . . .

IVOR Could have been Kierkegaard!

MUNDI Who?

IVOR *Fear and Trembling, The Sickness Unto Death!*

MUNDI Whatszat?

IVOR Fear! Trembling! Sickness! By Kierkegaard.

MUNDI Don't pull my leg, man. I'm in no mood for bad jokes.

IVOR You don't like a sick existential joke? (MUNDI *glares at*
IVOR *with a look that could kill.*) So . . okay . . what happened?

MUNDI What?

IVOR With Nothing . . . with *The Nothing* . . . I should say.

MUNDI Oh . . . yeah. Anyhow I get to this part where it says . .
. *it says* . . . it's all for nothin' That's it! You mean, we're goin'
through all this shit for nothing? – I ask myself. Is that it?
Living through all this for nothing?

IVOR (*playful, laughing*) Come on. (*Slight pause.*) Then what?

MUNDI I threw that fuckin' book against the wall, man. Like
this! (MUNDI *picks up "Being and Nothingness" and slams it to the
floor. Angrier.*) See! Now don't give me any more of this shit to
read. I seen enough. I know enough. I don't want to read any
more of that crap.

IVOR Calm down. Everybody's lookin' at you. The waitress is
lookin' at you.

MUNDI Ah . . . she doesn't give a shit. I could bust up this
whole place.

IVOR You're letting your anger . . . . get . . . . out of control.

Want some more coffee?

MUNDI No.

IVOR Take it easy. Slow down. You're not thinking clear.

MUNDI Don't give me any more of your bullshit, man. I'm sick. Really sick. I need a pill.

IVOR You've been trying to stay off that junk. Now look . . . you're missing the whole point . . . of the nothingness . . . . or the emptiness . . . if you prefer the Zen Buddhist terminology . . is that it's all just . . . . . . a phase . . . yeah . . . that's it . . . . an interim phase . . . an awareness . . . sort of . . . . see . . . between "knowing" in an uptight way . . then . . . not knowing . . . . confusion . . . . and then . . . knowing . . . really knowing again. Get it? Once you face that there really is a . . . nothing . . or emptiness . . or whatever it is, see . . . then . . it frees you to . . . to go ahead and choose yourself. That's it. See.

MUNDI Are you for real? What the fuck are you on, man?

IVOR (*more anxious – trying desperately to make himself clear to himself and to* MUNDI) The non-being of being choose the being of non-being. It's all right here. (*He holds up the big book.*) It's very simple, see. You . . . you . . . get beyond . . the . . the nothingness phase. You . . . you . . . *look* at the negation . . . the negativity all around . . . and you choose . . . . . you choose being – yourself – *against* the nothingness. It's like you're fighting off death, which is everywhere . . . can grab hold of you at any moment. *You choose existence.*

MUNDI Wha' for?

IVOR To live. You choose it – to live.

MUNDI (*sarcastic*) You got to choose to live? What are you, Billy Graham or Norman Vincent Peale? Sounds like religious malarky . . . . hocus pocus . . . to me . .

IVOR You don't understand . . .

MUNDI I'm telling you I need to get out of this life, man . . . I need a pill.

(*A pause. Enter* MR. NOBODY.)

Hey, who's that cat?

(IVOR *and* MUNDI *stare at* MR. NOBODY. MARLENE *looks up – drops her book. Exits in a fast run.*)

IVOR   Oh, that's my new friend. I met him playing chess in the park. He's interested in Sartre . . . only he has trouble talking. He makes sounds, though . . . . and can write. He doesn't like to give out his name or where he lives. Paranoid, I guess . . . probably with good reason. Somebody called him Mr. Nobody . . . a joke. Ha ha.

MUNDI   He looks really weird . . . like the invisible man.

IVOR (*signals to* MR. NOBODY, *who has been standing motionless up to this point*)   Sit down. Sit here. (*Pulls up a chair and keeps on talking about* MR. NOBODY *as if he could not hear.*) He used to be a reporter, I believe . . . . or maybe he was actually in the Air Force . . . as I understand it. I dunno . . near Salt Lake City or someplace . . . . near an atomic or hydrogen blasting test site. I think he was investigating . . . or got too close during . . . . anyhow, now he has . . . . as you can see . . . . he has no face . . . his hands and body were burned . . . charred black . . and he can barely speak. But he can eat a little and drink coffee with a straw though it is painful. He can make sounds. Would you like coffee?

MR. NOBODY (*slowly*)   Ooo ugh ooon – mn – nnuughguh!

IVOR   You see?

MUNDI (*anxious*)   What time is it?

IVOR   I don't know. Late afternoon. Workers should be getting off work soon.

MUNDI   I've got to split. Got to find somebody with ups. I'm having trouble . . I'm dead broke, too. I'd like to find somebody . . some sucker . . . I could kill . . . I'm so fuckin' angry, man. I can hardly control it no more. I can't find work. I guess I could wash dishes. I could . . .

IVOR   Calm down. Sit still. We'll order some more coffee.

Look. He is writing something. He can write . . . . but it causes him pain.

MUNDI What does it say?

IVOR It says "c-o-f-f-e-e." I'll order him some. He needs a straw. I'll order three. Where did she go? (*To* MUNDI.) You've got to face this thing . . . just stop running . . . get a hold of . . . yourself.

MUNDI (*sobs*) I can't. I can't face no more of this emptiness shit! You can.

(*Pause.*)

IVOR Look . . . . he's trying to speak . . . .

MR. NOBODY (*painful – almost a low-key piercing scream*) Ooo ahmmnhghtmmnn uuughst.

Blackout

Hollywood Palms

HOLLYWOOD PALMS

CHARACTERS:

DOREEN – *Heavily made up in a sheer peek-through nightgown and robe.*

DON – *A traveling salesman. He wears pajama bottoms and a white sleeveless T-shirt.*

STAN – *He wears a wrap-around terrycloth towel with white jockey shorts underneath.*

SCENE:

A 1950s-style Hollywood, California, motel room containing twin beds, a chair, a desk, a television set, and an oversized lamp. Newspapers, magazines, liquor bottles, an ice bucket, clothes, and suitcases are strewn about. A picture window looks out onto a second-story walkway with a swimming pool below. An adjacent room across the way is identical except for having only one large bed rather than two.

DOREEN *sits in a chair, her back to the window, while studying her face in an oversized compact mirror, sometimes using it for rear viewing.* DON *lies on the bed, his face behind an open newspaper. Muzak-type music plays softly in the background.* DOREEN *changes the station to tune in Julio Iglesias singing "It Never Rains in Southern California." She sits back down, files her nails in an agitated manner, looks in the mirror and adjusts her hair. Getting up again, she pours herself a double whiskey and adds cubes from the bucket.*

During this time STAN *remains in the "other" room, lying on his back on his bed in jockey shorts, staring blankly into a* TV *and drinking beer.*

DON Isn't it a little early in the day to be drinking a highball?

DOREEN It's not a highball, it's straight with ice . . . just a little
. . . pick-me-up . . . my nerv . . . ous . . . con . . . dition. I
had difficulty sleeping. During the night . . . I . . .

DON What?

DOREEN I had a dream.

DON What was it?

DOREEN I don't . . . I can't . . . remember. Anyways it's past
noon. I heard a church bell ringing.

DON Your face is fully made up. It's repulsive . . . preposterous
. . . you're wearing full face makeup . . . in the full light
of day. Blazing white sun is streaming in . . . through the
Venetian blinds . . . and you sit there overly made up like
some two-bit whore of an actress. Who do you think you
are, a fuckin' movie or TV personality? You're supposed to be
my wife . . . looking decent . . . respectable . . . in a way that
compliments my position.

DOREEN I prepared myself . . . my face . . . for poolside.

DON You didn't want your face to burn up . . . in the sun . . .
Is that it?

DOREEN That's right. That would be it.

DON You should employ a white sun-block cosmetic creme.
There are dozens of different brands on the market . . . in the
supermarket.

DOREEN I wanted to look . . . my best . . . in Hollywood. I
always dreamed of being in this town, seeing the stars, Judy
Garland . . . Marilyn Monroe . . . Betty Grable . . .

DON They're dead. You can't see someone who's dead. Now
you can only watch them in a film. You look like a tramp.
Take it off. Wipe off that shit with a washrag.

DOREEN Leave me alone. This is my goddamn vacation to do
what and as I please.

DON We are also here on business. Remember that? Business. Need I remind you . . .

DOREEN I know – but for me it's also a vacation – a chance to get away . . . from all that soot and grime in Secaucus, New Jersey, bad toxic air. Sometimes I could choke . . . oh, what's the use.

DON It says here in the paper that a wild coyote running loose on Mulholland Drive right here in Hollywood ate up . . . killed . . . devoured a baby . . . right near where Warren Beatty lives.

DOREEN What?

DON And here is another item about a great white shark swimming in the Pacific Ocean. It seems the shark took a bite . . . a chunk out of this guy's rear end. The shark thought the subject was a sea lion or maybe an otter. He was . . . the man . . . wearing a black rubber suit. Which made him appear . . to resemble a seal to the giant fish . . I suppose.

DOREEN Two days ago . . . on the color television . . . . a shark attacked . . killed a woman.

DON I wonder if it was the same shark.

(STAN *gets up and wraps a towel around his waist. He walks onto the balcony, leans over it, smokes a cigarette, and stares through the picture window at* DOREEN.)

DOREEN (*flirtatious*) A man . . that same man in the other room . . . is looking . . staring . . at me again.

DON Don't look back. Just ignore him.

DOREEN He is now taking off his wraparound towel. (*Smiling.*) He is wearing jockey shorts.

DON I told you not to look at him. The man is some kind of a Hollywood bum – a con artist, I can tell. There are thousands of them out here. They all come out here . . . aimless drifters. They're looking for a chance. Some kind of an over-the-rainbow success. Some might be . . considered . . dangerous. Thousands of them . . . every week . . . on

Hollywood Boulevard . . . they arrive in Greyhound buses
– or by train . . . or they thumb a ride. On the make . . . for
whatever they can get . . . their stupid hands on.

DOREEN (*dreamy*) He just went back . . slipped back . . into
his room. Now he's staring at me – again – through his
window . . . through his window . . . into my window. The
expression in his eyes is . . lascivious.

DON You should now lower . . close . . the blinds. Shut him
off. For all we know he could be a crook on the lam. He
could carry a concealed weapon like a revolver.

DOREEN A gun? You think he has a gun?

DON He might. He might have a gun . . it could be loaded.
(*Pause.*)

DOREEN (*getting up, nervous*) It certainly is hot . . in here. The
air conditioning in these second-rate Hollywood motels is
nothing to write home about. It must be over a hundred
degrees . . . outside. This place you brought me to . . . is not
exactly a Ramada Inn or a Sheraton Motor Lodge. Would
you care for a drink?

DON Shut up. We're not exactly on an extensive expense
account, you know.

DOREEN I asked you if you wanted a drink?

DON . . . In the morning?

DOREEN It's past noon. We are out of ice. I'd better go down
to the ice machine. Get some ice. That's it. I'll be right back.
Ice.

DON (*grabbing her*) Where are you going? Where the fuck do
you think you're going? Are you crazy?

DOREEN I said we are out of ice. Let go of me . . or . .

DON You stupid slut – bitch.

DOREEN Cool yourself down. Take a shower. We could meet
at poolside . . . later. You should get into a swimsuit. It's
Sunday. We can do whatever we want. I said I'd be right
back . . . didn't I . . with ice.

(DOREEN *goes out and stands by* STAN's *door looking in. Slowly she moves into the room.* DON *stares at them through the picture window.*)

DON Slut. Whore. Bitch.

Poster designed by John Eric Broaddus for two related plays,
"The Cake" and "An Old Tune," under the overall title
"Tropical Fever in Key West."

TROPICAL FEVER
IN KEY WEST

TWO RELATED PLAYS

Tropical Fever in Key West was commissioned by Crystal Field and George Bartenieff and first presented by Theater for the New City, 162 Second Avenue, on December 22, 1983. It was directed by Sebastian Stuart, with set design by John Eric Broaddus, lighting by Craig Kennedy, and the following cast:

The Cake
BILLY	John Uecker
JESS	Chris Tanner
FRANK	Jeremy Brooks

An Old Tune
RITA	Regina David
JIM	Harvey Perr
DR. VAN REEVE	J. P. Dougherty
BRIAN	Dorsey Davis

Jeremy Brooks (foreground), John Uecker (seated), and Chris Tanner in "Tropical Fever in Key West" – "The Cake." Photo by John Eric Broaddus.

THE CAKE

CHARACTERS::

BILLY — *The writer — in his mid to late thirties, handsome but with a gaunt appearance. He wears a neat Oxford beige shirt and pressed beige slacks with brown loafers.*

JESS — *A shy, sensitive, attractive young man in his early thirties. He wears a plain T-shirt, dungarees, and sneakers.*

FRANK — *In his early to mid forties, he is wearing disheveled, loose-fitting blue worker's pants and a short-sleeved baby blue dress shirt. His clothes give the appearance of having been slept in. He is unshaven and unkempt.*

There are costume changes in SCENE II.

SCENE:

Key West, Florida — the study-living area of a winter-vacation house with an archway opening to the left. A picture window (right) with wooden Venetian blinds and an air-conditioning unit. The view outside indicates palm trees and tropical shrubbery. Glass window-paneled French doors (center rear) lead onto a veranda.

The room is furnished as if it were taken directly out of a department store showroom with everything in perfect designer order, a desk and chair, a sofa, an overstuffed bachelor chair, a glass coffee table, a cocktail cabinet, a floor rug and ceiling fan.

Framed prints in the Miró manner; photographs of smiling men and theatrical women are on one wall along with framed citations and certificates of honor.

The stage should be well lit; and the walls and furniture should be in shades of sand white, wheat, and brown.

SCENE I

The time is the present.

Faint music in distance – Bach's Goldberg Variations on harpsichord – BILLY *is at desk sorting through papers. Enter* JESS *through the French doors. He closes the doors, enters and stands perfectly still, at attention as if waiting to be spoken to or ordered about. He is shirtless but has a T-shirt in his hands.*

BILLY *knows he is present but does not say a word while he pretends to be reading a document which looks like some sort of contract.*

BILLY (*angry*) To hell with it! (*Shoves paper into a drawer which he slams.*) I just won't sign it and that's it! That's all. (*Turns head. Nervous mood swing.*) Oh. It's you.

JESS You said I should come . . . in . . to . .

BILLY That's right. I wanted you to see where I do my work . . . where I write . . did you enjoy the hot tub?

JESS Oh . . . yeah. Relaxing.

BILLY We just had it installed. I don't know what it cost . . . though it was expensive. Your hair is still wet.

JESS Yes . . .

BILLY (*commandeering*) Put on your shirt. You could catch a cold with the cool air in here. I prefer it that way. Chilly. (*Slight pause.*) Well . . . sit down. Did you enjoy our little gathering of buffoons last night . . . the party?

JESS Oh . . . yes . . . I . .

BILLY I didn't. I have only contempt for them. They're just interested in one thing – money. I've got to put up with them. Business. A movie deal means . . . dollars. With film people . . you see . . it's all . . a matter of . . attitudes . . . wearing

attitudes . . performing, always . . performing . . on the
outside. Acting. You have to look like . . act like . . a success
. . . that is . . or . . Would you like scotch?

JESS What?

BILLY Some scotch? . . . a glass of scotch?

JESS Oh . . . yeah . . . yes . . . . sure. Why not.

BILLY (*mixing two large tumblers full and meticulously adding ice
with tongs*) There is gin . . . and 100 proof Smirnoff vodka
. . . but scotch is better . . a more acceptable drink . . . in the
afternoon. Besides Dewars sent us two cases of the stuff. I was
one of their distinguished literary drunks. I wore a plaid shirt
in the ad. Did you see it? Oh well, it doesn't matter. Water,
soda, or straight?

JESS Oh . . . straight . . . with ice.

BILLY Here you are, my boy. Your room is . . I hope . .
satisfactory? There is clean linen in the wardrobe.

JESS Oh . . yes . . it is . . . it has . . a splendid . . . a terrific view
of the water. I've never seen water so . . so . . azure blue . .
not up north anyway.

BILLY (*irritated*) Turquoise. It's turquoise blue . . or it might
be aquamarine. Anyway it has decidedly more of the color
green to it than blue. Have you finished unpacking yet? Your
suitcases.

JESS No . . not . .

BILLY Why not?

JESS I will later. I felt tired.

BILLY That's right. Driving all the way down here . . from . .
where was it . . then right into a full blast party. I'm glad you
decided to come . . . you can easily begin to feel . . become
. . . isolated . . . here . . (*Pause.*) . . you know . . (*Agitated.*)
. . the truth is I loathe vacations in idyllic spots such as this
is. I would rather spend time in a more run-down section of
a town . . . or Miami Beach . . . in a cheap sleazy hotel with
one bare light bulb hanging from a chain over an unmade

bed . . . than be staying . . here . . but everyone says this is
the place that a writer . . of my stature . . ought to be; and
that's why I bought this house at great cost. I guess . . it is
. . supposed to be important to keep up appearances. The
climate . . . . the climate here . . outdoors . . is sticky . . . thick
with the sweet stink . . . the overpowering smell of tropical
flowers. The air is so heavy with pollen . . . and humidity
that it could suffocate you . . . which is why I had to put in
. . . air conditioning . . . in every single room . . in order to
breathe . . (*Slight pause.*) I once spent a week at a Holiday Inn
. . near Newark Airport. I enjoyed that. No one knew where
I was . . I had disappeared . . it was the only time I felt any
peace of mind. They had a pool there. A cocktail lounge. All
of your needs are taken care of. What . . what did you say
your name was?

JESS Uh . . . Jess . . . or Jesse . . Jess for short.

BILLY (*vague*) It takes a while for me . . myself . . to remember
someone's name . . to associate the name with a body and
a particular face. I forget. I should have known it by now.
Sometimes my memory is becoming . . . creaky. It's not that
I'm old . . . but . . .then . . .I'm not exactly young either . . not
anymore. Ha. Ha. Mmm.

JESS (*changing the subject*) Those paintings . . that one there . . .
(*He points.*) . . . is . . . it is . . . ?

BILLY (*quick*) . . . abstract. I don't try to make any sense of
it. I wouldn't want to presume to . . interpret . . the artist's
meaning. Would you?

JESS Oh . . no . . I . . wouldn't . .

BILLY In any case I bought them . . . . the signed prints . . .
they are not paintings! . . . you see . . primarily as investment
. . . and to decorate the walls of this space. One day I was
in New York . . on Madison Avenue . . and . . . you see . . I
wandered into a gallery . . run by a dyke . . at least I think
she was lesbian . . . . she had a man's haircut and wore a man's
two-piece herringbone suit . . anyway, she had the same name

as a very famous . . the most famous . . American lesbian poet
. . which I thought was odd. (*Under his breath.*) What was her
name . . Gertrude . . Gertrude . . ?

JESS What?

BILLY Not that they were both lesbian – but that they . . the
gallery owner and the poetess used the same name. Not really
all that unusual I suppose but . . . in any case . . so . . .

JESS (*feeling he should be attentive and interested*) Oh . . . uh . .
what was her . . what was the gallery owner's name?

BILLY (*not able to remember, annoyed*) Oh . . . . for heaven's sake!
It doesn't matter now does it? In any case . . . as I was saying
she lectured at me . . intensely . . like a barking bulldog . .
intimidated me . . into buying these . . actually . . it was
only one I was interested in at first . . . but then I wound up
purchasing three. They are signed, you see . . . all by the same
artist. Two on the front, and one of them, I believe, is signed
on the reverse side somewhere . . (*Building intense irritation,
not wanting to admit to any ignorance concerning art.*) They are
kind of a triptych . . I mean . . they were intended to . . . er
. . . all . . . uh . . . go together . . in some way. (*Slight pause.
Building resentment.*) First off I left the gallery . . that day . . it
was raining. Pouring, I believe . . I had no intent to buy those
. . . I . . had some lunch and over coffee I decided to . . well,
anyhow, I went back and told her . . frankly . . I said I wasn't
really that crazy about the art work . . but . . ha ha . . I had
to admit that she had cajoled me . . into thinking of them as
a good future investment, which I suppose they are. They
are French . . . and abstract . . which I certainly prefer to
anything . . . realistic. Don't you?

JESS (*with some embarrassment and uncertainty*) They are . . it is . .
an interesting story . . I mean . .

BILLY But let's not waste our breath talking about Art. Let's
discover . . . find out . . . more about you. You said you were
from . . originally . . I mean . .

JESS Lancaster, Pennsylvania . . the farming region. It is . . the city is . . a very old place . .

BILLY Yes it is that. It is also . . Lancaster . . that is . . the name
of an English royal house . . Isn't it? Did you study the Wars
of the Roses? . . in your grade school . . history?

JESS No . . I . .

BILLY I did . . . but we are digressing. We were discussing
something else . .

JESS The city of Lancaster in Pennsylvania which is . . where . .

BILLY . . . where you come from. The Amish . . . Pennsylvania
Dutch . . German colonists . . Palatines . . the Mennonites
. . I know that area. I've driven through there . . . they make
pretzels, potato chips, and quilts . . . patchwork quilts. That's
it . . . and pickles. I remember pickles.

JESS (*as if in a reverie incantation*) On Sunday afternoons they
will stand . . all together in a field . . or on a hill and stare . .
stare . . just stare . . into the sun . . into space. I think they are
praying or something. They are very strict . . . their religion
. . but they mostly like to make money.

BILLY (*condescending*) Oh. But you are not one of those, are you?

JESS Oh . . . no . . . we come from Second Reformed
Protestant . . or Lutheran stock . . I think. My ancestry is
French, English, and German . . I believe.

BILLY (*somewhat seductive*) You haven't . . you're not telling
me anything . . not anything really . . about yourself. (*Pause.*
BILLY *stares at* JESS. JESS *stares at the floor nervously.*) How are you
doing with your drink?

JESS Oh . . . uh . . just fine.

BILLY We haven't finished it. Have we?

JESS Haven't we? I guess I've been nursing . . . sipping. Well . .
(*Swallowing.*) Here goes!

BILLY (*fixated*) Another?

JESS (*intimidated, nervous*) In a minute. Let me catch my
breath. I am feeling . . . . uh . . . dizzy . . suddenly dizzy . .
Sometimes I get these breathing attacks . . I . . uh . .

BILLY Are you all right?

JESS Yes . . . I'll . . . I'll . . . be okay. I guess it's just . . all
the excitement . . coming down here . . yesterday . . a new
situation and . . . meeting so many . . all those . . well-known
people . . and all . .

BILLY You need to calm down. You'll be just fine. Most of
them will . . . eventually . . bore the pants off you. The party
and the bar crowd down here I mean.

JESS What?

BILLY Nothing.

JESS (*circling the room*) Is that your . . .

BILLY That's it.

JESS (*idealistic and trying to flatter*) It must have been something
. . . just incredible, I mean . . receiving a prize . . an
honorarium . . such as that.

BILLY (*abrupt switch, a commanding tone*) Are you ready for your
second yet? (*Slight pause.*) You can fix it yourself. Since you are
here . . supposed to help me . . put my affairs . . my work . .
in some kind of . . order . . you may as well start by mixing a
highball.

JESS (*at the bar, trying to be coy*) Will . . . you . . have anoth . . . .
er?

BILLY You can leave out the ice this round. Add a little water.
Sometimes the sound of ice cubes clicking in a drink can
become irritating . . . that is if you are feeling somewhat on
edge anyway . .

JESS (*handing him drink*) Bottoms up. I don't usually drink . . .
in the afternoon . . except on Sunday . . . . at a Sunday brunch
or something.

(*Pause.*)

BILLY Have you ever felt . . . terrified?

JESS What?

BILLY Felt a sense of terror . . . of fear . . for no reason . . about

just finding yourself alive . . in the world. Have you ever read
Being and Nothingness or *Nausea* . . the novel by Jean-Paul
Sartre?

JESS No . . . I . . uh . .

(*Slight pause.*)

BILLY (*a stone-like gaze*) A man is walking along a beach and
picks up a pebble. Looking at it, he is overcome by a sickly
unfamiliar horror . . a terrible feeling of nausea. This feeling
persists . . . and there are other strange inexplicable episodes
of this kind . . . that follow. A general feeling of emptiness . . .
takes hold . . pervades this man. He is also a writer. During
this realization . . this awareness of the vast nothingness out
there . . he is unable to write a single word. But finally . . out
of boredom . . he decides to go back to his work. He decides
there is nothing else . . nothing else left for him to do. He
decides not to kill himself. What do you think about that?

JESS I try not to think too much about what is . . . unknown.

BILLY Why?

JESS I don't know.

BILLY You're a God damned fool.

JESS I'm sorry I . .

BILLY You said you wanted to become a writer . . someday.
Isn't that what you told me . . when we met . . or was that just
a line, a conversation filler.

JESS When I get enough experience . . life experience, I mean
. . . then I might try . . . but just now I . . .

BILLY Then you must read Genet!

JESS I thought it was Sartre.

BILLY The modern French existentialists . . . the absurdists
. . . that would be a very good . . an excellent starting point
for you. Well, we'll talk about that later. To begin with . .
I suppose . . there are certain things you should understand
such as . . . what specific role . . you are to . . perform . . here
. . in this . . (*At this point* FRANK *appears standing in the alcove*

with a look of terror and trepidation on his face.) . . what?

FRANK May I . . ?

BILLY (*perturbed*) What is it you want? Did I give you
permission to come up here? I thought I told you to remain . .
in your room. Go back down! (*To* JESS.) He has a backroom
in back of the kitchen . . . You have to go down a long
hallway . . then several steps . . uh . . to get to the kitchen.
His bedroom is somewhere off of there. I seldom go in. His
bed is always unmade and covered with grimy books. He is
supposed to stay down there . . . out of sight . . particularly
when I am at work . . or entertaining a guest. (*To* FRANK.)
You know you are only permitted in this domain . . this room
. . on very special occasions and on advance notification . . .
to me . . that you are coming. Do you understand? I told you
to stay in the kitchen . . in your room . . didn't I?

FRANK I thought . . I . .

BILLY Well, you may as well meet . . is it Jess . . or Jesse?

JESS Either one . . it doesn't really matter . . . I . .

BILLY He's going to be staying on . . . to help me through the
hell of the new . . the next project. Writing as we all know by
now is an arduous . . exhausting . . task . . an ordeal . . like
digging a ditch. Certainly you're not in any condition to help
anyone . . least of all yourself. Look at you! You're sweating . .
smelling . . . like an old wart hog, like a rabid dog. What have
you been doing, hitting the fucking bottle down there again?
You're filthy. You're letting yourself go . .

FRANK (*staggers a few steps forward*) I was . . uh . . listening
to some music . . . classical music . . . on the radio . . I just
thought I'd come up . . . and . . . I felt this panic . . like an
attack . . and . . (FRANK *falls down, passing into a dead faint.*)

JESS (*rushing over to* FRANK) He's passed out . . cold. What do
we do now?

BILLY (*angry, fastidious*) Nothing! Do absolutely . . nothing!
Leave him alone! Is he breathing?

JESS (*listens for a heartbeat*) Yes.

BILLY That's what I thought.

JESS Should we . . . should I . . try . . to get him to a bed . .
back to his room?

BILLY Don't bother. It is best . . at these times . . to ignore him
. . . let him stew . . in his own foul tomfoolery. He'll wake up
. . . revive himself . . . soon enough. The fact is, this affair is
nothing new. A bad . . a nasty habit. The fact is . . . he's of no
use to anyone anymore . . . and it does no good to try to be
of help to him . . or assist him . . . in any way. It would only
hinder . . .

JESS What . . . about a hospital . . getting an ambulance . . a
doctor?

BILLY We've been all through that . . incarceration . .
internment into a hospital . . the fact is he's been trying to
kill himself . . . slowly . . for some time . . an agonized . .
ending. No one knows what to do. Once he held a prominent
position on a newspaper . . as a critic . . . or something . .
and . . I think he feels . . now . . that I overshadowed him
. . he is dying . . . slowly . . to get back at me . . for my . .
what he thinks is my unwarranted success. I'm obliged to
watch . . . (*Sentimental rhapsodizing. Soft jazz music underneath.
Lights dimmer.*) We first met . . . in a bar . . . it was . . a kind
of underground hideaway in the Village . . a place that no
longer exists. We used to party . . into the night . . . into the
morning in those days . . we'd get drunk and wait for the
sun to rise. When I first met him he was very attractive in an
arrogant sort of way . . wearing a brown leather bombardier
jacket . . . Those were the fun days . . (*Jazz music off.*) . . now . .
I've thought lately of throwing him out . . . onto the streets . .
but then . . what? He has no money. I thought if I brought him
here . . out of the environment of a big metropolis . . he might
recuperate . . . and now . . . things are worse than ever . . . my
nerves are the ones that are failing . . . I don't know what to do
. . . where to go . . what to do . . what can you do?

JESS (*confused and frightened*) I don't know. I . . .

(*He stares at prone body. Lights out – harpsichord music up.*)

Scene II

The next day.

JESS, *in black leather pants and a black T-shirt, is tidying up and organizing papers. He opens blinds to let in the glare of the sun.*

Enter FRANK *carrying a white cake box. He is wearing a clean white shirt and black trousers as if he has made some attempt to look more organized. He has slicked down his hair and wears dark sunglasses.*

JESS How are you? I see you're feeling better today.

FRANK (*curt, defensive, angry*) What do you know about it? What do you know about my case? (*Pause.*) Here is a . . . I brought . . I bought . .

JESS A cake?

FRANK What's so unusual about a God damn cake . . damn it? It's his birthday today. Didn't he tell you? Doesn't he remember? Oh . . . maybe he'd like to forget . . . let the day just slip on by . . that way . . by forgetting . . he can maybe shave off a year or two. Did he tell you the number of years he's been on this fucking planet?

JESS I don't recall that . . . that it was even ever discussed . . . at any time . . I . . I . .

FRANK I think he pictures himself . . sees himself as a kind of Dorian Gray-Peter Pan young forever . . indefinitely postponing . . . time . . running out . . and I'm supposed to be . . .

JESS Yes?

FRANK I was about to say something really funny . . about my being the disgruntled distorted old fuck-up picture in the attic . . the other half . . the inner grotesque part of him . . but it wouldn't . . it doesn't make sense since my room here . . I've been deposited in as it were . . . in a small damp area

adjacent to the kitchen. You wouldn't keep an old painting
in a cramped, musty room. It wouldn't fit . . it might rot
there . . it might actually deteriorate . . in no time at all . . it
could . . possibly could . . begin to disintegrate. (*Slight pause.*)
Hmmm-m! But anyhow, that's why I got this stupid cake to
remind him that his sparkle-plenty-doll youth image is finally
beginning to fade. I hope I live to see his teeth fall out. (*Pause.
Staring directly at* JESS.) So you're next in line, I suppose.

JESS What?

FRANK Don't be coy . . or precious . . or act cute . . with me!
In line . . . being groomed . . to take over my place . . to
become a substitute for the roll I've been playing all these
fuckin' years. Do you know what that is? My role?

JESS No . . . I . .

FRANK Well . . you'd better find out. Did'ja go to college?

JESS I studied to be a schoolteacher but . .

FRANK It figures.

JESS What?

FRANK You'd probably like to go for a doctorate. Did he give
you that line about having difficulty with his writing . .
writer's block . . yet?

JESS No

FRANK . . to get you to feeling sorry . . . sympathetic . . to the
plight of the great distraught writer? Well . . it won't work.
Others have been brought in and they've all . . .

JESS All what?

FRANK . . left. I got rid of them. They couldn't stand . .

JESS I can believe that.

FRANK What dive did he pick you up in?

JESS It wasn't a dive for your information. He was giving a
lecture at State University . .

FRANK Lecturing? Ha! (*Slight pause.*) You think I can't spot a
tart . . a little whore . . a beach bum . . on the make . . when I

see one. Come here. (*Grabs him.*)

JESS You're out of your mind. Let go.

FRANK What back room, park, or . . .

JESS Let go. You're hurting. This has gone far enough.

FRANK I'll tell you one thing straight. Who do you think
wrote . . dictated . . . most of his early stupid so-called
masterpieces . . who do you think is responsible for whatever
success he's had . . . me! I'm like his double . . psychic twin
you might say . . alter ego I think they call it . . tossing ideas
back and forth at him . . then him at me . . until . . I began
to . . get the picture . . . see what was happening . . to me . .
working in that kind of arrangement . . used . . and then . .
somewhere in it . . I just got . . I felt . . I was used up. Most of
the better ideas were my own. You see what I mean? Used by
him. I did most of the actual writing there was to be done . .
see . .

JESS I don't believe a word of it.

FRANK He liked to take all the credit . . the glory . . . the
money when it came pouring in . . and I let him . . but no
more. And property. He bought property . . like this getaway
seaside house . . too. Well, now it's time for my fair share of
the game. (*Pause.*) So what are you gonna do here? Help with
the fan mail?

JESS What? (*Annoyed.*) I've been engaged . . sort of . . . as a
kind of secretary to handle certain areas of . . well social
aspects . . . things like that . .

FRANK What did he say about me?

JESS Not too much.

FRANK That I'm hopeless . . that I've become a hopeless case. A
schizophrenic. Did he refer to me in psychological textbook
terminology? Well, he may think that . . but he's got another
one coming . . . a surprise . . a birthday surprise. I got him a
surprise.

JESS Surprise?

FRANK Yeah. (*Holds up box.*) So what do you think this is? See it. See this. It's a cake.

JESS I see a box.

FRANK Yeah . . and it's tied with string . . and inside the box is a cake; but what do you think is inside the cake?

JESS (*sarcastic*) A bomb?

FRANK Close . . . but that . . an explosion . . would cause too much of a mess. It's a chocolate cake with raspberry creme filling. It didn't originally have raspberry creme filling . . . I added that and at the same time I added . . some . . some . . . strychnine. Ha. Ha. I thought of using a hammer . . on the head . . or a rolling pin from the kitchen like in the comics . . Maggie and Jiggs . . . Jiggs getting his skull cracked. Pow! . . but being his birthday . . a cake . . I thought poisoning was the best thing. It's an internal process . . you see . . the least offensive way . .

JESS You're really nuts, man . . . off the fuckin' wall. Really! (*Slight pause.*) Do you . . . uh . . . know where there's a phone around here?

FRANK What'sa matter? Yah scared? Do I scare the pretty boy?

JESS No . . . I need to make a call.

FRANK Try the corner. There's a bar . . there's a pay phone . .

JESS You mean there's no . . no phone in this house?

FRANK Up in his room . . bedroom . . upstairs. It's under lock and key. It's monitored to an answering machine . . "at the sound of the bell . . state your message!" He doesn't like to be disturbed by a ringing phone . . . and he only answers whatever calls he chooses, see . . and also it keeps me . . isolated . . I can't call out. I was making long distance calls . . Florida to New York . . he didn't care for that . . .

JESS I see.

FRANK (*angry*) See? What do you see?

JESS I don't know.

FRANK (*threatening*) Now don't say anything about the cake . .

JESS What?

FRANK (*more menacing*) The cake, stupid. Don't say a word or . .

JESS Or . . what?

FRANK I might decide to finish you off too after . . (*Slight pause. Excited.*) Here he comes. He's at the door. Now he's putting the key in the lock. It's turning. The lock is now turning. (*Aside.*) You better keep your trap shut.

(BILLY *enters wearing a lightweight summer suit, white shirt, tie, and white shoes. He carries a briefcase.*)

BILLY What the hell's going on? You're in here? (*Stares at* FRANK.) Looks like you decided to sober up for a change. Thinking of maybe getting your act together? (*Slight pause.*) I had a dreadful lunch. Nothing was accomplished. Nothing settled. Well . . don't just stare at me.

FRANK (*timidly*) I brought you something. (*He holds box behind his back.*)

BILLY (*condescending*) . . . what is it? What is it now?

FRANK (*suddenly handing him the box*) Here! It's your favorite . . . chocolate . . layer . . with . . uh . . . raspberry creme filling.

BILLY (putting the box on his desk and opening it with a scissors) Let's have a look.

FRANK (*false joviality masking hostility*) It's a birthday cake. (*Slight pause.*) Today's your fucking birthday. Hooraayy!

BILLY It certainly is not. Where the hell are you coming from? You've got the wrong month. Sorry . . but . . well . . don't look so God damn disappointed. It's not the end of the world.

FRANK (*nervous*) I thought we'd have a celebration . . I made coffee . . I'll go get it. Is it all right?

BILLY Yes . . go get it. If you must. I suppose I could use a cup. (FRANK *leaves. Calling out.*) Bring three . . three cups . . .

JESS (*nervous*) Where's he going?

BILLY The kitchen . . I suppose . . . . probably for a drink . . . he hides a bottle under the sink. He thinks I don't know

it. He knows he's not allowed to drink here. I can't bear
watching him get "pissed" in my presence. (*Slight pause.*) Now
. . would you care for a cocktail? A martini? No, it's not the
correct hour. Is it? In any case my writer's block seems to be
lifting . . an idea has begun to enter into my head . . or rather
a plot . . . with characters . . . It's dim, but something is trying
to enter in, I think. I thought I might . . . we might . . thrash
it out . . together . . is that okay with you?

(*Mood shift.*)

Go to the typewriter. No. Wait. I hear something . . a
clattering noise. What is it? Listen. (*The sound of dishes
breaking.*) What do you suppose he's doing? No, never mind
about the typewriter. Suddenly . . I'm not feeling . .

JESS I . . . uh . . . I wanted to tell you . . uh . . well, I don't
think he's too well . . feeling very good . . today.

BILLY You don't think . . ?

JESS (*uncertain*) Really . . I don't think you should . . uh . .
eat . . any of that cake he brought in. I think he might have
tampered . . done something . . . er . . ah . . unusual to it. He
said that.

BILLY What . . . is this some kind of a . . . ?

JESS (*concern*) He asked me not to tell you about it.

BILLY What? I'd like to know . . let's not have any mysteries
. . . or games.

JESS (*bluntly*) I think there may be strychnine . . . or something
. . I think he . . might have . . added something . . some
poison or foreign substance to that raspberry creme filling . .
in the cake.

BILLY That is preposterous! Certainly . . . most . . preposterous
. . hilarious! He is always inventing these ridiculous little
games . . . neurotic sub-plots . . in order to bring negative
attention to himself . . narcissistic infantilism. Ah . . . ha . . ha
. . he certainly is willful. Don't you see? You must see. He's
now trying to be divisive. He knows that I've brought you in

. . asked you to stay here . . to help . . me . . and already that vicious persnickety foul mind is at work. He can't stop.

JESS He said he was the author . . actually wrote your . .

BILLY (*crying out*) My words! My words. Yes. (*Slight pause.*) Come, now. I think we should treat this realistically. I think we shouldn't get too involved in this . . this chicanery. We'll just ignore . . not pay any mind . . . any attention to the whole thing. That's what the doctors said . . that is the best way to handle the entire affair. We'll humor him . . . in a detached way. You're looking pale. What is it?

JESS I . . don't know.

BILLY What's the matter?

JESS I suspect . . .

BILLY You're letting the ravings of a lunatic get to you. Look. I've been all through this. It is important not to let him know he's getting to you . . frightening you. He's been in and out of several hospitals. The doctors have always maintained that if he harms anyone . . it will be . . most likely . . himself. That is the way it works. That means he turns all his subliminal rage and anger onto . . onto himself . . you see . . On several specific occasions he's tried . . once he swallowed sleeping pills . . another time . . he slashed open his wrists . . with a Gillette razor blade. It's only a matter of time. I'm sorry you have to find out about this now but if you're going to . . work . . stay . . here . . in this house . . there is probably no way of your not knowing . . it's only a matter of time . . (*At this point there is a shift in which* BILLY *seems to be talking about himself.*) If anything . . they said . . he will probably murder himself . . an accident, a drowning . . a drunken fall down a flight of stairs. A moment's inattention . . a blank out of the mind . . a sudden gap . . . one thought is no longer connected to another . . . you see . . the process of thought is . . is . . interrupted . . . out on a tangent . . . it can't get back . . make a return . . and wham! Like a sudden car crash . . and he's a dead duck! That's it. He will be a dead duck. (*A refocus back on* FRANK. *Building hysteria.*) He has to be watched . . but no one can watch him all the time now, can we? What are you suddenly so wrought up . . so . . nervous about? Calm down! (JESS *is coughing and retching.*) Now you must quiet yourself. Remain serene. I brought him here . . we came to this island of sunshine and palm trees swaying . . for a rest. Yes, that's it. Now here he is . . he's coming . . . back up. Try to look . . . to act . . normal. If he sees . . notices . . that he's upset you . . he'll . . . do something rash . . .

(FRANK *appears in the archway carrying a large silver service tray with a fancy coffee pot, cups, saucers, spoons, cake plates, forks, a creamer, a sugar container, napkins, and a large cake knife.*)

(BILLY *continuing, commanding.*)

No need to stand there like a cigar-store Indian What have we got there now?

FRANK (*smiling*) It's coffee. I used the best china . . I thought you wouldn't mind, this being a special occasion.

BILLY Maybe our house guest . . would prefer tea . . a pot of Chinese tea . .

JESS (*flustered*) Uh . . . no thanks I . . . uh . . would prefer . . .

BILLY (*directing*) Set it down. On the coffee table. Here. Coffee table. (FRANK *sets down tray and begins to put cake on a large plate.* BILLY *tries to make small conversation.*) Is it a coffee table or is it a cocktail table? Let me see. A cocktail table would have to be somewhat higher wouldn't it? I believe . . I think . . originally they were called a cocktail table . . a low-lying table . . to be set in front of a sofa . . . and then . . and then . . all of a sudden . . . at some point they were referred to as coffee . . coffee tables . . not cocktail! Maybe it was after Prohibition . . . (*Abrupt mood switch.*) Put it down! Put it down, I said! Let's get this ceremony over with. Don't irritate me. You've got my nerves on edge with that smiling . . that inner laughter . . hostility of yours. Pour the coffee. (*Polite attitude. To* JESS.) Would you like coffee? There's no tea. He didn't make any tea. (*Drinks coffee.*) It seems to be hot. At least the coffee is piping hot . . for a change. Coffee must be steaming hot . . never lukewarm. Disgusting! Have you ever gone to a restaurant where a meal was ruined by serving lukewarm coffee?

FRANK (*hands* JESS *a cup of coffee with a leering smile as if on a* TV *commercial*) Here it is. It's coffee time . .

JESS I think I would prefer a whiskey. A glass of . . .

(JESS *pours himself a drink – with ice.*)

FRANK (*slowly cutting the cake – to* JESS) Would you want cake? Would you care to join us in a piece of . . delicious sugar-sweet cake . . . (*Joking.*) . . just like your mommy used to make!

JESS (*almost spilling his drink and gagging*) No . . no . . cake . . I . .

FRANK (*coy*) I'm going to eat a piece. Would you like some? Huh? It's your favorite filling . . and chocolate too . . you like chocolate . .

(FRANK *hands* BILLY *a large piece and cuts one as well for himself.*)

BILLY (*slightly suspicious and uncertain but still playing "the game"*) Where does this cake come from?

FRANK It's a Cuban cake . . that is . . I got it at the Cuban bakery down the street. It cost six dollars.

BILLY Where would you get six dollars? I didn't give you six dollars.

FRANK Huh?

BILLY Who would give someone like you . . . oh, never mind! Did you steal it?

FRANK (*mishearing the question*) I went this morning . . . I got it in the . . uh . . morning.

BILLY (*aside to* JESS – FRANK *is engrossed in eating the cake*) You see. It's all . . he likes to play . . these . . practical jokes . . There is . . there was . . nothing to worry about . . whatsoever . . nothing . .

FRANK (*to* BILLY) Here is your fork . . and a napkin.

BILLY (*humoring him*) That was very thoughtful of you, now, wasn't it?

FRANK Shall I light a candle too?

BILLY Not necessary. It's not yet dark enough for candlelight.

FRANK (*childlike*) I could put a candle on the cake. (*Slight pause.*) Are you happy . . happy . . with your happy birthday? (FRANK *begins to laugh in a soft, gurgling-underneath childish manner.*)

BILLY (*eating cake*) Don't be silly . . you're making a spectacle of yourself . . and in front of our new house guest.

FRANK Mm-m-m-m mm-m-m! Yum!

JESS *moves toward the French doors and stands perfectly still in a shaft of yellow light. He holds his drink in his hands but does not drink it. His hand trembles nervously causing a slight clicking of ice cubes in his glass of whiskey. He stares intently, almost with contempt, at* FRANK *and* BILLY, *who by now are softly laughing with one another, eating cake and "into" their own insular game. There is a small circle of light on these two protagonists on the sofa which gradually disappears. Lights fade, and the last light to go out is the luminous light on* JESS, *who is now staring out the window.*

Blackout.

Soft harpsichord music up.

Regina David as the inebriated tanked-up ex-band singer Rita mixing up a Red Parrot Zombie cocktail at her outdoor ironing board bar in "An Old Tune," the second play in "Tropical Fever in Key West"

Harvey Perr and Regina David in "Tropical Fever in Key West" – "An Old Tune."

J. P. Dougherty as the Doctor and Dorsey Davis in uniform in "An Old Tune." Photos by John Eric Broaddus.

AN OLD TUNE

CHARACTERS:

RITA — *A robust woman who wears turquoise pedal-pusher toreador pants, a loose-fitting see-through blouse, sling-back high-heeled ostrich-plume bedroom shoes, and dark glasses with rhinestone chips that peak-point up at an oblique angle. Throughout the play she takes these glasses on and off as if she were sometimes hiding behind them. She is overly made up as if she thought of herself as a retired movie star just about to take to the Las Vegas nightclub circuit; red lipstick, orange-tan makeup, blue eye shadow, pencil-thin brows, and mascaraed eyes complete this image along with peroxide-yellow hair which is worn in a 1940s clump-of-curls with the longer back hair tucked into a crocheted snood. She sports a large diamond ring.*

JIM — *He wears an oversized rayon Hawaiian print shirt, a small straw fisherman's hat, green Bermuda shorts, white socks, and black loafers with gold chains.*

DR. VAN REEVE — *He wears a cream-colored Panama suit, white shirt, a black tie, pointed white shoes, and a planter's hat. Somewhat eccentric in his manner, he speaks in a distinct Southern accent. Carrying a small black doctor's bag, he seems to be an apparition that has stepped out of the Old South.*

BRIAN — *A young, handsome, slight but well-proportioned, bright-eyed sailor. Dressed in his white Navy sailor's outfit, he has the gait and manner of a brash small-town Midwestern boy.*

NOTE: *While* RITA *and* JIM *are ostensibly retirees, they are an "early" retired couple by comparison to the more usual octogenarians of Florida. In this sense the actors portraying them need not be old themselves but representatives of a "condition."*

SETTING:

*The lawn to the front has white-painted wrought-iron furniture on it
with the cushions covered in a 1940s fabric of a tropical leaf or bird
pattern. Also on the front lawn are several metal, plastic, or wood
cutouts of life-size white whooping cranes, pelicans, and egrets. Old
rusted toys, machinery, rakes, empty liquor and wine bottles, as well
as other garage debris are scattered across the lawn. Sections of a large
rusted-out 1950s red Buick are to stage left (these may be literal old car
parts or painted flats).*

*On a low-lying garden table are several half-full bottles of liquor: rum,
vodka, and Seagram's Golden Gin; and containers of orange, papaya,
and cranberry juice mixes, maraschino cherries, and sliced oranges. A
white plastic ice-cube container and a wind-up phonograph machine are
on this same bar-entertainment table.*

*Directly in the background is the front of a coral-pink Florida stucco
house which is cracking and in a state of deterioration. Two short steps
lead up to a small cement porch, which is painted turquoise. Tropical
foliage and hibiscus flowers surround the house.*

*There are also an orange tree, a mango tree, a lemon tree, and a palm
tree, which is stage center near the furniture arrangement and under
which the characters sit for shade.*

*The blinding white heat and light of the sun changes to yellow-white
and yellow, until it is finally sunset orange – and in the last segment
of the play, at twilight, there is a purple-blue light. This is the stage
lighting color pattern.*

Music – opening – Frances Langford vocal, "My Cabin of Dreams."

*Soft background guitar music under opening and closing sections –
background music also during alligator story.*

TIME: *spring of 1983*

As the play begins we see RITA *and* JIM *sitting on two garden chairs
under a palm tree (stage center), the table slightly to the back of them.*

RITA *appears to be somewhat nervous; but is attempting to pull herself together as if she were about to make a prepared speech before a ladies' luncheon.*

JIM, *her husband, is in a stupor, half asleep.*

RITA *stares at him with disgust and then looks straight ahead in the direction of the audience. The soft sound of a Hawaiian guitar, perhaps from a nearby bar, is heard in the background.*

RITA (*as if talking to a neighbor – in this case, the audience*) I can't imagine why we left Secaucus, New Jersey, eighteen years ago, to come to this miserable out-of-the-way place . . . but where else was there to go? (*Pause.*) By the time you drive down here by car through Key Largo, Bahia Honda . . . across several bridges, endless coral reef waterways, and islands . . . keys . . as they call them . . . you arrive in Key West, Florida, which is the southernmost tip . . . then you are practically in the tropics. Almost in the lap of Cuba. In fact this place is now overrun with Spanish-speaking Cubans chased out by the Communists. And . . . of course . . . it is well known as a vacation playground for fashion-conscious queer men. Don't get me wrong. I have nothing against men with a penchant for other men . . who am I to say who is to do what . . but these men are into what they refer to as . . . . property improvement . . . . the fixing up . . . . the upgrading . . . of once dilapidated property . . . into luxurious "guest houses" . . . which means that old-timers . . . the old fucks . . get their butts kicked the fuck out onto the street. Ha ha. See what I mean? That is one reason why you hear a lot in this town . . . or read in the papers about the fag-bashing of queers. In fact one very famous one who is a writer lives . . . or did live . . . just across the street, though I could never figure out why a world-renowned celebrated author would choose to live in the run-down part of town . . . although his house by comparison to the others in this neighborhood is immaculate . . . restored to its original grandiosity. Many's an evening I'd be sitting right here on the lawn and I'd watch him in a

natty white Palm Beach suit . . with a white Panama hat . .
staggering home in a stupor . . falling flat on his sun-red face
before he could make it to the front door. Usually, finally,
he would manage to crawl in on his own . . and sometimes
he would be taken in by a younger man dressed entirely in
leather, boots, pants, jacket, hat . . . and gloves . . . looking
every inch like one of those motorcycle storm troopers or an
angel of Hell. Oh! Sometimes there would be a broad smile
. . . a tip . . . of his hat and a cheery hello. or a waving of the
hand . . . but that was usually all the communication he could
muster up. Cadillac limousines would pull up to his house
driven by uniformed chauffeurs . . . and once he was . . . I did
see him . . . on a television game show – "To Tell the Truth,"
I think it was called. I understand he left a great deal of cash
behind but none to this vile town he called his runaway home
– and I can understand why! (*Pause – breathing heavily. In a
determined manner.*) I spend a great deal of time these days . . .
in the interior of my mind . . . and I watch what goes on. I
know it's all coming down . . . that it's only a matter of time.
If you wait long and hard as I have been doing – the enemy
will finally come forward and show you his face.

(*Lights down.*)

(*Lights up.*)

JIM What time is it?

RITA I don't know.

JIM It must now be late afternoon . . judging from the position
of the sun . . the sunlight.

RITA You were dead-asleep.

JIM I know. (*Pause.*) Where is the paper?

RITA Here it is. Still in its plastic pouch. Why do they put a
newspaper in a plastic bag?

JIM Makes it easier to throw and . . . in case of rain.

RITA It hardly ever rains here.

JIM It does . . . it does rain . . . during the rainy season . .

RITA   But this is not the rainy season.

JIM   It would be nice to experience a violent hurricane . .
winds blowing . . the waters thrashing . . . drowning waves . .

RITA   It could sweep us away . . .

JIM   We could hide indoors.

RITA   The hurricane could take us away . . . out to sea.

JIM   Should we move inside now?

RITA   There is no air-conditioning. We would suffocate today.
Our air-conditioning system is emitting some kind of poison
ether . . . into the air . .

JIM   I loathe air conditioners.

RITA   And our TV has become a blur. The picture . . . is . . .
now a series of jumping zigzags . .

JIM   Good. I prefer it that way. I hate looking at it these days.

RITA   (*fanning herself*) This interminable heat . . . is unbearable.

JIM   It's not the heat, it's the humidity. The humidity is ninety-
five percent of the air . . . as if we were under water. We
should have gills.

RITA   I can barely catch my breath. I could choke on the
sickening smell of all these tropical flowers and shrubbery . .
kapok trees . . . hibiscus.

JIM   Calm your nerves. Where have you put your pink pills?
Mix yourself another drink. When do we eat?

RITA   Nothing is in the Frigidaire. There are some canned
Planters salted cocktail peanuts somewhere.

JIM   It would satisfy me if I could have some of those deep-
fried conch fritters and some yellow lime pie like we had in
the White Cockatoo Restaurant once. Remember? Could
you prepare a dish like that?

RITA   That is really a tall order. I can barely move around . . . in
this heat.

JIM   You're just a lazy bitch if you ask me. I'm lucky if I get a
chopped chicken liver sandwich around here. We should have

moved long ago to Miami Beach . . into one of those stucco
hotels. There are dozens of restaurants there serving . .

RITA You're at it again with what we should or shouldn't have
done . . . (*Slight pause.*) Why don't you kill yourself – and do
the world and yourself a big favor.

JIM (*anger, moves toward her threateningly*) Shut your fat face!

RITA You're drunk again. I can see it. Stay away . .

JIM Somebody should fuck your stupid brains out . . . to shut
you the fuck up . . but not me. Sometimes I . . .

RITA You? You couldn't get it up. Ha. Ha. You would die if . .
(JIM *suddenly falls into a semi-sleep.*) What now? Asleep again
. . . or is it that you are drunk or are you . . . dying . . what is
it? (*Half to herself.*) You . . . we . . may as well be dead as living
out our lives in this residential tropical jungle where nothing
ever happens. You couldn't stand the northern winters . . . the
cold. Or was it your heart? Was that the reason we eventually
left the north? Was it a heart attack? Yes, you developed a
heart condition. Some kind of a weak artery. Blood could no
longer be pumped into your immense animal heart. Now you
are connected to . . . what is it . . . all kinds of plastic inner
tubes . . . a battery-operated pacemaker . . . is that what they
call it? Kept alive by science . . . beating away inside of you
every second . . . . thump . . . . thump . . . oh God. Help us!
The doctors said you had expired . . . you had actually been
pronounced dead . . . for three whole minutes . . . but then
they revived you. What was it like? Can you remember?
Did you feel . . anything? Then you were forced into early
retirement. The Cuckoo Bird Seed Company of Harrison,
New Jersey, put you on a permanent leave of absence with a
pension . . . into retirement . . sentenced until death. Retire
to what? To this? Sometimes I wish it would just hurry up.
Death . . . the final termination . . the cessation of all this
suffering. "All labor, all worldly cares are laid to rest" . . that's
what they said over the body of my twin sister Helga. She
wasn't really a twin. She was a year older . . . but they always
called us the twins. (*Laughs.*) In her casket she looked like a

wax dummy of herself . . . all the blood drained out. I think
she contracted some kind of cancer . . of the terminal variety.
I hardly recognized her in that air-conditioned funeral home
in Jersey City. "Come back!" I screamed out. I thought . . I
almost thought . . it was . . myself lying there . . stiff . . finally
they had to carry me away . . out of that place I was blacking
out . . the stench . . the perfume . . . of those floral wreaths.
Funny . . I never really loved her. I hated her guts. My father
liked her better than me and . . . favored her . .

JIM (*waking up*) Huh? What . .

RITA (*depressed and angry*) Dying . . . . death . . a joke . . you
live and then . . . .

JIM (*out of a stupor*) Where am I? (*Pause.*) You don't know
what you're talking about. You're off on that morbid train of
thought again. It's no use discussing it. It's obvious to anyone
that we are living on the edge. That's why no one comes to
visit. The subjects you focus on are depressing to the average
visitor. Not to mention myself. Look at yourself. You're like
an old whore. Didn't you used to be a singer or something?
A pop vocalist? Didn't we meet originally in some kind of
saloon?

RITA The Jumpin' Joint in Newark . . or was it called the
Jumpin' Jive? One of them hundreds of lounges they got in
that war-torn town.

JIM I thought it was Kitty's Koon Kat Club. You had
practically bottomed out on booze by the time I came along.
Your voice could hardly hit the middle notes. It sounded like
the rasping croak . . the last gasp . . . of a dying bullfrog. Ha.
Ha.

RITA Yes . . . . I was a little off . . . . tired out when we met
. . . . but I still had some of my looks when we first met.
When you first saw me you said I had million-dollar legs . . . .
like Betty Grable. Do you remember that? (*Anxious, building
crescendo.*) Remember our honeymoon? You had a red Buick
roadster. We drove all the way down the coast of New Jersey

. . . from Newark . . the old shore route. We went to Asbury
Park, the Berkeley-Carteret Hotel . . remember the merry-
go-round there? . . . and the ride on the lake inside the giant
swan boat . . . . and then driving down old highway 9? We
had coffee and a homemade doughnut at the Manahawkin
Diner . . . . and then we spent a night at the Traymore Hotel
in Atlantic City. Swing and Sway with Sammy Kaye was
playing on the Steel Pier. Remember the diving horse. A girl
on a diving horse . . . diving into the ocean . . . . from the
pier?

JIM (*oblivious*) No. It was the booze and drugs that finished
you off . . . as far as being a vocalist. That's what ruined your
voice. The voice I never heard . . . except on a record. Ha.
Ha.

RITA When the band broke up . . I didn't know what to do
. . I . . . they said . . the record company . . my voice was
too thin to promote me as a solo attraction. I didn't have the
personality of Dinah, Doris, or Peggy Lee . . . Why dont'cha
put one of 'em on . . . . the old records . . one of the old tunes
. . ?

JIM I'm not in any mood . .

RITA (*childlike, boastful*) I made fifteen 78 rpm recordings, some
with Orin Spivak and his orchestra on the Okeh label. We
played all the hot spots . . . but that was before I met you . . .
some of the solos weren't bad . . . but it was in the area of
promotion that I suffered.

JIM Your voice was gone when I met you. I'm tired of listening
to those scratchy recordings . . old out-of-date songs.

RITA Please. It would be nice to hear one of the old songs.

(JIM *winds up the Victrola. We hear "It's Like Reaching for the
Moon," vocal by Frances Langford, with the Victor Young Orchestra.*
RITA *is in ecstasy.* JIM *appears to be racked with pain.*)

RITA That one made it to the Top 25 on the Hit Parade. I sold
thousands of Victory Bonds, and when the soldiers heard that
song . .

JIM That was years ago . . . before . . before . . now . . .

RITA Now?

JIM No one would recognize you now even if they saw you. You don't look like the person I used to know. You don't resemble . . you don't look anything like . .

RITA At least I had fun in the old days, I have memories, something to remember . . . besides selling Cuckoo birdseed. How did I ever come to get mixed up with the likes of you? . . if only I could have had a baby . . then . . maybe if . .

JIM The birds need to be fed . . and you needed someone to rescue you from . . .

(Bird sounds.)

RITA What?

JIM You are free to fly off whenever you choose. There is no cage . . or chain tied around your neck. That's for God damn sure.

RITA Where to go? What to do . . . that is the problem. I supposed I could go to . .

JIM Where would you go? What can you do? You couldn't even be a hostess . . . or cashier . . or hat check . . in a nightclub.

RITA Stuck here in this tropical swampland quicksand. Mosquitoes. Flies. Gnats.

JIM This is an ideal place to be . . according to all the brochures . . the sunshine . . the pink and red hibiscus flowers . . the Royal Palm trees . . the night-blooming cereus . . .

RITA The dead-end Road to Florida . . . starring Betty Hutton . . or was it Dorothy Lamour in those pictures. Remember the road to this . . the road to there with Bob Hope and Bing.

JIM Now she's an old hag in an oversized sarong with a ukulele, squawking like an old green parrot, just like you.

RITA Who is?

JIM Aw . . shut up. Where's my magazine? Where did you put

my God damn magazine?

RITA Here it is.

JIM That is not my magazine. That is the newspaper.

RITA Oh. (*Pause.*) I think it's in the house . . . next to your
chair. You had it in your hand when you fell asleep. Earlier
this afternoon. Then you got up and came out here; and asked
me to set up the bar . . . even though it was not quite yet
cocktail hour.

JIM . . . what time is it?

RITA I don't know.

JIM Is it time for my walk? It's not time to walk, is it?

RITA Not yet . . . the walk takes place in the evening just prior
to bed.

JIM What's in the news?

RITA What?

JIM The news . . what is there today in the paper? Today's
news? (*Pause.*) Where did you put my bifocals?

RITA You left them in the house . . . on the table . . . . with the
magazine . . next to . .

JIM Oh . . . in the house . . .

RITA Should I get them?

JIM No. Don't bother . . you tell me then. What is going on . .
read it to me . . something might happen if I were to go into
the house by myself.

RITA What? What could possibly . .

JIM My heart . . . . it could stop. There is some pain . . . .
today . . I . . .

RITA (*superficial*) Oh. Shall we have another drink then?

(*She reads the paper. Mixes drink. Fade lights. Lights up.*)

It says . . let me read it to myself first . .

(*Pause. Reading.*)

JIM What?

RITA Wait. (*Reading.*) A man in Boca Raton . . . where is that?

JIM North.

RITA (*she mostly reads to herself and then paraphrases*) A small pond in the back of this man's house. He has lived there for almost nineteen years . . . it says . . and . . . and . . . (*Reading.*) . . . here is a picture . . . . there never had been any sign of . . . any . . . life . . in that man's backyard pond. This part is peculiar. On this particular night . . on . . the day before yesterday . . . that would be Sunday – wouldn't it? His wife heard their pet Pekingese yelping and sent the man to go downstairs . . . from their bedroom . . . I guess . . . to have a look around . . . . thinking a prowler might have gotten into the house, I suppose . . . .

JIM Yes? Then?

RITA Anyway he opened the kitchen screen door and the dog ran out into the back yard barking and . . .

JIM And?

RITA The man followed suit . . . let's see . . (*Reading.*)

JIM And . . you're not reading it aloud . . damn it.

RITA I'm telling you . . . . It seems the dog was severely bitten . . and it died . . and . . oh no!

JIM What?

RITA He was . . . this man . . . then attacked . . . thrown to the ground . . and thrashed to death by what they say must have been a giant alligator or crocodile.

JIM Did anyone see it?

RITA No but . . traces . . large lizard feet markings . . and imprints of a tail . . from the lashings were later found on the ground as well as on the torso of the man . . and bites too! That's what it says right here. See. (*Shows him the paper.*)

JIM That is stupid. The man looks like a fool!

RITA When his wife came into the back yard with a flashlight wondering . . naturally wondering . . what all the cries and commotion were about . . he . . the man . . she found him . .

torn limb from limb.

JIM And?

RITA They say . . in the police report . . that the alligator just
disappeared . . . walked or . . slithered away . . later when
frogmen searched the pond the monster was not anywhere to
be found.

JIM That is a preposterous story. Since no one saw this . . so-
called beast . . . from the deep . . . it probably never happened
. . never was there . .

RITA What?

JIM It's a made-up affair . . like one of those television movies.

RITA But . . How can you . . ?

JIM (quick) It could only have been the wife. She must have
done it. Probably an insurance policy is in it somewhere.
She must have killed the dog . . . the man . . . by herself . . .
beat her husband . . who was probably inebriated anyway
. . . with a shovel . . . and a rake . . into a stupor . . until he
stopped breathing. In. Out. In. Out. Thud. Stop. Just stopped
breathing . . .

RITA What about the imprints on the ground?

JIM I don't know. That's an easy task . . . an easy enough
deception with the proper equipment on hand.

RITA But why? Why would she . . ?

JIM Out of sheer boredom. Either that or the entire episode is
a complete fake. A made-up affair. After all, no one saw the
alligator . . or even an iguana.

RITA . . . this area is filled with . . known for its alligators,
snapping turtles . . . all kinds of reptiles and giant lizards . . .
everywhere. Swamps, dark ponds . . . everglades with huge
vultures, salamanders, and . . crocodiles.

JIM The crocodiles are almost extinct. We read that last week
in a National Geographic in the doctor's office. Crocodiles
certainly have become among the endangered species.

RITA (anxious, questioning her own sense of reality) No. It is not true. It must have happened I'm sure . .

JIM (*more aggressive*) Journalists, newspapers, like to create
exaggerated accounts . . . invent stories . . around simple
everyday incidents. Lies . . . and more lies . . more and more
every day. Incredible fictions . . . . staged disasters . . . . .
to keep the world . . the gaping public . . amazed and filled
with the necessary . . the required terror and fear. Meanwhile
nothing has happened. The man . . died . . probably . . .
of . . it probably was just a massive coronary . . . like so
many others . . . and the wife . . . or someone else cries out
"alligator." Phfftt! There is no pond in the back of the house.
None . . and no alligator. You have to look into these things
and . . . investigate . . from your own . . from a detached
point of view to get at . . . what the real truth really is. The
man could have been a secret agent that had to be eliminated
by the CIA for Christsake!

RITA Wasn't our very own pet parrot . . the red . . Polly wants
a cracker . . strangled to death and eaten by a wild kinkajou?

JIM Not a kinkajou. There are no kinkajous in Florida. I
believe those pests are native only to Mexico, Central or
South America. Besides, they are too small . . . to attack a
large red macaw. It was, if you will remember correctly, a
standard backyard raccoon.

RITA Was it . . was it a raccoon? It could have been a monkey
. . a wild monkey.

JIM You know it was a rabid raccoon . . . who bit our Polly!
Now shut up. Leave me alone. Let it be. You are driving me
crazy with these false accounts . . .

RITA It could have been you . .

JIM What?

RITA Devoured by an alligator, then . . . what would happen to
me? It could've . .

JIM Oh shut up now! Enough. Silence. Mix yourself a drink.
Isn't it almost time for happy hour? Probably the old bastard
was better off dead anyhow. Ha ha.

RITA What?

JIM Too much bickering with a wife . . and suffering. The
alligator did him a favor if it did him in.

RITA Oh.

(*Pause. Making conversation.*)

Where would you find an alligator . . . if . . . I mean . . . if
you were looking . . for one . . . if you wanted to see one?

JIM You could go to the Everglades. They say . . . I hear they
are quite abundant there. Some have been captured . . just to
be on display . . for the amusement of tourists.

RITA How far away are the Everglades? . . from here?

JIM Not far . . . not far at all . . . . You could go to the town
of Flamingo . . in the Everglades . . near Shark Point . . . they
would be there . .

RITA Would you see a flamingo there?

JIM Where?

RITA In that town . . called Flamingo. Florida.

JIM I think those birds are almost extinct in these parts. You
seldom see a flamingo now . . . except in a zoo.

(*Light fades.*)

(*Light up.*)

RITA (*drunker, happier attitude*) Here is your drink. It is just
about time for the . . the Happy Hour! (*Laughs childishly.*) I
remember the happy hour . . . in the old days . . sometimes
the happy hour would go on for hours and hours . . even
days . . I remember singing songs like "Enjoy yourself . . . it's
later than you think . . . enjoy yourself . . if you're still feeling
pink." Remember that one? Ha. Ha. I sang it with the band.
Remember?

JIM You're smashed. You've completely crossed over . . into . .
incoherence.

RITA Not yet. Not yet . . there . . . not smashed. Control. See.
See. (*She falls.*)

JIM You'll wind up back in that loony bin again if you're not
careful . . if you don't watch your intake. Where was it . .
Marlborough State Asylum . . in New Jersey? Or was it the
women's shelter in New York City? I had to come and get
you . . out. The booze had soaked into your brain. You had
become incoherent . . . on a runaway binge. Permanent brain
damage . . . That's what they said. It took them months to
dry out your wet brain. Now you're back on that fuckin' piss
again. You can't stop; and you're going nuts again . . on me.
You're gonna wind up dead . . . that'll be it! Ha ha. Stone
cold dead.

RITA I'll outlive you. It's you . . . you're the one who can't stop.
It's you . .

JIM (*vague*) Is there a women's shelter in New York City? I
know there is a men's shelter there. Absolute scum! Lost! Lost
forever! The look in their faces . . . in New York City . . . is
blank . . empty . . If you look in their faces . . just behind
the eyes . . . you will see nothing . . . no pain . . . no more
anxiety . . . they have crossed over the edge . . not living
and not yet dead. What do you think about it? Do you think
about it?

RITA Think of what?

JIM Not living and not dead. An interim point.

RITA You're talking into the air . . . trying to scare the hell out
of me. You know my nerves are . .

JIM (*continuing in a half-drunkalogue*) It becomes like a
nightmare. The days are without end . . .

RITA You're the one who needs to quiet down your nerves . . .
learn to relax. Relax. Your heart could burst . . . that thing
that is inside you . . . could explode . . . if you keep getting
yourself all worked up . . excited . . why get so excited . . . .
huh?

JIM (*coming down*) You make me sick. Just looking at you now
. . you've become an old floozy . . . but then I never knew
you in your so-called prime. I bet you put out for soldiers,

sailors . . . anything that came along . . . that walked in pants.
At those war bond rallies. Miss Victory. Miss Ammunition.
What did they call you? Weren't you once a pin-up girl . . .
during those war years . . one of them tarts . .

RITA Some letters did come from overseas asking for an 8x10
glossy . . . . something to remember me by . . . keep up the
old battlefield morale . . . the fighting battalions. (*Crying.*)

JIM Don't cry. I can't stand your wailing self-pitying tears.
(*Humoring her, singing.*) "Comin' in on a wing and a prayer"
. . Didn't I go fight the Japs for Uncle Sam? Didn't I? Huh . .
didn't I? The yellow menace. We were instructed to blow 'em
up. Ha. Ha. Now they're runnin' the world, TV sets, cars. Ha.
Ha. Now they're on our side . . . just like us.

RITA What do you know about . . . . (*Still sobbing.*)

JIM About what?

RITA About the love. You never loved anybody in your life.

JIM Why bring love into it now . . you bitch . .

RITA You don't know a thing about anything. You never
experienced any . .

JIM Shut the fuck up. (*Grabs her by the throat.*) Shut up now! Or
I'll shut you for good!

RITA You're choking me. Ugh! Ugh. Get off! Your heart!
You son of a bitch . . . bastard . . you've become a vicious old
alligator yourself . . you are . .

(*Enter* DOCTOR.)

DOCTOR Ah-hem! Mmahm huh Oh! Hello . . . excuse . . is
everything . . . uh . . ?

RITA (*getting up, attempts to make small talk*) Oh . . . uh . . . uh
. . . Doctor . . . excuse me. I fell down. I mean . . sat down . .
Can we offer you something? A drink? . . . we were fooling
around and . . . the heat . . . what do you think of this heat?
You could have a stroke in this weather! (*To* JIM.) Get up! Get
up! He is having trouble. He fell . . . uh . . . I was tryin' to
help him . . and I fell . . to . . to help him up . .

DOCTOR Here, let me help. (*Pause.* RITA *sits down.*) I was just around the corner. I drove my Pinto and . . . well . . . you had called up yesterday for your tranquilizers . . . . anti-depressants . . Triavil . .

RITA Triavil . . yes, my Triavil.

DOCTOR That is the medical brand name . . uh . . . well . . . here they are! (*Hands her a bottle of pills.*)

RITA Uh . . . thank you . . yes . . I'm . . I am . . running out.

DOCTOR I thought I'd drop them off . . . save you the trouble of coming into town . . . and since I was out this way. Your supply has run out, isn't that what you told me? Run out? Remember on the phone?

RITA Just a few left . . . . but I could also use something to get me to sleep nights now . . . lately my nerves have been . .

JIM (*caustic*) Wrought up. Her disposition lately has been . . . her nerves have been acting up . . . to the point where she will wake up in a panic . . . sometimes screaming . . . calling out in the middle of the night!

DOCTOR I see. Well, we'll see . . . what we can do about sleep.

RITA Lately I've been on edge, feeling right on the very precipice, Doctor.

DOCTOR Now, now. We must try to remain calm . . . at ease. There is nothing . . . absolutely nothing . . I can assure you . . . to be frightened of. Believe me.

RITA (*sighing*) Oh . .

DOCTOR The main thing is . . consistency . . to be consistent. Two pills every four hours. That's what the prescription calls for. No variation. No forgetting. You should wear a digital watch with a timed beeper . . . an alarm . . . to help you remember. We all have a tendency . . . sometimes . . at times . . . to forget . . our . . . responsibilities . . to ourselves. That's it! We don't want you suffering a setback . . . a type of severe anxiety attack . . from which you might not . . . recover . . . gain back your faculties. I've seen it happen . . now . . . you'd

be surprised at the number of cases – I have encountered in
my practice – of those who sink into a permanent . . a manic-
depressive state of mind. A thought disorder. One thought
. . . you see . . . does not . . . it no longer connects with . .
bridges to . . into . . the other. Then what? Oh! Ho! Then we
are certainly in some real trouble. (*Slight pause. To* JIM.) And
how are you faring, my good friend? You are due for another
examination. Where have you been? In hiding?

RITA   The heart is still pumping? I believe . . Is it . . . is your
heart still pumping?

JIM (*steely*)   Yes.

DOCTOR (*examining the bar*)   And drinking . . What have we got
here . . . ?

RITA (*nervous*)   It's . . uh . . . huh . . the happy hour. We're
having our happy hour. Would you care to join . . . ?

DOCTOR   Remember what I said to you . . . in moderation . .
about just moderate imbibation! But the wrong combination
of pills, alcohol and . . . whammy! . . ha ha. You'll find
yourself out in the cold . . yes . . and forever. It's no joke.
Look at what happened to Elvis. An imbroglio. The
wrong combination. He blew up like a poison stingray . .
an oversized bloated blowfish. He no longer looked like
or resembled himself. He had moved somewhere that was
beyond all recognition to his fans . . family, and bodyguards.
He could no longer perform . . . and firing a gun into his
TV in his den in the middle of the afternoon. No one could
discuss anything with him. His behavior had become . . well
. . shall we say . . erratic! His attendant doctor was a cousin of
mine from Tennessee. We grew up there together. These guys
don't know when to stop! They can't stop! If they don't get it
. . the necessary boost . . one place – they'll go someplace else.
A euphoric all-enveloping sense of boredom sets in. There is
very little if any . . sensation left . . in the true nerve body.
Success . . . the little realities of everyday life . . . none of it
comes to mean a God damn thing! Now I can't stress this
enough! There comes a time when we must all pay the piper.

Now, you may think I'm joking, sermonizing up here . . . but
. . you see . . . as a doctor . . . I've seen a lot of 'em wind up
in . . well . . heh . . heh . . cheap . . . . meaningless . . . and
then . . (*Slight pause.*) But . . . well . . . what can I tell you
. . . ? Look at me. Now I personally stay in shape by playing
a daily game of tennis at my men's club, though I should not
recommend that to either of you. Ha ha. Oh, well. I should be
taking off now. I have other cases to attend . . . (*Starts to leave.*)

JIM Oh . . . uh doctor . . if . .

DOCTOR (*turning around*) What is it?

JIM (*seductively*) If . . . just for a moment . . if you could stay just
a moment longer. We hardly see anyone . . these days . . . and
I was . . . yes . . just about to play . . I wanted you to hear one
of the little lady's old records if you have just a minute or two
. . that is if . .

RITA (*loud, agitated*) No! I'd rather you didn't . . . just right
now!

JIM Perhaps you would have . . share . . a drink with us. I do
believe it is . . . we are well into the happy hour. Aren't we?
Isn't it happy hour time?

DOCTOR My watch says five of six, which I do believe is
correct.

RITA Imagine that. I thought it was closer to four . . . . but it is
so easy . . . so very easy to lose track of time . . . in the state
of Floridah . . . only ninety miles from Cuba . . . from Fidel
Castro . . the Communist dictator.

DOCTOR I suppose just one wouldn't hurt . . . uh . . . ha . .
ha . . . just one for the . . uh . . road. I do have a dinner
engagement with a young . . . uh . . . what is it you're
drinking?

RITA (*mixing drink*) We like to mix one-fifth of tropical papaya
juice with one-fifth Tropicana orange juice or Dole pineapple
juice . . another one-fifth Ocean Spray cranberry with
one-fifth each of Jamaican rum, Seagram's Golden Gin and
Smirnoff vodka. If you don't have rum you may substitute rye

. . bourbon . . Canadian Club . . or Wild Turkey.

DOCTOR (*befuddled*) Sounds like an extra fifth in there
somewhere . . but I'll try a taste . . . . uh . . for the road. The
proverbial road.

RITA (*like a cocktail waitress – smiling*) It's quite a bright
concoction. We then add a maraschino cherry, orange bitters,
and . . and . . uh . . a wedge of orange. We like to call it a
Red Parrot Zombie . . after our pet bird . . we had a red
parrot once. Now dead, I'm afraid . . he was murdered I
think by vicious neighbors. Here you are . . . (*Hands drink to*
DOCTOR) Now . . . the record.

JIM I thought you didn't want . .

RITA (*still at loose ends*) For the guest. I want our distinguished
doctor to hear what I sounded like . . in my better days . . ha
. . ha. Yes. Shall we have a toast. A toast to happy . . happier
days. Wait, let me take a tranquilizer . .

RITA, JIM, DOCTOR (*together*) Cheers . . bottoms up . . happy
days!

(*They all sip and stare into space. Record plays – "It's Like Reaching*
for the Moon," vocal by Frances Langford, with Victor Young
Orchestra. RITA *pulls it off at mid-point at the exact moment when*
BRIAN THE SAILOR *appears.*)

RITA (*coy*) Are you looking for someone?

BRIAN I guess . . I lost my bearings . . as to which way to . .
uh . . . get back . . into . . town . . the station base. I mean. I
made a pilgrimage here to see His house across the street. You
see . . in college . . I studied Him . . in Literature I . . and . .
well then. That is the house? Isn't it? His house?

RITA That's it, but it's been shut down.

BRIAN Seems to be empty of all contents from the look of
things. No books. No typewriter. No furniture. Doesn't seem
like anyone is living in there now . .

RITA It isn't presently occupied.

BRIAN I thought someone might have put up an honorary

plaque . . . on the house . . an honorarium.

RITA They say the disposition of the house is unsettled . . . in some kind of lengthy litigation.

BRIAN It should be turned into a museum.

RITA Tourists come by . . . from time to time . . though most would find it difficult to locate. We are somewhat out of the way here . . . from the center of things . . of tourist attractions . .

BRIAN Yeah.

DOCTOR You say you are interested in literature?

BRIAN I was interested in . . studying . . the short story . . in college before entering the Navy. I wanted, I thought, I might become a writer myself like . . . Him . . . like he was. They . . I mean the Navy . . made it very attractive. I mean now I can get my degree through doing a four-year stint in the service; but now I've switched to a computer-programming course. More practical. I mean . . . computers . . . are what the future is supposed to be all about . . . technology . . see . . . it's . . . uh . . . the "techn-no-uh-log-ic-al" age. Yeah. Phew! Sometimes it's a hard one to spit out. I guess literature . . it might be . . dead, words. That's what my military instructors tell me. Nobody reads much what with television and video games . . . information . . . you see . . can all be . . . uh . . . processed . . so . . books . . may soon be . . becoming obsolete. I mean you can learn now all you need to know through your computer. It will give you all the answers. Computer programming. Heh. Heh.

RITA He devours newspapers . . . and magazines . . any kind of information . . but I'd rather look at a good comic when I can find one. My father told me . . when I was a baby girl in New Jersey . . that trying to read a book was a waste of my time. "Why fill your pretty little head with all those ideas? It's ideas that complicate things . . . create problems." That's what he told me. In the hospital . . I was in the bins for a while . . they told me not to think so much. "Thinking too much is what got you into trouble in the first place!" They said. They

told me I should not think too much or go too much into my
feelings . . that I should concentrate on what I . . uh . . can do
. . or make . . like crafts . . . basket weaving or . . . sewing . . .
but I can't do any of them . . (*Suddenly in panic.*) Would you
care for a drink, sailor boy? A . . .

BRIAN I am a little dry. I walked a long ways . . . to find this
place. I looked up His name . . . His number . . and address
in the phone directory. I even tried the number thinking
someone would pick up. They said . . the operator . . that
the phone . . it was no longer in working order. Out of
commission. Heh. Heh. I sure would like to have met Him.
Yes sir . . (RITA *hands him a drink.*) Oh. Thanks. But that's the
breaks.

DOCTOR What?

BRIAN I mean . . . his being dead . . . and gone . . before I got
stationed down here.

RITA He put a revolver into his mouth and blew out his brains.

DOCTOR No . . . I think he was choked to death. It was a
strange . .

BRIAN (*with enthusiasm*) You knew him?

DOCTOR Yes . . . I was his personal physician . . down here,
that is . . . among others . . . he had others watching over
him. I used to dread hearing that desperate voice on the other
end of the phone saying, "Get me a little combination of this
to help me to make it to Morocco . . get me a mixture of that
for New York City" . . or . . he was running himself ragged
jumping from one place by plane or train to another trying to
stay on top . . of the game . . . in search of . . what? Elvis was
the same way.

BRIAN (*excited*) You knew Elvis?

DOCTOR (*feeling flattered and bloated with self-importance*) I
certainly did. Yes! Ha. ha.

BRIAN (*like a child, innocent*) Could you tell me about Him . . .
what he was like.

DOCTOR (*in control – calmly*) There is nothing to tell. In the end he just wasted himself away. He became like a monster. You wouldn't have recognized him. Have you seen a picture of him . . in the end?

BRIAN (*ignoring what was just said*) I would like to have met someone with that kind of ability to . . . rouse up, up the whole world. Yeah! That's it. Hey . . . what's in this drink, man?

RITA Just a little Southern concoction. I call it a Red Parrot. A Red Parrot Zombie. Ha. ha.

BRIAN Sure is mighty strong stuff . . . well, I have to get into town. Supposed to meet some guys . . . some of my buddies in town. I'd like to go . . maybe . . to see Sloppy Joe's. I hear that's famous as a hangout for famous writers . . they say . . . and actors hang out there. Real tough shit! Oh, excuse me, ma'am. (*Slight pause.*) I haven't been stationed here that long. A long ways from home . . . Iowa. Iowa . . everything is real flat out there in – Iowa. Not much happens. I joined the Navy . . really . . to . . well to get away I guess . . from . . from just being bored . . I guess. I wanted to find adventure. Boy. I found it. I'm finding it.

DOCTOR (*interested, excited*) You've found adventure?

BRIAN You might say that. There are some pretty weird people . . . down here . . like . . in this town . . . but I don't exactly mind it . . . it's different. I've been around a lot lately, I guess you could say . .

RITA Where?

BRIAN Well . . let's see . . there was Chicago, Illinois, Savannah, Georgia, and uh . . . a bunch of us just went to Disney World. We met Donald Duck. I actually shook hands with Mickey Mouse himself on Main Street, U.S.A.. and . . wow . . thousands of white doves . . . real white doves of peace flew over Cinderella's Magic Kingdom Castle. They raised the American flag and played the Star Spangled Banner. Walt Disney is a real American hero. We didn't get to

Epcot. that's next! That's what really interests me – computer technology – and industry. Yeah. We need to stay ahead of the Communists, you know, the Reds. Good thing we landed first on the moon. That is important . . who controls the world from what vantage point . . I mean. Anyway . . . I . . thanks for the drink . . I should head into town. It's my night off . . I thought I'd . . arouse . . . play around. Have some good times.

DOCTOR I could give you a lift . . my Pinto is just around the corner.

BRIAN I'd like to do some sightseeing . . . look around.

DOCTOR (*seductive*) I wouldn't mind driving you around . . the area . . here . .

BRIAN You're really okay. That sure will be nice. A ride around . . what's in that bag?

DOCTOR Oh . . . mostly pills . . of one kind or another. That is my specialty. The world of pills. Most people need something to keep them going . . . feeling motivated . . and . . . well, that's my job . . doctor . .

BRIAN (*excited*) I'd like to see the sun set at the tip of Key West point . .

DOCTOR (*moving in*) I know just the spot. Well . . we should be off then.

BRIAN (*like a little boy*) I'm real happy to meet you folks. Where did you get all these birds?

RITA (*vague*) Who can remember. They just turned up, I guess. (*Suddenly formal.*) It's our pleasure to meet a Navy man. Are you religious, young man?

BRIAN (*anxious*) Oh . . . yes . . . I believe in Him. I was raised Catholic but He is the only real thing . .

RITA Who's that?

BRIAN You know . . Him . . . . Jesus . . . I talk to Him sometimes. When I get the blues . . really lonely. He's helped me through some tough spots.

RITA (*perturbed*) Oh. Are you sure you wouldn't care for just one more little drink for the road, Doctor?

DOCTOR Oh, no. Don't bother yourself. You both should take it easy . . wind down . . at day's end. Ha. Ha.

BRIAN (*to* DOCTOR) Maybe we could pick up a six-pack along the way?

DOCTOR (*laughing*) Or a bottle of Puerto Rican rum – from the Last Chance Liquor Store.

BRIAN With Coca-Cola. Could we get a bag of ice and could we . . . . we could pick up some chips? Potato chips?

DOCTOR We could hit a few highway bars along the way . . . even stop at a hot dog stand – along . . or . . on the way back . . . whatever you like. See the sights. Hit the hot spots.

BRIAN Do they have a drive-in movie down here? Do you . . . does anybody sell any loose joints? Well . . . so long.

DOCTOR See you in my office, Rita. Next Tuesday . . with your hubby . . . call in for an appointment now. Bye bye.

(*They exit. Pause.*)

RITA Gone.

(*Lights down. Slowly – lights up to a pale orange which gradually changes to a twilight purple-blue and then into a darker cobalt blue as evening approaches in the last moments.*)

RITA (*sighing*) It sure was nice of the good doctor to come all this way . . out of his way . . to see us . . just to have a look . . at how we are . .

JIM Not that far.

RITA . . . and to meet a fighting man . . someone from the Naval base . . a young man.

(*Slight pause.*)

JIM (*nervous*) Would you say . . do you know . . if the doctor is a married man . . or is he a bachelor?

RITA I believe he is a confirmed bachelor . . from what I have heard through the grapevine . . though I never asked if he had been . . at one time . . . that is . . with a wife. Such a gentleman of the old school. So . . . so . . polite . . so . .

JIM (*cranky*) Such an old fox . . . a meanderer . . if you were to ask me. (*Slight pause.*) So what happens now?

RITA What?

JIM What will happen to us now?

RITA Oh. (*Slight pause. She shifts the train of thought so as not to encounter any difficult or painful subject matter.*) The sun is going down . . a bright orange-red . . like a bloodshot eye . . Ha . . ha . . There is nothing . . nothing . . like a tropical sun in descent . . the southernmost tip of Florida. How I love this place. There is nowhere more beautiful . . anywhere in the whole world. Evening will come very soon. (*Singing.*) "When the gold of the day meets the blue of the night, someone waits for you" . . ha . . ha.

JIM What then?

RITA What?

JIM Someone waits . . for . . should we move inside? It might be getting cold at night. There seems to be a slight breeze heading this way . . moving in . . off the ocean.

RITA (*hopeful, dreamy*) We could take that . . uh . . walk . . if you feel up to it. We might even find a restaurant that is nearby . . not too far . . that is open and . . and we could order a piece of that Key Lime pie you always crave. You think you'd enjoy that? (*A slight pause.*) Would you care to go . . if we could find a place . . not too far away . . in walking distance?

JIM I think I might . . I think I could . . make it.

RITA If we went . . if we go . . I could order up a frozen peach daiquiri . . . from bar service . . . or one of those exotic Cuban drinks . . . piña colada . . I think they call it . . made with pineapple . . and . . coconut milk . . and with rum added. Shall we try it? To go? (*She moves toward him, helping him up and then helping him to walk.*) Put one foot . . one foot . .

in front of the other . . slow . . that's it! You see. Slowleee. (*He momentarily slumps as if to fall.*) Oh my, God! There now. Are you all right?

JIM I'm all right. Get off me. Ha. ha. Not yet. Not yet dead . . . deceased. Just one of those momentary setbacks. You'd like to see me dead and buried . . . but not yet. Not yet ready to go.

RITA (*distracting him, moving slowly forward*) There is a mild breeze . . . and . . look up . . . the sky is filled with stars. (*Slight pause.*) Shall we go? Shall we move on . . . move ahead . . one . . two . . one foot in front of . . . in front of . . the other.

JIM *does not reply. The lights turn darker and darker as music ensues. Recording of Frances Langford singing "My Cabin of Dreams" – orchestra: Sam Koki and his Islanders.*

Blackout.

The music continues at curtain call.

THEATER For The NEW CITY / Bartenieff-Field present

OF IDENTITY

A new play by **ROBERT HEIDE**
With REGINA DAVID · ROBERT FRINK · DARYL MARSH
Set: John Eric Broaddus   Lights: Michael Warren Powell

JANUARY 9~26 ~Thurs Fri Sat & Sundays at 8:00 PM
Reservations: 254-1109 —— Tickets $4 —— TDF
THEATER For The NEW CITY ~ 162 2nd Ave at 10th St

CRISIS OF IDENTITY

Crisis of Identity was commissioned by Crystal Field and George Bartenieff and opened at Theater for the New City on January 9, 1986. It was directed by the author, with set design by John Eric Broaddus, lighting design by Michael Warren Powell, and the following cast:

BEATRICE	Regina David
ARTHUR	Robert Frink
KIRK	Daryl Marsh

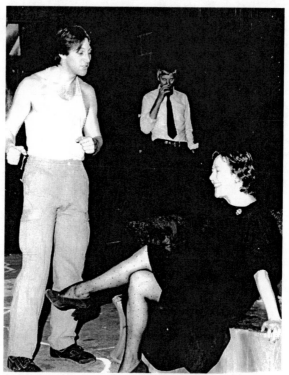

*Darryl Marsh and Regina David (foreground) and
Robert Frink in "Crisis of Identity"*

Crisis of Identity

CHARACTERS:

BEATRICE — *Formerly an actress (stage-film), with dyed red or bleached blonde hair, she now wears too much makeup and is almost too well groomed. It is as if — now in her middle years — she is still attempting to create the idea of the perfect cosmetic image which had helped her to face a movie camera or a theatre audience. Her fitted black cocktail dress (or suit), high-heel shoes, a pearl necklace (or gold chain) complete this outward image which is meant to contribute to the concealment of the hidden terrors and conflicts just beneath the carefully maintained surface. Bursts of nervous energy sometimes take the form of jerky unexpected movements, physical tremors, or sudden outbursts as if she were some wild animal or bird trapped inside of a cage.*

ARTHUR — *A modest but stern-looking figure of a man. He wears a business suit, shirt, tie, and black shoes. During the course of the play he loosens the tie, takes off his jacket, and rolls up his shirt sleeves.*

KIRK — *A swaggering man in his twenties or thirties with an imposing though not overly developed physique. There is a feeling of seediness about his manner, probably coming from too much carousing about in various nefarious nighttime activities. He wears fitted dungarees, black shoes (or white tennis shoes), a T-shirt, and a leather jacket. He also wears half-size open-finger gloves, which he removes, putting them in his jacket pocket shortly after arriving. He carries a small revolver in his jacket pocket.*

SETTING:

The stage set is spatial, almost the feeling of a bare stage. Yet there is a sense of depth created by many small rectangular shapes that are open as well as one large open rectangular framework upstage. The backdrop is a composite of geometric and jagged shapes meant to represent the cityscape of Manhattan as seen from the windows of a modern glass skyscraper apartment building.

The interior of the apartment is "high-tech," with an indication of floating stairs that go off into other levels and exposed theatrical lighting units which are an essential part of the overall design concept. The furniture, the chairs, a two-seat low-lying couch, coffee and end tables should be constructed from wooden blocks, with the seating units covered in black vinyl or leather. A cocktail cabinet should be a higher rectangular-shaped piece. Liquor bottles, glasses, and an ice bucket are the objects the cabinet-bar-service contains. The colors used are primarily black, gray, and cream with just a touch of green.

Though this is an open spatial room there is an element of confinement and coldness that might also be found in an institutional setting.

The time is the present in the evening.

Music ensues. The lights are dim, coming up gradually.

BEATRICE *sits alone on stage blankly staring front forward.*

She is finishing up a drink and sets the glass down on the coffee table.

BEATRICE (*half to herself*) There is very little about this place that is familiar to me though I know I have been . . lived here before. Sometimes it is difficult to remember where I have come from . . . where I have been . . . or where I am now. Today. I sometimes have this tendency to forget myself . . that I exist. There are these lapses of time . . time lost . . time free floating . . in which the pieces . . the fragments do not assimilate . . it's as if one day . . one particular day . . . the world had stopped spinning on its axis – having hurled itself into oblivion . . having sacrificed itself to the wind . . . into the void . . . a no-return ticket . . into nowhere space . . and now it seems . . a kind of all-encompassing stasis . . an inexplicable emptiness surrounds and engulfs me . . . and is inside of me like a wormy spider . . . at the very center . . into the heart of everything I previously held up . . supposed . . to be real. At times I am disappearing into myself. No route of escape. No escape hatch. If only I could jump. (*Getting up.*) It's as if I were suspended in space as in a dream – a dream of my own making. In this dream I act and interact with strangers . .

(ARTHUR *enters.*)

ARTHUR Last night I dreamt I held your head in my hands . . the hands . . . that held it . . . . my hands . . were amputated. I hadn't expected you back so soon.

BEATRICE I arrived this afternoon.

ARTHUR You should have . . you might have . . let me know you were coming. (*Slight pause.*) Your room is exactly as you left it. I think . . you will find that . .

BEATRICE Yes, I know.

ARTHUR Ah, yes . . Any . . er . . ah . . calls come in . . ?

BEATRICE (*anxious*) I left . . I mean I took . . . the phone off of the receiver. The incessant ringing . . the noise . . . irritated me . . . Do you mind? I had a headache . . from . . . the sound of the wheels . . of the train . . . against the rails. The shaking back and forth, to and fro.

ARTHUR You came by train?

BEATRICE I had difficulty sleeping. Even with pills, when I did manage to sleep, I would have this nightmare – jump up – wake up! in a cold sweat . .

ARTHUR About what?

BEATRICE What?

ARTHUR Isn't that a long journey . . a long time . . across the country . . California to New York . . by train? You could have come by air . . .

BEATRICE There had been flight warnings . . warnings of turbulent winds, dense fog, and . . I thought I could use the extra time . . . time to think.

ARTHUR Oh. I suppose you'd like a drink?

BEATRICE I could use one.

ARTHUR (*noting the glass, sarcastic*) It looks like you've been hitting the bottle already. (*Half to himself.*) You don't waste any time.

BEATRICE (*angry*) What? (*Slight pause.*) Oh, what's the use. I see that nothing . . nothing . . has changed. I guess it was too much to expect civil . . .

ARTHUR You know where the cocktail cabinet is. You can get it for yourself.

BEATRICE What happened to the help around here?

ARTHUR They had to be let go.

BEATRICE When?

ARTHUR Never mind . . I couldn't bear the way they stared . . gawked at me. (BEATRICE *goes to the cabinet to mix a drink.*) Fix me up one while you're at it! My nerves are right on the very edge . .

BEATRICE What will it be?

ARTHUR The same. The usual.

BEATRICE With ice?

ARTHUR Of course, ice!

BEATRICE Quit snapping at me!

ARTHUR It doesn't matter.

BEATRICE What?

ARTHUR Ice − or no ice.

BEATRICE Oh, well . . . here you are. You do seem unusually tense. Is it the trial? I read the news report at breakfast − on the train. Pressure . . undergoing the pressure of an investigation into your private . . your financial . . dealings . . your . .

ARTHUR (*cutting her off*) I'd rather not talk about it! (*Slight pause.*) You know, for someone I haven't seen or communicated with in . . . isn't it over a month? . . you have had very little to say thus far of any consequence.

BEATRICE What is there to say that hasn't been said between us?

ARTHUR About what you've done . . where you have been.

BEATRICE Why put the burden on me? It was to have been a
trial . . . a trial separation . . wasn't that it? . . and we agreed
there was to be no telephone conversation or communication
by mail during that time . . and when . . . and if . . I returned
. . we were not to talk about unpleasant subjects . . . old
memories . . the past . . like . .

ARTHUR You're still in a state of shock. I can see it. I see it.
Think it's been easy for me?

BEATRICE You're starting again . . you can't . . you won't . . let
up!!

ARTHUR You've got to face it!

BEATRICE What? Face what? You don't know what you're
talking about.

ARTHUR The death. It couldn't have been a suicide. It must
have been a terrorist attack. Bomb blast – an explosion. That's
the only explanation . . the only thing that makes any sense.

BEATRICE What are you talking about. Small planes . . .
single-engine planes crash all the time . . into the side of a
mountain . . or mid-air . . . into another plane that has gone
off its course. Those are the chances you take. Disaster . . the
possibility of disaster can occur . . happen at any moment
. . . in any circumstance . . and without warning . . without
reason.

ARTHUR (*stiffening*) Then we should change the subject.

BEATRICE (*going on*) I gave birth to him. It was not an easy
birth. Traumatic. His future . . the future . . was supposed
to be in front of him. My only child. A son. Eventually . . .
he was to fulfill . . your position . . . in the world. I don't
understand. Was it a rainy night? Was there fog . . . a density?

ARTHUR I think it was . . . yes . . . and some kind of
misinterpretation as to the position of the vehicle in terms of
altitude. Something like that. The flight pattern was disrupted
. . then . . they were . . they found themselves in front of a

mountain . . then . . How is your drink?

BEATRICE Is he dead then?

ARTHUR Yes. Have you accepted it?

BEATRICE (*blank*) Yes, I think so.

ARTHUR I see you've emptied your glass. Shall you have . . .
will we have a proper cocktail?

BEATRICE (*half smiling*) I don't see why not? It is we who must
go on . . who must pretend to know what it is we are going
on for. Isn't that it?

ARTHUR There is no sense in philosophizing . . rationalizing
. . going over and over the same ground. What happened was
meant to happen – clearly – it's as simple as that. We must
bury the dead. Here is your drink. You're back much earlier
than I expected.

BEATRICE (*half drunk*) I came back thinking there must have
been something I'd forgotten. Now I don't . . I can't . .
remember what it was . . what it is . . that I have been looking
for. Do you?

ARTHUR You are exhausted. These things . . . it takes time to
recover. You've got to pull yourself together.

BEATRICE (*sadly*) What will I do?

ARTHUR I don't know. (*Slight pause.*) You could go into a
repertory company somewhere . . try taking up acting again.

BEATRICE A return to . . . the boards . . . Ha. Ha. . . that's not
so easy.

ARTHUR You said that you once were happy . . . in that
profession . . that you found enjoyment . . .

BEATRICE That was a long time ago. Now . . I would be
too frightened . . . . terrified. It would be difficult now to
remember . . words. Then there is the movement. Walking.
Talking.

ARTHUR It's a thought. (*Slight pause.*) Well, how did you find
California?

BEATRICE What?

ARTHUR The desert? Didn't you go to the desert for a rest
.. cure .. Was it ... hot?

BEATRICE Dry. It was very dry there. Everything dries
up in the sun. Yes .. hot. Sun-drenched. White hot ...
unbelievable .. particularly at noon. It is dangerous to even
venture out into the sun .. out there ..

ARTHUR (*dreamy*) Out where?

BEATRICE In that place .. the place that I have come from ...
the place we have been discussing. And then at night ... at
night ..

ARTHUR What?

BEATRICE It is suddenly cold.

ARTHUR What else?

BEATRICE Dried-up brown palm trees that are very tall and
offer no shade .. no comfort .. whatsoever. No relief from
the sun. These tall trees ... as they call them ... and the
surrounding brush .. can ignite ... actually catch on fire
... burst into flames .. suddenly .. phew .. just like that.
Combustion. It is as if you were in hell.

ARTHUR Really?

BEATRICE Then ... during the rainy season .. there are these
mud slides with houses actually ... literally ... that slide
into the sea. But that is another area. The west is very vast.
Wherever you go .. it seems .. there is some catastrophe that
has happened or is about to happen – one or the other.

ARTHUR But you had been there before .. in that state .. of ..

BEATRICE Yes .. but this time it was ... it seemed like a
different place.

ARTHUR Didn't you meet anyone ... see anyone you know?

BEATRICE I didn't seek them out and I wasn't sure if they would
still be there if I looked them up. I was afraid .. I didn't want
to be disappointed.

ARTHUR Oh.

BEATRICE One day I drove . .

ARTHUR You drove?

BEATRICE Yes.

ARTHUR In a car . . ? You drove a car?

BEATRICE Yes. I wanted to see . . to have a look at the scenery.

ARTHUR What did you see?

BEATRICE Sometimes you would go over a mountainous hill
. . . very high up . . and then at other times it would be flat.
You could see the horizon beyond. And the ocean – and sea
otters swimming about or just sitting on rocks.

ARTHUR Did you see any wild animals out there? Such as . .
the great black bear? Or the American or Indian buffalo? (*He
sings.*) Oh give me a home . . where the buffalo roam . . .

BEATRICE No usually they are . . . in hiding . . . although I did
see a coyote. I think that's what it was. It was some kind of
a large wolf . . walking . . just walking on a dirt road. There
were several homes along the road. It wasn't in the wild. It
must have been lost.

ARTHUR Coyote have been known to kill babies . . left
unattended.

BEATRICE Yes, I know.

ARTHUR They will sneak into . . enter . . a house . . through
an open window or a door left ajar and if they see a baby or a
young child they will make a meal of it . . . sometimes even
finishing off the bones along with the flesh.

BEATRICE Revolting.

ARTHUR Domestic dogs are no better. I heard of Doberman
Pinschers going mad . . out of control . . . when they don't get
their way . . . when they don't get what they want . . . then . .
they attack their owners . . . they go right for the throat.

BEATRICE I can see by the drift of things that I should not have
returned.

ARTHUR Perhaps you should have gone further . . . farther
away.

BEATRICE Where?

ARTHUR You could have traveled to a tropical island in the Pacific
. . like . . Tahiti . . . . or you could go by boat to . . to Australia.

BEATRICE What on earth would I do there?

ARTHUR Where?

BEATRICE In Australia?

ARTHUR I don't know but if it's wild animals you wanted to see
that would . . . that would most certainly be the place.

BEATRICE I have no urgent desire to seek out wild animals.

ARTHUR There . . in Australia . . the wild animals roam about
freely. You would be amazed . . Free . . on the land. Some
of the animals found there are almost prehistoric creatures
. . . but there they are . . . running . . . stomping . . . jumping
about on the plains. Not shut up behind bars in a zoo. Now
that would be the place . . . the place you should have gone.
Australia. But you have to go . . outside the cities . . . into the
wilds. Weird animals and tribal ape-like men, strange dogs
. . dingo dogs . . and monkeys – all over the place roaming
. . . just roaming about. Now that would be exciting . . . an
adventure.

BEATRICE I think I would prefer to see them . . . these beasts
you find so fascinating . . contained . . . shut up in a zoo.

ARTHUR Even in a zoo . . . placed in confinement, they have
been known to turn on . . . to kill those that have tried
to contain them . . . when they have the opportunity. A
moment's inattention – and – wham! (*Laughs.*) You can be
dead as a door nail. A goner! Ha! Ha! But we . . we . . are
the more cunning. We have the key . . . the . . er . . uh . .
intelligence . . the ability to keep them under control with
a whip . . . a gun . . if necessary . . or we can withhold their
food . . their water . . starve them. You mustn't forget . . we
have a powerful superstructure at our command.

BEATRICE (*joining in on his fantasy*) Yes, we . . . of the human
animal species . . that is . . can outwit those that are our
enemies . . . who continuously stalk after . . . have their mind
on . . what we have . .

(BEATRICE *takes a small container of pills out of her handbag, which
is behind the sofa. She pops several of them into her mouth and
swallows them down with liquor.*)

ARTHUR Now what have we here? Pills?

BEATRICE My prescribed tranquilizers . . nerve pills . . . to keep
my anxieties . . thoughts . . . buried . . . to hold the terror at
bay . . particularly at night when . . .

ARTHUR Are you insane . . stupid . . mixing these with
alcohol? Want your heart . . your brain . . to explode? Want
to have a stroke – become comatose – a non-thinking brain-
dead vegetable like Karen Ann Quinlan or Sunny Von Bülow
. . hooked up to a machine. I saw it on the TV.

BEATRICE Sometimes oblivion . . . darkness . . . blotting it all
out seems preferable . . to this endless charade . . . blackness . .
seems . .

ARTHUR You should have journeyed into China . . . taken
a world tour. That's what I would have done. China. The
Chinese . . have a great deal to offer. Their thinking is more
. . advanced . . in some ways; but now it seems they want
what we have, TV sets, cameras, Coca Cola. Still there is a lot
there that remains undeveloped.

BEATRICE I understand in the cities . . . they ride everywhere
on bicycles . . . and in the countryside too. Bicycles
everywhere. Can you see me on a bicycle?

ARTHUR Those Orientals will take over the world.

BEATRICE Are they?

ARTHUR They will work day and night . . . to grab up . .
whatever they can. They have learned . . wisely . . from us.

BEATRICE (*tired of the game*) You are stupid!

ARTHUR (*grabbing her*) Don't you ever refer to me as stupid . .

BEATRICE Let go.

ARTHUR So we are back where we started.

BEATRICE So it would appear. Well, what shall we do – have another drink? Eat? I think I'm getting hungry.

ARTHUR I wouldn't care for food. No . . . the very idea of it makes me nauseous.

BEATRICE Shall we turn on the television.

ARTHUR While you were gone the big tube blew . . . just fizzled out . . I was almost glad . . in fact . . relieved . . . all those horrible reports . . . the late night news . . . just as I was trying to sleep. Men and women smiling their empty toothpaste white smiles while describing earthquakes, volcanic eruptions – one horrific event after the other – worldwide plagues, terrorist bombings and attacks of boats and planes . . shoot-outs at shopping malls . . or hamburger restaurants, desperate lost persons wandering the streets, sleeping in terminals, and carrying plastic bags filled with God knows what . .

BEATRICE No identity to call their own.

ARTHUR Desperate . . desperate . . crazed persons are at loose everywhere . . like wild animals.

BEATRICE You're shouting! You're going out . . . of control. You need to calm down.

ARTHUR What has happened to the world we once knew . . . the order of things . . the order we took for granted. The world . . such as it is . . . such as it has become . . no longer makes sense.

BEATRICE It's you that have become absurd. The world goes on as it always has

ARTHUR A senseless flux.

BEATRICE And what about yourself. Now it's fraud . . or embezzlement . . . which is it? Are these the charges brought up against you?

ARTHUR Shut up!

BEATRICE Forced to resign The toxic chemical corporation of America. You can't fight that. Have you thought about life in jail? Confinement. What will happen to me? Have you thought about that?

ARTHUR I said keep your trap shut or . . .

BEATRICE Did you think you could go on . . . undetected in your schemes, manipulations, and maneuvering? Did you sign those bad checks?

ARTHUR (*grabbing her*) I told you – I will not discuss it. This is a matter for lawyers.

BEATRICE Is that why you sent me away – to avoid embarrassment? (*He jumps at her.*) Get off me or I'll . . .

ARTHUR (*menacing*) Or you'll . . . what?

BEATRICE Go ahead and kill me . . . kill me if you must . . . only do it quickly. You're like a mad, ravenous, raving beast.

ARTHUR Ah-h-h! I should . . . just do it . .

(KIRK *enters, stands and watches.*)

BEATRICE (*startled by another presence*) Who are you? How did you get in?

KIRK (*holding up key*) A key.

ARTHUR (*straightening himself out*) He has a key.

BEATRICE (*straightening herself out*) Oh.

ARTHUR This was to be a surprise . . . my very own surprise.

BEATRICE Surprise?

ARTHUR I thought I'd . . . I thought you'd enjoy having someone else around the house. I knew you wouldn't have a dog. I thought of getting a dog . . a bull mastiff, a Doberman, a Great Dane . . but . . you don't care for dogs.

BEATRICE (*suddenly desperate and confused*) Are you my son?

KIRK What? Is she crazy?

BEATRICE He does . . . he does bear a certain resemblance. He looks like someone I used to know . . like . . our long-lost son that disappeared . . . was it in the war?

KIRK I was in the Marines. Was your son a Marine?

ARTHUR I hired him on for protection.

KIRK Security. I offer security.

BEATRICE Security?

KIRK Yes — that's what I do.

BEATRICE You mean you work in a bank?

KIRK Well, no . . I worked at a lot of other places though.
My last job was in security in a disco. A security man. I've
handled all kinds of situations, all kinds of people . . who get
out of line. I'm a black belt in karate too . .

BEATRICE You are . . you seem . . strong.

ARTHUR He's only just been in this city . . for a month? Isn't
that it?

KIRK Yeah. That's right.

ARTHUR He's going to stay here with me . . . I mean . . . till
things . . the trouble . . blows over. I needed . . well . . a
bodyguard to fend off those that are on my trail . . . that are
after my ass. He's a very capable fellow. Aren't you?

KIRK (smiling, ingratiating) I'm the best. Yah wanna see my gun?
It's not a toy. (He takes out his revolver.)

BEATRICE Oh! Yes! Oh no! Put it away. It frightens . . . me . . .

KIRK I wouldn't use it . . uh . . unless I had to — but I know
how. If I want to. Believe it.

BEATRICE My son was a daredevil. He had a gun. He was killed
. . . the war . . . Saigon or Nicaragua or some far-off place like
that. He was shot down in a plane.

KIRK Oh. Tough luck.

ARTHUR (to BEATRICE) You're getting your facts, your stories
confused again. The truth is he had become a drug-runner.
Cocaine. Or was it marijuana? A no-good bum. I don't know
for what reason. He was on a run going across the border into
New Mexico in a small carrier plane. There was this crash . . .
or it could have been sabotage.

BEATRICE It's a complete lie . . all lies. My son was a hero!
He doesn't believe me. He was my only son. He served his
country well. I was proud . . . if he had been involved in what
you say he had been involved in, it would have been your
influence . . . your criminality . . what it is . . that which
you impose on others. It is you that must bear whatever guilt
exists . . or shame . . for . .

KIRK I'm not . . I've never been afraid of death . . . of taking
risks . . I've seen a lot of suckers conked out . . and for good
. . because they didn't have their wits about them.

BEATRICE I believe you. Wherever did he discover . . find . .
you?

KIRK An ad in the newspaper.

ARTHUR He had placed an ad in the newspaper.

KIRK I was kicked out of my room. He's offered to help me out
in exchange for . .

ARTHUR Services. And now that you have met . .

BEATRICE Have we?

ARTHUR Well, in a sense . . you'll get to know one another
soon enough.

KIRK Mind if I put on music?

BEATRICE Music . . ?

KIRK Dance music. I'm studying . . learning . . ballroom . . .
dancing. Fred Astaire Dance Studio. I figure I needed it . .
for my special skills in this city. You know. New Year's Eve.
The Waldorf. Roseland. I've always wanted to go to those
places. The bossa nova, samba, disco, fox trot . . that's what
they teach. I get this free lesson. You like Glenn Miller? I saw
"The Glenn Miller Story" on TV with James Stewart and
June Allyson. Sad. Sad.

BEATRICE Glenn Miller was killed in a plane crash – and Buddy
Clark . .

KIRK Yeah. Buddy Holly. Otis Redding – Jim Croce . . all
cracked up. Here . . . (*He puts on phonograph.*) It's my practice

record. Fox trot. It's easy. Wannah try?

ARTHUR (*laughs*) Go ahead.

BEATRICE Well . . why not? I haven't danced in . . . well . . since . . (*They dance.* ARTHUR *reads book during record interlude.*) Phew . . . I think I've had enough.

KIRK I'll turn it off.

ARTHUR I'll be going upstairs to my room. Kirk, will you be coming along?

KIRK Yes, sir, I will . . soon . . . but I'm . . I was feeling hungry. Food. Ha. Ha.

ARTHUR Where were you? I expected you earlier on in the day.

KIRK Prowling around. Looking around . . . seeing the sights. I went to the top of the Empire State Building. I'm still a tourist.

ARTHUR Did you get the tickets for the game?

KIRK Tickets?

ARTHUR The game Saturday. We mustn't miss that.

KIRK Oh yes, I'll be sure not to forget . . tomorrow . . . I'll pick them up.

ARTHUR I missed you. Well, I have work to do . . in preparing my case . . I think you will find – in the refrigerator . . a bucket of Colonel Sanders chicken – a container of cole slaw . . milk. You need milk . . for your bones.

KIRK You think of everything.

ARTHUR Whatever you need – my boy – it's yours for the asking.

KIRK Yes, sir!

BEATRICE (*coy*) You're going to spoil him.

KIRK What about beer?

ARTHUR We are always well stocked in that department. Always plenty of Budweiser, Miller, Blatz, Schlitz, Heineken's. Here you are. (*Hands him a beer can from the cocktail cabinet.*)

KIRK Thank you, sir.

ARTHUR You needn't call me sir.

KIRK How do you prefer to be addressed then?

ARTHUR We'll talk about that later . . well, good night. You'll
come up then later to tuck me in?

KIRK Sure, if you like.

ARTHUR I need you to be close by while I go to sleep.

KIRK You can count on it.

ARTHUR Are you sure?

KIRK Yes . . er . . sir. I mean . .

ARTHUR Give me the old military grip on that!

(KIRK *and* ARTHUR *shake hands to the point of pain and then
subsequent release.* ARTHUR *goes upstairs.*)

KIRK (*to* BEATRICE) He's a strange man.

BEATRICE Yes, he is.

KIRK And powerful – in the world of business . . that is.

BEATRICE Yes. He has made a lot of deals in his time.

KIRK He told me about his tower . .

BEATRICE His tower?

KIRK Oh, you may not have heard about it yet. He plans to
erect a great tower . . . wipe out an entire city block . . of
buildings just to build this big tower.

BEATRICE I see . . . a sort of monument to himself. Like a big . . .

KIRK I guess so.

BEATRICE You haven't told me about yourself.

KIRK Not much to tell. I told you I was in the Marines . . .
four years. Before that . . . my family . . . they moved around
a lot . . . Texas, Chicago. My old man was a military man
too, Navy . . . he was killed . . but it wasn't in battle. He was
bumped off . . . something to do with gambling. A gambling
debt he owed or something like that. My old lady, I don't
know where she is. Probably holed up drunk in some hotel in

California or someplace. I worked at a disco in Houston . . .
then . . I came up here. Thought I might get into modeling
or acting . . . into a TV soap in New York or something. What
do you think?

BEATRICE I was once an actress.

KIRK (*excited*) Really?

BEATRICE Then I married . . . and . . .that screwed, seemed to
put a damper on my career, though my career had never been
particularly illustrious.

KIRK Could you help me?

BEATRICE Help you what?

KIRK Act. You know what I mean? Think I have star potential
like Robert Redford or Charles Bronson?

BEATRICE It's possible. Anything is possible.

(*Slight pause.*)

KIRK (*relaxing with his beer*) Hey, I've met some pretty weird
people in this town . . since I hit town I . .

BEATRICE What do you mean?

KIRK Oh . . people wanting to be tied up . . you know . .
stuff like that. Or who want you to get dressed up in leather
outfits. Private parties. I aim to please but some people can go
too far – you know what I mean?

BEATRICE I think so.

KIRK Your husband – he's a pretty cool guy. He likes to call all
the shots; but I know how to handle him. (*Slight pause.*) What
about you?

BEATRICE Me?

KIRK Yeah . . . you!

BEATRICE I seem to have taken up the escape of travel. At one
point I began to feel nervous like an animal in a zoo. Trapped.
Confined. I needed to get out. Get away. Break loose. Now
I'm back.

KIRK I'd like to go to Morocco.

BEATRICE In Africa? Why would you go there?

KIRK I hear people are really off-the-wall insane there . . .
completely stoned out all the time on hashish − cocaine −
opium − you name it, you can get it, whatever you want there
. . without a big hassle . . .

BEATRICE Sounds intriguing. I wouldn't mind getting out of
this town.

KIRK You could get really lost there . . in a place like that . .
yeah.

BEATRICE Yes . . lost. That would be nice . . to just . . . drift . .
for a while. This may sound silly but . . .

KIRK What?

BEATRICE I'm glad you turned up here. I'm feeling less tense.
More comfortable already.

KIRK You're crying. What is it?

BEATRICE I can't help it . . . it's just that I'm happy you've
arrived here. I was feeling so lonely . . It's silly . . .

KIRK It's not silly − we all need somebody. I was to be
the surprise, you know. I could be the something . . the
somebody . . you were looking for all along.

BEATRICE I don't know what's come over me. I feel − dizzy.

KIRK You're trembling. You need to just relax . . . take it
easy for a while. Breathe deeply. I am also . . . I neglected to
mention an expert . . . and a registered . . masseur. I can help
you . . offer up relaxation. But first . .

BEATRICE What?

KIRK (massaging her shoulders) You must take a deep breath −
breathe in deeply and then . . let go. It's easy. In and out. Yes,
that's it.

BEATRICE Your hands are on my neck. You're hurting me.

KIRK Relax.

BEATRICE Did he hire you as an assassin . . a murderer . . to do
away with me . . .

KIRK What?

BEATRICE (*half smiling*) I wouldn't put it past him. I know he'd like to get rid of me. Once . . once . . there was something . . between us . . but now . . I don't know.

KIRK I'm only here to assist . . . to protect. We all need help . . . learn to help . . one another.

BEATRICE Yes, help . . . help . . and protection!

KIRK Nothing to be afraid of – breathe deep. Deeply . . now . .

BEATRICE Breathe deep. Deep. (*The two begin sexually fondling one another and* KIRK *slowly moves on top of* BEATRICE. ARTHUR *enters in bathrobe, pajamas, and slippers. He is carrying a half-size bucket of Colonel Sanders Southern fried chicken.*) It's you . . . I thought.

ARTHUR Food . . . I thought . .

KIRK Hungry . . . that we might be hungry.

ARTHUR Out of the ice-box . . . frigidaire . . Here. (*Puts it down.*) Eat.

BEATRICE (*eating*) Oh. Yes. He is a good . . . a good provider.

KIRK I could eat a horse.

They all chuckle as they gather together almost as a family.

Vivaldi music ensues.

Blackout.

Time Warp

TIME WARP

An elderly couple living in a high-rise complex in Coney Island. A formica-top chromium kitchen table, haphazardly arranged 1950s-style decor.

ARNIE

BERTHA

TIME: *the present.*

ARNIE I feel rotten . . my head hurts . . . too much of too much.

BERTHA What?

ARNIE A headache.

BERTHA Put your feet, immerse them, into a bucket of cold water . . then jump into . . . a bucket of hot . . . each for a full five minutes . . . in all the process of in and out should last about a half hour. Do not take any medication. The results will be amazing.

ARNIE You're cracked. Where is my coffee?

BERTHA Get it yourself. If it is over-perked it becomes bitter.

ARNIE Is Christmas finally over?

BERTHA . . . and the New Year.

ARNIE Why don't you put down that paper?

BERTHA I like to keep myself informed.

ARNIE You should listen to the radio. You will get an instant world and local report . . on the radio that's not in the . .

BERTHA It's mostly the tedium of weather, the mindlessness of sports, and then there are the all too intermittent commercial breaks.

ARNIE Those can be a relief.

BERTHA From what?

ARNIE Panic. Pandemonium. I don't know. Like those on television . . they can be of help. I bought myself a sound alarm wristwatch. It is due to arrive in the mail. You have a heart attack . . . a stroke . . or something . . and you push this button . . . and you call out for help . . .

BERTHA Ridiculous.

ARNIE You call out for help to some way station out there . . . and they send out an alarm . . . and then . .

BERTHA Then what?

ARNIE A rescue operation . . help is instantly on the way. I saw it on TV.

BERTHA A waste of good money . . . that's for certain. An outfit like that should be investigated by the government. How much did they charge you?

ARNIE I don't recollect the exact amount. I called the 800 number.

BERTHA What are you reading?

ARNIE There was a shootout . . on the streets . . three babies were caught in a crossfire . . . of bullets.

BERTHA Dead?

ARNIE One survived: but will have to live in a respirator . . a sort of iron lung or something.

BERTHA It's falling apart out there . .

ARNIE Where? What?

BERTHA Civilization.

ARNIE Oh, that.

BERTHA It must be the beginning of the end. That's all I can deduce from it. What else is in the news?

ARNIE A giant panda bear gave birth to a baby panda through artificial insemination.

BERTHA What else?

ARNIE The air we are breathing seems to be contaminated unless we can reverse the process.

BERTHA You should not open the window.

ARNIE I never do.

BERTHA The air is filled with strange invisible bugs. Thank God for radiator heat and electrical appliances like my Frigidaire refrigerator and the air-conditioning unit.

ARNIE And don't forget my retirement benefits . . checks that arrive mysteriously in the mail . . each month.

(*Lights slightly up.*)

BERTHA Why am I in this ongoing state of pain?

ARNIE Where is it now?

BERTHA Everywhere . . . it seems. I can't seem to get a hold . . a grip on things.

ARNIE You should remember not to overexert yourself.

BERTHA I never do. I walk at a snail's pace now . . almost a crawl. I never carry bags home from the store.

ARNIE You could slip and fall onto the ice. It is better not to go out. You should order in. Then there is the danger of being hit on the head from behind . . . when you are not looking and when you least expect it.

BERTHA Of course we don't have eyes in the back of our head . . .

ARNIE But nevertheless . . .

BERTHA What?

ARNIE (*continuing*) A woman was raped in this building just last week by two men pretending to be city inspectors. She was held at gunpoint. She had opened her door just a crack. A mistake.

BERTHA What will happen to us?

ARNIE That is a question you should keep to yourself. You can't expect me to seriously contemplate a question like that. It is a day-to-day thing. You know how it is. You ought to pay more attention to your appearance now . . which is becoming haggard . . . look at yourself in the mirror. You used to use beauty creams . . put on makeup, lipstick. A pat of dry rouge.

BERTHA I think the clock stopped.

ARNIE You forgot to wind it. Your forgetfulness and your anger . . . are beginning to get the best of you. If you're not careful you'll explode. How long can you go on – living in terror?

BERTHA I don't know.

ARNIE You should wake up.

BERTHA Wake up?

ARNIE To reality. You're letting your symptoms . . your illnesses get the best of you. You need to find some kind of inspiration . . you could read a book.

BERTHA My eyesight is going. It's all a blur.

ARNIE Hope. Find something to do. Don't give up.

BERTHA One must try . . . I suppose.

ARNIE You could talk to a priest. Find hope there. When do we eat?

BERTHA Soon. The Polar Bear Club is taking a swim today. I can see them running into the water from here.

ARNIE It must be really freezing. I wonder if it will be on the news tonight?

BERTHA It is a yearly event.

ARNIE It is always the same thing.

Media Circus

A News Bulletin Intermediate Report

Media Circus, part of *Greed/Flood – an Organic Virtual Reality*
by Tom O'Horgan, was presented in October 1995 at Here Arts
Center, 145 Avenue of the Americas. It was directed by Tom
O'Horgan with the following cast:

Don Diaz   Peter Craig
Debby   Radha Kramer

Media Circus

Topic: *Disappearing Towns of America*

Characters:

DON DIAZ – *A television newscast anchorman with a somewhat Republican presidential attitude, at times coy and charming in an "Our Town" boyish manner – or stuffy and arrogant in his conservative posturing coupled with a blanked-out-on-camera stare. He wears the usual blue-gray suit, blue oxford shirt, striped tie.*

DEBBY – *A perky, overly made-up young blonde weathergirl in a fitted red dress who speaks in an incredible fast reporter's staccato while maintaining a show-business smile no matter how great the disaster being reported.*

The glaring light and the cameras are focused on these two, who are always on "alert." They sit next to one another.

SOUND: *Intermittent gunshots, crashing waves, car crashes, and explosions in the background.*

DON Welcome to tonight's special TV media circus report. This evening we ask the question on our Disappearing Landscape series: What has happened to small towns across America? Thousands of towns across the country once had a Main Street with luncheonettes, dry goods stores, ice-cream parlors, barber shops, butcher shops, shoe stores all run by Mom and Pop who also lived in the back of the store – or upstairs – who lived in a community where everyone knew one another, worked together, went to the movies and church

together, striving toward a better way of life in hometown
U.S.A. Today with suburbanization and drive-in shopping
malls run by giant conglomerate corporations, millions
have deserted the sweet little American towns leaving them
to a new modern-day economy based on the drug market,
car theft, and including street muggings, rape – a general
atmosphere of violence and crime! Once thriving towns,
some of which were burnt down and looted during sixties
race riots, are now in total ruin with certain strategic areas
paved over to accommodate a Burger King, a McDonald's,
a Roy Rogers, or a Wendy's where a boxed hamburger and
a cardboard container with French fries suffices for a meal.
A drug war shoot-out occurred recently at a McDonald's in
California leaving nine dead, some of whom were eating or
had just eaten a Big Mac. The killer, surrounded by police,
then turned the gun on himself. Tragically sad to say, today
no one would dream of walking down Main Street without
gun in hand, and no one can shop in town anyway since
most storefronts are boarded up. Those that insist on staying
open must invest in heavy metal gates and keep a gun handy
under the counter – in case of armed robberies, which are
not infrequent. Now we know no one lives in the drive-in
shopping malls so you are relatively safe – sometimes – and
whatever is going on is recorded by security cameras. The
answer, it seems, is to buy or rent your videos and just stay
home. That's it, folks. Why go out when it's not safe out
there? Today even the police are at a loss and are often shot
just for the fun of it or for no apparent reason by angry thugs
high on booze or drugs. Well, Debby, that's our special media
report. Now what's happening out there with the weather
It feels cold in here; but then . . . ha . . ha . . we are air-
conditioned.

DEBBY   Well, Don – since global warming has taken hold out
there, there's not much good news, but here goes anyhow.
Folks in Sea Girt, New Jersey, are currently on alert for
Hurricane Zelda which is heading up the coast from North
Carolina where many homes have been swept out to sea – and

now 25 persons are known dead. Sea Girt residents fear the worst and are evacuating with many families staying in inland schoolhouses and some in abandoned movie theatres. I tell you . . out there . . it's a real mess. Right now the pounding Atlantic Ocean is crashing over the Sea Girt sea wall and onto the already eroding muddy roadways – some of which are closed to traffic already due to high winds and flooding – and another earthquake measuring 4.5 on the Richter Scale has hit the L.A. area. Still cleaning up after the last one – many residents – including movie stars – are threatening to leave the L.A. area permanently. Some fear the entire state or a large coastal portion of it will eventually fall into the sea – given one more jolt! However, U.S. government officials have called this idea ridiculous – and meanwhile looters are having a field day in L.A., though some have been shot or beaten with billy clubs by the police in an attempt to stop the looting. Mysteriously, though this is only October, Colorado and Montana are enjoying ten feet of snow. Good for skiing but meanwhile many roadways remain blocked. Yes, the weather patterns are crazy and in our immediate area we are hoping – praying – for rain following the worst drought of a summer without relief. You could literally not breathe anywhere. Remember? The numbers are still coming in on how many died in Chicago.

DON Well, that's our special evening report. Tune in tomorrow A.M. when we promise to read an excerpt from the Unibomber's Manifesto. This station made a deal with the mysterious bomber, who has promised not to blow up the station if we read his special essay on the dangers of the techno-computer society he says should be done away with in favor of – well, who knows what. Thanks for listening to our report on the Blighted Towns of America.

DEBBY As of tonight no one has claimed the winning lottery ticket – and the jackpot is now at 10 million. Hurry up! Yes *you* could be a winner. But you must buy a ticket.

TOGETHER Goodnight.

(*Commercial break.*)

DON Oh . . . suddenly I have this awful itch on my foot.

DEBBY You need Baby Gold Bond medicated powder . .
(*Holding up can.*) . . available at all Rite-Aid drug store outlets.

DON (*taking off shoe*) Ooooo –

DEBBY Oh . . no . . foot odor! You need Dr. Fink's rub-on
ointment too! Oh wow – unbelievable. Put your shoe back
on.

DON I guess I better buy a tube of Dr. Fink. (*Puts shoe back
on.*) Now let me ask you – and our TV viewers – a serious
question. Have you tried new Ovaltine yet?

DEBBY Oh, yes. Don – I had a glass of cold Ovaltine this
morning. I love the fact that Ovaltine is non-fattening and
rich in vitamin supplements.

DON Well, Debby, for a chocaholic like me it's the rich
chocolatey flavor that gets me every time. Ovaltine was for
years the favorite drink of Captain Midnight.

DEBBY And radio's Little Orphan Annie too.

DON And her dog Sandy too. Even a dog loves Ovaltine.

DEBBY We all remember Little Orphan Annie Ovaltine shake-
up mugs. For a dime with an Ovaltine label they would send
you your very own mug.

DON Ovaltine is a nostalgic drink – and so much better than
Nestle's Quik. So much more chocolatey.

DON/DEBBY (*together*) Drink Ovaltine – today. You need it for
your health in these hard times. Ovaltine will make you feel
good! And the flavor. Mmmmmm!

I Shop: Andy Warhol

A MELODRAMA

I Shop: Andy Warhol was part of *Bang for Your Buck!*, a benefit honoring director Robert Dahdah, presented by Peculiar Works Project (Barry Rowell, Katherine Porter, and Ralph Lewis) on May 15, 2007, at the East 13th Street Theatre. It was directed by Nancy Robillard with the following cast:

PAUL	Chris Mirto
ROBBY	Lars Preece
ANDY	Ellie Covan
CANDY	Michael Cross

Andy Warhol, Ingrid Superstar, and Robert Heide

I Shop: Andy Warhol

CHARACTERS:

PAUL — *a young, muscular hustler type*

ROBBY — *a gaunt playwright*

EDIE — *short silver hair, short '60s pullover silver dress, earrings (long)*

BOBBY — *a '60s rock star dressed in black, frizzy blond hairdo in the Afro style, dark glasses*

ANDY — *silver wig, black and white striped T-shirt, black leather jacket, black dungarees*

CANDY — *a smart '60s tailored dress, a diamond pin, a fur, high heels, blond shoulder-length hair*

VICKI — *a scruffy "beat" outfit, baggy pants, jacket, and an oversized cap*

THE SCENE:

An anteroom connected to a large loft. Walls are covered with tinfoil and large photomurals of Liz Taylor, Elvis Presley, and other personages. There is a three-cushioned plush couch center stage with a large circular coffee table just in front of it, on which there are ashtrays, fashion magazines, liquor bottles, glass tumblers, and piles of 8x10 showbiz and fashion glossies. A handsome, well-built young man is half asleep on the couch with his legs stretched over the coffee table. There is a liquor bottle on his arm, and a Physique Pictorial magazine covers his mid-anatomy. He wears only white Jockey briefs. Another man is asleep behind the couch on the floor. He wears a black sweater and charcoal black pants. The lights are dim, and the faint sound of music is coming over the radio. It is the voice of Bob Dylan singing "Just Like a Woman." The time is winter 1967.

In a flash EDIE *comes in wearing a short fur chubby coat.*

EDIE Shit. It's fuckin' cold out. It's freezing in here. What are
you doing with no clothes on?

PAUL (*still half-asleep*) What?

EDIE Give me a swallow.

PAUL Here.

EDIE So where the hell is he?

PAUL On the phone . . someplace . . maybe in the office . .
business.

EDIE I thought the cameras were supposed to be ready to roll.
What am I . . . . a nobody? No one tells me anything. I suppose
I should put on some makeup.

PAUL You look fine.

EDIE You haven't opened your eyes, sweetheart. How the fuck
do you know how I look?

PAUL You always look okay.

EDIE I have a hangover. There are dark circles under my eyes.

PAUL So have another drink. It's early morning. Nobody's here
yet.

EDIE Then why am I here?

PAUL Could be a mistake. I could use some more sleep though.

EDIE Fucking again all night?

PAUL Bitch. (*He grabs her and pushes her onto the coffee table,
jumping on top of her.*)

EDIE Is this supposed to be a rehearsal for the great love scene?
Save it for the cameras . . . pretty boy. I see you're dressed
for work . . . or undressed . . . I should say . . you'll get
pneumonia parading yourself . . .

(*A head appears,* ROBBY'*s, from behind the couch. He turns off the
radio and turns up the lights.*)

. . . now who the fuck are you?

PAUL (*sarcastic*) He's the playwright . . I mean he's a screenwriter now . . . he thinks. He says he's written a special part for you. He thinks it's supposed to be filmed today. Here.

EDIE Says who?

PAUL I don't know. It will happen when it happens.

ROBBY But Andy said . . .

EDIE (*angry*) "Andy said" . . . I'm supposed to be the star around here. Get it straight. It's my picture that's in *Vogue* magazine this month. They're calling me "Girl of the Year" – what a joke. That prick. I've been paying for all the dinners lately too. Can you believe that? Wanna see my Gold Charge Card? (*Dumps carry-all bag on the table.*)

PAUL What's this? (*Picks up small gun.*)

EDIE What does it look like? It's a tear-gas . . . or mace gun . . or something. It came in the mail from my mother. It's for self-protection. Give it to me.

(*They struggle with the gun.*)

ROBBY Hey . . you guys . . wait . . it might go off. Put it down!

(*They break off.*)

EDIE My anxiety . . . my nerves . . are frazzled . . . right on the edge . . today. I don't think I can perform. I don't think I will perform. Shit. Why should I? (*Pause.*) Got any uppers? I'm feeling down . . . depressed . . . the pits! I can't go on like this.

PAUL Okay, Miss Mess, wait till Fatso gets here. She'll give you a stab . . .

EDIE Oh . . . come on . . . the secretary? She's probably comatose somewhere. I haven't seen her for weeks.

PAUL Here's a couple bennies to wind you down.

(EDIE *swallows them with some liquor, then sways back and forth.*)

EDIE I feel dizzy. I must be tired.

PAUL Or burnt out . . . better sit down.

ROBBY You wanna see the script? My script?

EDIE Script?

ROBBY For today . . . I think you'll like the part. It's built around you . . see . . well . . . you remember the 1940s film actress Lupe Vélez?

EDIE Who?

ROBBY She was called the Mexican spitfire . . . in the movies. Well, in real life she was in love . . . carrying on with Tarzan played by Johnny whatshisname. Once he couldn't go on as Tarzan because she covered his body with big purple hickies . . . see . .

EDIE Eew. Cute. Do go on. Don't let me interrupt your fascinating synopsis. Is that the word? (*Aside to* PAUL.) Who is this creep?

ROBBY Anyhow it turns out she's pregnant?

EDIE Who?

ROBBY Lupe.

EDIE Oh . . .

ROBBY By this just-a-gigolo boyfriend of hers who then decides to jilt her . . well . .

EDIE Well?

ROBBY She decides she's had enough and writes him a letter – a sort of farewell suicide note.

EDIE You've got to be kidding?

ROBBY But then she realizes . . . well . . . in true Hollywood fashion . . . she has to go through with it.

EDIE What?

ROBBY The actual suicide ritual . . see . . she gets herself into this silk pantsuit negligee kind of outfit.

EDIE Sounds fantastic. I like that part.

ROBBY She figures . . well . . (*Acting it out.*) . . I'll be found in my Hollywood bed . . . dead. She visualizes the morning headline. TRAGIC SUICIDE . . BEAUTIFUL LUPE DEAD – just as if it were all happening in a movie . . .

EDIE My name is Edie.

ROBBY I know who you are, sweetheart. Anyway, she has her maid prepare her a last dinner . . . or last supper, as it were. A Mexican dinner made with lots of hot chili peppers and spices . . she's Mexican . . you see . . so . .

EDIE We'll have to change that . . .

ROBBY Following the dinner she drinks a glass of wine with a handful of Seconal.

EDIE Well . . . so what?

ROBBY She . . . uh . . . well . . . she doesn't die . . on the bed like she planned it out . . . like in a glamour pose . . . she hoped she'd be discovered like a beautiful corpse.

PAUL Can I play the Tarzan role?

EDIE What?

ROBBY He's not in it but we might write you in.

EDIE What then?

ROBBY She has to throw up then and vomits all the way to the bathroom – sticks her head into the toilet bowl . . . and . . . that's how they find her. Her head stuck in the toilet.

EDIE I can do that role. Where is the script? (*She looks at it*) . . . but I can't memorize lines. (*Starts to tear it up but instead she throws it at him.*)

ROBBY But . .

EDIE You heard what I said. I can never memorize lines. I can . . . barely . . uh . . . contain my own thoughts these days. We'll improvise it. (*To* PAUL.) It will open with a sex scene. You and I are in bed . . . but we've already had sex so we don't have to go through the motions. I know about the baby to come but don't mention it. You leave and then I sit down to write a suicide note . . . see . . very little dialogue. It will be more cinematic. (*Mood switch.*) Where is he? I can't wait around all day. (*Breaks down, sobbing.*) He makes me sick.

ROBBY Who?

EDIE You know who . . . Andy. (*Bursts into tears.*) I've tried to get close to him but he . . . he's like a zombie . . he doesn't respond. He never says anything.

PAUL He doesn't care about love. He's ultra cool . . . see. Hip . . to . . .

EDIE (*exploding*) I wasn't talking about love . . . was I? I mean . . . I'm telling you I just can't go on like this. (*Enter* BOBBY. *Mood switch, sweet.*) What are you doing here, honey?

BOBBY You said I should pick you up here. Don't you remember?

EDIE I did? (*Pause.*) Oh. Did I phone you?

BOBBY The car's downstairs. We can split. Are you ready?

EDIE Maybe . . . (*Pause. To* PAUL.) Look – just say . . . tell him I couldn't make it today. My nerves are shot.

PAUL Tell who about what?

EDIE Tomorrow. I'll feel better tomorrow. We'll make it tomorrow. Believe me. I can pull it together. Have you met . . .

ROBBY (*flustered*) I have all your records. I really think . . . your . . . especially . .

BOBBY Skip it. Let's get the fuck out of here.

EDIE Where are we going?

BOBBY We'll head for Connecticut. It'll be quiet.

EDIE I could sure use a rest. A long rest. Really I . .

BOBBY (*to* PAUL) So where's Andy?

PAUL I don't know. I thought he was in the office . . but I guess he left . .

BOBBY There's nobody there. I looked. Tell him I'm looking for him. Tell him to stop fucking around . . . spreading stories about me . . . around . . . all around town. See. If he keeps this shit up . . . I'll . . . never mind. I'll tell him myself. (*To* EDIE.) C'mon. Now you're shaking.

EDIE I don't feel . . . well. My nerves. I've been . . . on the very edge of the precipice . . . for weeks . . . exhaustion . . . I can't sleep . . . I can't stay awake either . . I . .

BOBBY Let's get the fuck outa here. You look like you need rest.

EDIE I don't really need to rest. What I really need is a
manager! Somebody to handle my affairs. Money. I've signed
checks all over town. I need money. I'm running out of luck.
My credit is running out . . . too.

BOBBY (*childlike*) I said I'd take care of you. Didn't I say I'd take
care of you . . ? Trust . . . just trust me. You hear . . . me . .

EDIE It's hard to trust anybody, probably you least of all . .
you . . I'll go with you anyhow. Nowhere left to turn. (*Starts
singing, dancing, twisting, and gyrating.*) Nowhere to run to baby
. . . nowhere to hide . . . got nowhere to run . . here comes
your nineteenth nervous breakdown. That song was written
for me – and I didn't even get a percentage. If I stay here I'll
hit bottom for sure . . . in no time flat. This is nowheresville.

BOBBY There's champagne in the fridge . . . in the car . . we'll
have a toast . . on our way.

EDIE Toast to what?

BOBBY To life . . . to a new day. Who the hell cares? Let's go.
I'm getting out.

(*He leaves. She follows.*)

PAUL Man, what a dumb mixed-up chick.

ROBBY I kinda like her. She reminds me . . kinduv . . of Judy
Garland or Marilyn Monroe.

PAUL Yeah, I know what you mean . . but

(*Enter* CANDY.)

CANDY Did I hear someone mentioning Marilyn? Where was
Edie going? She seems to be a wreck . . . the poor thing . . .
she's paying the awful price of stardom I guess. Too much of
too much.

PAUL Who knows?

CANDY She coming back?

PAUL I think she's split.

CANDY What about the picture?

PAUL I dunno.

CANDY Maybe I could do the part. I mean if she takes off . . .
she must be in love. Do you think they'll marry? Like my
hair? Yesterday I was Carole Lombard, today . . . I'm Kim
Novak. I put a lavender rinse in my hair. Kim loved lavender
. . the color lavender. Lavender walls . . lavender silk sheets,
dresses. Everything lavender. Have you seen that bitch Jackie?
My nemesis? I don't mean Jackie O. She's pretty. Anyway, my
mother . . get this . . . said I looked like Pat Nixon when I left
the house today. Can you imagine that? I felt like slugging
her. She thinks Andy should pay to have my teeth capped. Do
you think he will?

PAUL I wouldn't count on it.

CANDY Cynical today, aren't we? He will want me to look my
best . . . in front of the cameras, won't he? Why don't you get
dressed for a change?

PAUL I'm hot.

CANDY I'll say. Like my nails?

PAUL Want a Coke? (*Hands her a Coke.*)

CANDY Where is everybody?

PAUL I guess they're hung over . . . from the big Salvador Dali
party last night. Edie must have been up all night. She never
made it in this early before.

CANDY Well, I always get my beauty sleep. She doesn't
look too well. For someone who's supposed to be the girl
of the year I mean. I'm being photographed for a German
publication . . . der . . . I can't pronounce the second part.

ROBBY Spiegel?

CANDY That could be it. Are you a reporter? Would you
like to write about me? You should. I'm going places. You
could make your name . . . if you wrote an article about me
somewhere . . I mean now . . before I get too big and can't see
you.

ROBBY I wouldn't want to be accused . . . somehow . . . of
hitching my wagon to a star. Yah know what I mean?

CANDY Oh, don't be a jerk. Did you ever hear my Joan Bennett imitation?

PAUL Oh, not that . . again!

(CANDY *stares them both down.*)

CANDY Well, this is Joan Bennett in "Scarlet Street" to Edward G. Robinson. I'm hoping to do this routine in my new film. He's keeping her . . . in a way . . . but he's trying to be cheap about it . . . sort of like Andy. "An actress needs a thousand dollars just to have a decent wardrobe; why these producers won't give me a second look, silly. It's jewels, furs, perfume . . . making the right impression." And then I do Kim Novak. "I don't wanna go to the picnic ma!" Ha. Ha. Like it? Think I could do it on the Joe Franklin Show?

ROBBY I don't see how you can miss . . on that one.

(*Enter* ANDY.)

ANDY Oh, hi! What are you kids doing here?

PAUL Edie was just here and left. She said she wasn't coming back.

ANDY Oh, she always says that. She'll be back.

CANDY I thought we were supposed to film from that script "Slut" . . . is that the title?

ANDY Oh, you're a day late. We did that yesterday with Jackie. Where were you?

CANDY Her again. I can't believe . . she told me it was today.

PAUL You should never trust a drag queen . . from the Lower East Side.

CANDY I'll wring her evil . . and thick . . neck . . . wait till I see her at Max's, that two-bit tramp with her glitter lips.

ANDY I just don't know what to do today.

PAUL We could make some flower prints.

ANDY I really don't feel like working. Maybe I'll do some shopping.

PAUL I think Edie's in rough shape.

ANDY What am I supposed to do about it? She's had two
suicide attempts in three months not to mention the nervous
breakdown in between. She needs a good doctor. (*To* ROBBY.)
What do you think about Edie? Think she'll do it?

ROBBY What?

ANDY Kill herself?

ROBBY Who knows.

ANDY I hope she at least lets us know so we can film it. (*Pause.*)
Guess what. I think someone's tailing me. Someone's been
watching my house too. I think they followed me here.
Today! Where is everybody? Look out the window.

PAUL What?

ANDY (*terse*) You heard me. Look out the window. (PAUL *looks
out.*) See anybody?

PAUL Nah. It's your imagination. There's nobody.

ANDY Well, it's giving me the willies . . . and hang-up calls
too . . . and breathing . . into the phone. I wonder who it is?
I wonder how they got my number. Gee whiz. Wanna go
shopping with me, Candy?

CANDY Can we stop at Tailored Woman?

ANDY How about the Ritz Thrift Shop?

CANDY I could use a new sable.

ANDY Rhymes with Gable.

CANDY My favorite leading man. (*To* ROBBY.) Did you see "The
Misfits" where Marilyn looks up at him and then up at the
stars and calls out "help" . . just "help" . . just like that. Can
you imagine? When Gable died, Marilyn felt that she'd killed
him. It was both of their last picture. Imagine that! They
say she was having a full nervous breakdown on the set. She
hid in her trailer . . . with Paula Strasberg. Paula wore a big
black picture hat with a long veil – and dark glasses to protect
herself from the sun. I think all those emotional memory
exercises were too much for her – don't you? She was so
fucked up . . her and . . . Jimmy . .

ROBBY Jimmy?

CANDY Jimmy Dean. Jackie thinks she's Jimmy Dean sometimes . . . when he's not Barbara Stanwyck. Who would want to be Barbara Stanwyck? Such a hard woman. Anyhow, Marilyn left all her dresses to . . . guess who? The Strasbergs. Imagine that. It makes no sense. They don't know anything about glamour.

ANDY Where should we have lunch?

CANDY I like the Russian Tea Room. Tennessee goes there . . . and Truman . . and Hedy. Tennessee said he's writing a play for me. What do you think of that?

ANDY Oh really. He said that?

CANDY I told him I should play Blanche. Don't you think that makes perfect sense?

ANDY (*sighing*) You'd be perfect. Really. Everyone who played it so far has been just so boring.

CANDY Except for Vivien Leigh . . and she had a breakdown too . . . playing that part. What we actresses go through to give a convincing performance.

(CANDY *and* ANDY *exit.*)

ROBBY Is she for real?

PAUL He's changed the idea we've all had.

ROBBY About what?

PAUL The gender thing. Don't be stupid and middle class, man. This is the sixties. Everything's changing. Nothing is what it was before. That's what Dylan says. (*Noise.*) Hey wait. (*Goes up to a curtain.*) I thought I saw something . . . move . . behind there.

ROBBY Could be one of the cats . . . no?

PAUL No. Wait, I'll get dressed. There's something . . . somebody. (*He puts on black dungarees and a T-shirt.*) Keep still. (*He pulls out a switchblade.*) If somebody's behind there . . . just stop playing stupid games, you hear me?

ROBBY Why get excited?

(VICKI *steps out – a kind of "dark man" character.*)

VICKI Drop the knife. I have a gun . . pointed right at your face.

PAUL Now where did you get that?

VICKI I found it. Ha. Ha.

PAUL Is it loaded?

VICKI Never mind. If you all shut up and behave I might just put it in my pocketbook. See. (*Puts gun in handbag.*)

PAUL Are you all right?

VICKI I was sitting in the bathroom closet for what seemed like . . . hours . . not able to even move . . just sitting . . staring . . thinking.

PAUL Are you sure . . . ? What are you on today?

VICKI I think I'm beginning to see things . . . as they are . . . for real . . . for the first time. I know what I have to do. See.

PAUL What?

VICKI I can't say exactly but . . . did you ever read Sartre . . . I think he really knows what it's all about . . . being and nothingness. Don't you? Some things got to change . . . something has got to . . . (VICKI *passes out.*)

PAUL She's out cold!

ROBBY What's her problem?

PAUL She's drugged out of her fuckin' mind . . . again. What a spaced out . . . Really. She's a freak. She feels he owes her some money or something, I think. She's gotten kinduv really way-out obsessed with this idea she has that she should be paid for some idea he supposedly stole from her. He doesn't want her around anymore. See. She did some kind of writing and now she thinks she's due a percentage or something. I think it was a film idea or something.

ROBBY She seems real dangerous.

PAUL Nah . . . she's just nuts . . but this place . . well, it's not exactly back-home-normal or anything. It's sort of a hotel for wayward children . . see . . everybody's fucked up . . . just trying to make it somehow. They're all nuts.

ROBBY What should we do with her? Wake her up? Call an ambulance?

PAUL Let her be. She'll sleep it off. It's just drugs, man. The wrong combination, I guess. I'll empty out the shells. Once she wanted to play Russian roulette with this thing. With about five people. Scary. Real weird shit. Got a cigarette.

ROBBY Yeah. (*Lights two cigarettes.*)

PAUL Where'd jah-cum from?

ROBBY Ohio. Now I live downtown.

PAUL Howdja get here?

ROBBY I don't remember.

PAUL You live in the Village?

ROBBY Yeah . . . well . .

PAUL Got anything to drink down there?

ROBBY Where?

PAUL In your apartment?

ROBBY I guess . . . some Five Roses whiskey, I think.

PAUL Wannah go?

ROBBY Well . . . I . .

PAUL I could use a stiff drink . . or two. This place, it's bone dry. We can grab a cab, can't we? I got ten bucks. Got any money?

ROBBY What? Oh. Yeah . . .

PAUL I'm thinking of changing my name. Got any ideas?

ROBBY Well . . . let me think . . .

Curtain.

MUSIC: *"19th Nervous Breakdown"*

Andy Warhol, Edie Sedgwick, and "The Death of Lupe Velez" (original title)

This "Lupe" film scenario was requested by Andy Warhol for Edie Sedgwick. Warhol wanted a treatment in which a star would consciously participate in her own demise. Andy felt that Edie – in 1966 his superstar Girl of the Year – would one day commit suicide. He once remarked to me, "I hope she lets us know – so we can film it."

Ultimately Edie, who played the part and who felt the Rolling Stones' "19th Nervous Breakdown" was written about her, was no longer the life of the party and a victim of drugs and alcohol. During the filming of "Lupe" Edie had trouble memorizing lines but performed well as a star-on-the-brink in the film. At the time Edie liked taking rides (in Bob Dylan's limousine) through Central Park to relax, stopping at places like the Ginger Man or Tavern on the Green, running up tabs drinking Bloody Marys or vodka martinis. She was a true party girl, and it was fun to accompany her on these forays.

Charming, innocent, and truly crazy, Edie was a great beauty who behaved as if she were above and beyond the rest of the crowd. Even Andy often admitted he didn't know how to handle her; but he felt she certainly created a splash.

In my own mind Edie is one of those unforgettable people who though gone seem to live on forever.

LUPE

A SCREENPLAY

Edie Sedgwick as Lupe

NOTE: *Edie Factory Girl*, a book compiled by Nat Finkelstein and David Dalton (published in 2006 by VH1 Press), contains writings about Edie by Dalton, Finkelstein (one of Warhol's chief factory photographers whose lavish color photos of Edie fill the book), and others who tell their fantastic factory stories including Billy Name, Danny Fields, Gerard Malanga, Bibbe Hansen, Marianne Faithfull, Ultra Violet, and Robert Heide including posthumous quotes from Andy Warhol about Edie, whose untimely death from an overdose occurred in 1971 in Santa Barbara.

LUPE

*The scene is the interior rooms of the adobe-hacienda-style bungalow
called Casa Felicias on North Rodeo Drive in Beverly Hills. The
rooms are a bedroom with an oversized bed covered with satin sheets
and pillowcases, a large deco blondewood vanity with a full-size round
mirror, its surface covered with a combination of cut-glass perfume
bottles, full and emptied liquor bottles, cold cream jars, and numerous
vials and pillboxes containing barbiturates, uppers, downers, laxatives,
and other make-it-through-the-night "helpers." Large vases filled with
florist-perfect flowers create the atmosphere of a funeral parlor rather
than a bedroom. Smoke emanates from pots of incense burning at
various points in the room. The bed appears to be a death-bed with
flowers and rose petals strewn across it. Venetian blinds are drawn.*

*The adjacent room is filled with bamboo furniture covered in tropical
floral print fabric, sofa, chairs, side tables, lamps, coffee table, and desk.
A life-size painting over a pseudo fireplace of "The Star" who dwells
within dominates this living area. A spotlit table is set in an alcove
with the dinner-for-two remains of a Mexican-style supper. The lights
are dim in these rooms with the exception of the bathroom, which is
dominated by the glare of a fluorescent bulb. A bathtub has a shower
curtain covered with tropical leaf pattern and cranes.*

The character of LUPE *is based on a comedic film actress who has fallen
on hard times.*

At the first opening LUPE *is curled up in bed, wearing a negligee,
clutching a movie magazine in one hand.*

She suddenly awakens in a jolt as if out of a nightmare, and looking around the room moans.

LUPE Oh, shit. I can't!

*She arises slowly stretching then putting her head in her hands as if
pondering what to do next.*

She pours herself a glass of wine and then takes a sip.

*Picking up one of the atomizers from her vanity, she sprays perfume
onto herself and onto the bed as if to rid herself and the bedroom of the
smell of too much liquor consumed the night before.*

At the vanity she applies lipstick and false eyelashes.

*Looking about the room she picks up a framed 8x10 black and white
photo of a handsome actor or gigolo and hurls it angrily to the floor.*

*She switches on her glow-in-the-dark radio, and we hear the song "In
my adobe hacienda . . . there's a touch of Mexico . . . "*

With glass of wine in hand LUPE *dances around, sometimes tripping
and falling down, laughing, then dancing again.*

Swaying back and forth, LUPE *goes back to the vanity and swallows a
handful of pills.*

LUPE I need to be up. I must always . . . forever . . . I must be
   on the upswing. It is important to look good . . . be a winner.
   That son of a bitch. I'll show him. I am the star. I don't need
   this crap – what can I do? Who the hell cares.

LUPE *switches the radio to another station which is playing popular
music in the Mantovani style. The sweeping violin soundtrack is turned
low for the purpose of relaxation and background as if the life being
lived in the little house were a role in a movie.*

In another mood swing LUPE, *now gulping the remains of the wine and*

*setting the glass down, pours herself another drink with ice in a different
tumbler, perhaps a mixture of tequila with orange juice.*

LUPE *laughs.*

LUPE This is it. I know it. Think I'm stupid? I know what's up.
I know what's going on. Think I'm stupid? You got another
thought comin' your way if you see me as finished. Not
through yet. No way. Fuck you! That's what I say. Lupe says
– go fuck yourself. I'm gonna write this down. I'll show that
son of a . . .

LUPE *sits down at the desk, pulls out writing paper, and with a
fountain pen stares straight forward, then writes.*

The inner voice of LUPE *is heard as she writes with pursed angry lips.
Tears fall down her cheeks.*

LUPE (*voice-over*) "Harold – may God forgive you and forgive
me too but I prefer to end my life and the baby inside me.
How could you Harold fake such love when all the time you
never did want us? I see no other way out for me so goodbye
and good luck to you. Love – Lupita!"

LUPE *folds the paper and seals the envelope.*

*She wanders about the house, room to room, as if in a trance and as if
having a last inspection.*

LUPE (*begins to tremble*) A drink. I must have . . . I need another
drink. A Tequila Sunrise. That's what I must have. It will
make me feel better.

*She mixes the concoction in a chromium cocktail mixer, shaking it
furiously. She pours the yellow-orange drink into a proper long-
stemmed cocktail glass, holding it up to the universe.*

LUPE This is it. Yes. Smooth. Should I call Louella? She could

interview me. A last word. What a joke. What could I say?
(*Pause.*) It is hard to say goodbye. I don't like farewells. I
should smile. This will be "The End," the final scene, the last
act. Where does that leave me? Ha. Where's the director for
this scene? I always knew I would play it out – alone. My fate.
(*Singing and then humming.*) "In my adobe hacienda . . . there's
a touch of Mexico . . . "

LUPE *heads for the bathroom.*

*She opens the medicine cabinet and fills her hand with pills which she
swallows with her drink. Taking another handful she throws the pills
on her bed.*

*She takes the envelope marked "For Harold" and lays it on one of the
bed's pillows.*

LUPE That's it. I will die in beauty like Juliet . . . like Camille
. . . like Garbo . . . that's how they'll find Lupe.

LUPE *takes a large wooden Jesus cross off the wall, lies down, and
clutches it to her chest, murmuring a prayer in jumbled Spanish.*

*Suddenly jumping up, she rushes to a table and uncovers a platter filled
with taco chips covered with cheese and salsa, obsessively eating these,
with some of the food falling onto the floor.*

Rushing about giggling and crying at the same time –

LUPE (*screaming*) Oh, my God.

Running to the bathroom, LUPE *falls down gagging, choking, and
vomiting head first into the toilet and reaching to pull the flush
mechanism.*

LUPE *falls limp, her head stuck in the bowl.*

AFTERWARD:

There is the sound of a Spanish guitar in the background along with the barking, yipping, whining, and whimpering of a tiny dog. This dog barking though persistent seems to come from a faraway place or another psychic dimension.

LUPE (*voice-over*) It wasn't meant to be that way. I didn't think I would really be dead. The Hollywood and world press including Louella, who had interviewed me three days before for a *Modern Screen* layout all in my little adobe hacienda – all taking the final pictures. I thought they might discover me – a Sleeping Beauty or like Snow White surrounded by roses and lilies. But there was no prince to wake me up. Too bad! I got stomach-sick I guess with the hot spicy food mixing it up with the pills – oh, yes, and my drinks. I remember from my bed I rush to the bathroom. I'm thinking where's that rat Harold Raymond to save me or my former love Tarzan – my Johnny Weissmuller? How I love him still after many years gone by. So long. My dog – who will take care of my little baby Chihuahua? Oh, well, maybe Louella will take him home. I guess she'll mention me on her Sunday radio broadcast. Where was Leon Errol or my friend Jimmy Durante when I needed them? (*Singing.*) "Where is the song of songs for me?" . . . That was my song – I sang it in . . . but I don't remember the name of the picture. I made so many movies, silent, talking, singing. They called me the Mexican Spitfire because of the way I could kick and scream. It was all good for a laugh, but my life became a mess. So many bills to pay and a house I could not pay for and no money – and – no love. Yet they said I was in demand. I didn't want to die – I only wanted to be wanted. Love is a bag of tricks. If I could go back I would scratch love out. Just make more movies and have some fun. I'm sad about the baby, but with no husband – only a rat who disappeared . . . what would happen? What's next? Where do I go from here? I feel like nowhere – no place to go . . . no place to live and play. So . . . then . . . what?

MUSIC: *"In my adobe hacienda . . there's a touch of Mexico."*

Stephen Shore

Robert Heide watching the filming of Andy Warhol's film of "The Bed," 1965

Sam Shepard (left) with Robert Heide (in fedora) on the rooftop of the Caffè Cino in 1966

ABOUT THE PLAYS
(AUTHOR'S NOTES)

Hector

My first play, *Hector*, was inspired by Alvina Krause, my theatre professor at Northwestern University School of Speech. An expert teacher, actress, and director, Professor Krause had herself been exposed to Method Acting masters like Michael Chekhov and Stanislavski. In class she demonstrated her sense-memory exercises and performed monologues from a variety of plays with spellbinding authority. As she walked into a turbulent storm, you could feel the rain hitting her face and a strong wind blowing against her body. She was never harsh or critical, and I quickly learned how to be simple and understated in acting. My colleagues Lanford Wilson and Marshall Mason, who also studied with Alvina at Northwestern, agreed with me about how great a teacher she was.

Hector was produced in 1961 by Jimmy Spicer, the general manager of the Living Theatre, and Lee Paton, who had produced the long-running Ionesco plays *Jack, or the Submission* and *The Bald Soprano* at the Sullivan Street Playhouse. For the Living Theatre's Monday Night Series, *Hector* was presented on a bill with other one-acts including Jean Cocteau's *Marriage on the Eiffel Tower* and Kenneth Koch's *Pericles*. For my first time out I certainly felt I was in good company! Director Nick Cernovitch, who was also a theatrical lighting designer, cast a tall, robust actress named Jean Bruno in the role of Professor Krause. Jerry Tallmer, the theatre critic for *The Village Voice*, described her performance as "magnificent" and praised the play.

Hector was later performed off-Broadway by Henrietta Strom and directed by Lee Paton at New Playwrights, the theatre Lee had created and built in what had once been a grocery store on West Third Street in the Village. Strom was incandescent in the play, but for a variety of reasons it opened in previews but not to critics. In March 2008 *Hector* was revived by Peculiar Works Project at the Theater in the Gershwin Hotel starring Gillien Goll.

Gillien Goll in "Hector." The giant white dog was executed by Stephen 'Hoop' Hooper.

The set for *Hector* is simple: an ornately carved wooden throne-like chair with books and papers strewn about everywhere, and an old faded Oriental rug. Next to the chair sits a four-foot-high amusement-park plaster-of-Paris game-of-chance prize, a bulldog statue named Hector. The professor addresses the audience (her class), speaks out her thoughts, or quotes poetry in a reverie; at other times she addresses the silent dog-statue or cries out in pain.

I thought of *Hector* as a kind of everyman-everywoman play with Death as an absent character both feared and to-be-embraced. At play's end, wrapped around the dog on the floor, she is either asleep or dead. When directing the play it is important to understand that the actor is sometimes attempting to address Death – the unknown – and at other times the classroom/audience. Movement is important, as all of this ought to be not just words but a dance of death. In the final moment a light flickers on her face, then on the dog, and then it is dark.

West of the Moon

Following *Hector*, Lee Paton asked me to write a play that she could direct to accompany an absurdist anti-war/anti-violence play she had optioned, *The Blood Bugle* by Harry Tierney Jr., whose father was famous for having written the Broadway musical *Rio Rita*. (*Hector* was also to be a part of this repertory, and Henrietta Strom was depicted in a *New York Times* illustration as Professor Krause, but it played only in previews.)

After the official opening of *West of the Moon* and *The Blood Bugle*, the production went awry. The seven uptown newspaper critics slaughtered the two plays. On opening night Lee Paton was confronted before the curtain by critic Judith Crist, who asked her, "Where the hell did you get the money to put these on?" Commenting on the reviews, Jerry Tallmer wrote that he had never before seen such savagery and butchery in print. The critical remarks included the lines "Robert Heide will never write another play" and "Robert Heide should break his typewriter over his hands." I was dumbfounded and felt – well, that's it!

Soon after, I ran into playwright Edward Albee and producer Richard Barr at the San Remo. When Barr asked me, "What are you going to do now?" I had no answer. Later I was invited to join the Albee-Barr-Wilder Playwrights Unit they established to nurture playwrights at the Van Dam and Cherry Lane Theatres. I quickly realized that in the *New York Times* and the other leading newspapers of the day, any reference to homosexual or gay life was verboten. An exception was the Broadway hit *Tea and Sympathy*, in which Deborah Kerr rescued a young man with these forbidden tendencies from himself by unbuttoning her blouse and luring him into her boudoir.

In *West of the Moon*, a down-and-out, aging hustler named Luck meets a young man during a rainstorm in a doorway. Luck begins to talk about his wild adventures working for a male escort service as a masseur/prostitute for men who enjoyed high positions but had to play the game with complete anonymity and without too much trouble or personal involvement. By now Luck is dealing drugs on the street, and when he spots the young man he proceeds without a second thought to seduce and corrupt. The actors in the production at New Playwrights were the seasoned professionals Joe Ponazecki and Paul Giovanni.

Decades later Peculiar Works did a series of what they called classic plays from the 1960s on the streets of Greenwich Village. *West of the Moon* was acted by two young men on a Grove Street stoop. I was amazed and delighted to see that somehow *West of the Moon* had come of age.

The Bed

Following the productions of *Hector* and *West of the Moon* I found myself at sea with no direction and no compass to point the way. One night at the San Remo Tavern on MacDougal Street, a hangout for dissolute drunks like the old-time bohemian writer and Village character Maxwell Bodenheim, "beat" poets Allen Ginsberg and Jack Kerouac, playwrights like Edward Albee, Arnold Weinstein, and Jack Gelber, and a bevy of actors who liked to drink and drug and stay up all night, I began to feel that I was in some kind of passageway into a different realm. Warren Finnerty, who had played a junkie shooting up on stage as if for real in Jack Gelber's jazz-play *The Connection*, a big success at the Living Theatre on Fourteenth Street, handed me a tumbler filled with apricot nectar and a purple concoction that turned out to be mescaline, a psychedelic extract from peyote mushrooms. Like that crazy girl Alice who, finding herself in Wonderland, swallows from a glass labeled DRINK ME, becoming at once tiny and then elongated and super-tall, I found myself in a state of other-worldliness. In the Remo I entered a glowing yellow light bulb, then seemingly floating out of it wound up on MacDougal Street with some friends who were escorting me home. I remember having a great time drifting in and out of neon lights on the street. Stopping and looking up at a black sky filled with stars, I felt and said to myself, "Hey, there is no time – I'm just in this eternity."

It was then I decided I would write the play that Joe Cino had asked me to write for two blond men. "Make it just like *West of the Moon*," he had cheerfully suggested. This time around I thought I would develop a situation taken out of my own experience wherein two men trapped in an existential time warp cannot get out of bed. Using the bed as the play title and the focal point of despair, drugs, and disillusion, I experimented with time in the philosophical sense of Jean-Paul Sartre's *Being and Nothingness*, in which Sartre details concepts such as "the being of non-being" and "the non-being of being." In coffee houses in the Village, H. M. "Harry" Koutoukas and I read aloud from that Big Book, sometimes well into the early morning hours. Naturally, we both dressed all in beatnik black, as they did in the Left Bank in Paris, sipping black coffee and smoking cigarettes.

So I went home and wrote *The Bed*, which took about a week. I handed the manuscript to Joe, and he gave me a date in March, suggesting I ask Robert Dahdah to direct. This time slot changed when a fire destroyed the interior of the Caffè Cino on Ash Wednesday, March 5, 1965. *The Bed* opened instead on April 26 at the Sullivan Street Theatre as part of a fund-raising benefit to re-open the Cino, on a bill with *Little Tree Animal* by Oliver Hailey, *Three Sisters Who Are Not Sisters* by Gertrude Stein, and *Humilities* by Diane di Prima.

Jim Jennings and Donald Brooks played the two men fueled by liquor and drugs and caught in a time-warp. With Dahdah's precise sense of prolonged time co-mingled with non-time, the actors had a field day, twice just staring at the audience during the full-volume playing of "Any Way You Want It," a three-minute song by the Dave Clark Five. The benefit, under the aegis of Ron Link, the stage manager for *The Fantasticks*, was successful, and when the Cino re-opened, the play was re-scheduled by Joe to open on July 7.

The original cast for the production at the Cino was Jim Jennings and Walter McGinn. At a pivotal point in rehearsal, Walter refused to get out of the bed even though that was what the play-text

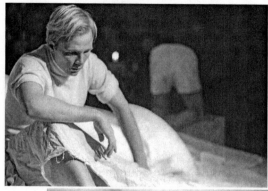

*Jim Jennings (left)
and Larry Burns
(below right) in
"The Bed" at the
Caffè Cino. Photos
by Nat Finkelstein.*

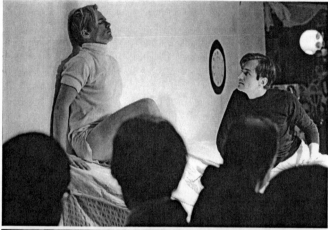

called for. A method actor, Walter told Robert he could not find
the motivation. Just days before the opening, after much anguish,
Robert felt he had to fire the taciturn actor. To the rescue came
Ann and George Harris, who with their large family were the
"first family of Off-Off-Broadway." They recommended an actor
named Larry Burns, whom they had known in Florida before
moving to New York. Larry was perfect in the role and during
the course of the play did get out of the bed, to go to buy a
bottle of Coke and a pack of cigarettes. A momentary escape from
existential despair and ennui.

The Bed had a good run at the Cino with a couple of return
engagements and was subsequently taken all over town by Robert
Dahdah with the same two actors into church basements or
wherever there might be an opening slot. An entirely different
production directed by Neal Flanagan was staged at Speedy's
Old Reliable Theatre Tavern on East Third Street in the late
1960s, featuring a young black actor and a young Yiddish actor
with an Afro hairdo, both of them nude. A few years later two
acting students performed The Bed for Kim Stanley's acting class
in the Village. I was thrilled to meet her, as she was, along with
Geraldine Page, one of my favorite actresses. It was great to see
the play in her studio setting and later to have coffee with her
at Jeanne's Patio on Greenwich Avenue. My friend and theatre
cohort Ron Link got us seats for several previews and the opening
night of Lee Strasberg's production of Chekhov's The Three Sisters
performed by Stanley and Page with Shirley Knight. The memory
of that production stays with me as among my greatest theatrical
experiences.

During the original run of The Bed at the Caffè Cino, Colin
Wilson, the much-talked-about author of The Outsider, showed
up several times to see it, and we became fast friends, getting
together to discuss existentialism, Sartre, Heidegger, Nietzsche,
and Kierkegaard. Colin compared The Bed to Sartre's No Exit.
Andy Warhol also came to see the play on a number of occasions,
ultimately deciding that he wanted to film it, which he did, at
Richard Bernstein's loft on the Bowery, using Jennings and Burns,

Stephen Shore

Andy Warhol filming "The Bed"

with his assistant Danny Williams shooting additional close-up footage. The film was screened by Jonas Mekas at the Filmmakers Cinemateque at the Forty-First Street Theatre in 1966. As of

Stephen Shore

Larry Burns and Jim Jennings in Warhol's film of "The Bed"

this writing Warhol's split-screen version of *The Bed* with overlapping dialogue is being digitized by the Warhol Museum in Pittsburg in conjunction with the Museum of Modern Art and the Whitney Museum of American Art in New York for posterity along with a host of other Warhol movies.

All hell broke loose back then when theatre critic Eleanor Lester, who had given a rave in *The Village Voice* to *The Bed* at the Cino, went on to write a comprehensive article featuring *The Bed* and describing the whole Off-Off-Broadway scene for the *New York*

Times Sunday Magazine. I still savor her quote: "Heide brings two singularly appropriate characters literally lying in the bed of their dissolution. Two men on a bed when 'sex is dead' and 'God is dead' is what the play is about. Here is the ultimate hang-up, psychologically and metaphysically, and the playwright focuses hard on the essence of the matter. The playwright clearly establishes that what we are witnessing here is the anguish of existence." Following Lester's *Times* piece, Off-Off-Broadway came of age, and everything "underground" opened up with a new kind of superrealism very different from the naturalism of Broadway.

The Bed has been performed in many places recently. Michael Feingold directed a version at the Here Theatre in Soho. It was performed at Yale, and the Caffè Cino itself was re-created at that Ivy League university with cafe tables, chairs, and cappuccino served. Part of the Warhol film of *The Bed* was also screened. Theatre

Jerry Marsini and Derek Jamison perform "The Bed" on Seventh Avenue in Peculiar Works' site-specific production "Village Fragments"

professor Jeff Grace directed the play at Knox College in Illinois, also re-creating the Caffè Cino setting with strings of twinkling lights. In 2015, on the play's fiftieth anniversary, the Great Beast Theatre in New Orleans, directed by Agnes Knows aka Edmond Garron, produced a way-out version with mattresses strapped to the actors' backs.

The most remarkable image in the annals of *The Bed* for me was seeing the bed pulled by ropes up Seventh Avenue with the two men on it acting in motion. This Obie-winning site-specific 2006 production was directed by Tim Cusack and produced by Barry Rowell, Catherine Porter, and Ralph Lewis for Peculiar Works.

Why Tuesday Never Has a Blue Monday

The genesis and inspiration for the hour-long *Why Tuesday Never Has a Blue Monday* was a New York psychotherapist I went to named Robert Akeret. Sessions were held in a penthouse apartment on the Upper West Side in a room filled with potted plants and trees. A beautiful blonde woman – his wife, Ann – would show me in. The doctor would already be seated across the room from where I would sit and squirm as he gazed into my mind with his penetrating eyes. A tall, handsome man, he had a warm. affirmative smile on his face when he greeted me.

Some time after the closing of her theatre, New Playwrights, Lee Paton had called me in a terrible state of anxiety. We arranged a coffee meeting. She was living with a young man named Billy Hollywood, a lighting designer, who had a drug addiction and went into terrible rages at the slightest provocation. Lee was overwrought, had gained a lot of weight, and was in need of help. We first went to a doctor I knew named Karl Goldman, a psychology professor at NYU. In his apartment on the top floor at 123 Waverly Place, Karl had a salon where he collected interesting and sometimes disturbed young artists, playwrights, and poets whom he encountered in bars, in the park, or on the streets. A father figure of sorts, Karl provided the beer, wine, and coffee and each week made a mammoth meatloaf for the hungry and broke. Having escaped the Nazis back in Germany, where some of his relatives were killed in the death camps, Karl had never been psychoanalyzed, nor did he then practice in that sense, but he loved to pontificate on almost anything, tossing out phrases like "free-floating anxiety" in a random manner. When Lee and I met with him one afternoon, he insisted that as creative, artistic individuals we might best relate to an existential type of therapy espoused by Rollo May in his case-study book *Existence*. That is how we both got to Akeret, whose mentor was Rollo May.

Lee did better than I did with Akeret (we always referred to him by just his last name). He seemed to be uncomfortable with men, but it might have been that I felt uncomfortable with him. He would say, "Your father still has his hands on your throat," and this was certainly true, as in our sessions I seemed to have difficulty finding words.

Lee met a dancer named Daniel Nagrin, and Dr. Akeret with his wife came to the wedding held at Lee's loft on Bleecker Street. Nagrin was ambitious and hoped Lee could help him achieve his goals in the world of dance. Ultimately the marriage fizzled, and he ran off with a younger woman, leaving Lee again heartbroken. Later, with Akeret's encouragement, she became a painter and also a playwright-performer in her own right, working hand in hand with Theater for the New City and master puppeteer Basil Twist.

I stopped seeing Akeret some time after the wedding. He published several successful books. *Photoanalysis* psychologically examined in detail ordinary family snapshots and the way people positioned themselves as they posed for the camera. In *Not By Words Alone*, he confessed to the mistake of having an affair with a patient he called Mary Faye, who was a friend of mine. Mary Faye, who was quite elegant and beautiful, thought they would be married, but he returned to his wife, and Mary Faye felt betrayed.

A movie magazine ran an article about the actress Tuesday Weld entitled "Why Tuesday Never Has a Blue Monday." I used this title for a play I wrote for La Mama. The subject of the play is an actress having an identity crisis while appearing as Joan of Arc in Shaw's *Saint Joan*. She is experiencing difficulty differentiating between her stage role and her actual life, and she and the doctor act out a sexual fantasy with one another. I am sure I wrote this in some sense about Mary Faye and Dr. Akeret.

While I was writing the play, I read a newspaper article about the strange death of Karl Goldman, who had been specializing in seriously disturbed cases; one of those patients, a former prisoner, had apparently murdered him. Fascinated by the writings of R.D. Laing and the cult surrounding Carlos Castaneda, Karl felt he could share the world view of the schizophrenic personality by entering directly into their realm. Being overly permissive, he allowed a patient to put him in handcuffs and lead him to the bathroom, where he was drowned in the tub.

The director of my play, my friend Ron Link, had seen many therapists, been in and out of Payne Whitney a number of times, and was thoroughly familiar and in tune with the subject matter. Marilyn Roberts, a kind of blonde-goddess-Marilyn Monroe herself, played out the neurotic scenes with gusto, with a tall handsome Patrick Sullivan as the doctor – they were in my mind the perfect duo. At Ron's request Ellen Stewart, who had been a clothing designer for Saks Fifth Avenue before becoming the impresario of La Mama, created a shimmering white hand-sewn gown for Marilyn, later in the run replacing it with a stunning bright red one.

After its premiere at La Mama, *Why Tuesday Never Has a Blue Monday* was presented at the National Catholic Theatre Conference presided over by critic John Lahr, where it received the National Catholic Theatre Award. In 1971 it was published in an acting edition by Breakthrough Press under the aegis of *Show Business* theatre critic Joyce Tretick.

Moon

With my play *Moon* set to open at the Caffè Cino in mid-February of 1967, I thought of the time I had spent in the Playwrights/Directors Unit conducted by Harold Clurman at the Actors Studio. Harold would say to the assembled group, "Just do it," and with that in mind, I decided it was a good idea to direct *Moon* myself and just jumped in. I was friends with Victor Lipari and Jacque Lynn Colton, two members of Tom O'Horgan's La Mama Troupe, and they joined me in this endeavor along with Jim Jennings, one of the actors in *The Bed*, and John Gilman, who, newly arrived in town from San Francisco, had been introduced to me by Joe Cino at Mother Hubbard's on Sheridan Square. An attractive, sensitive actress named Jane Buchanan showed up at the Cino. She was the perfect match to play opposite Victor in the lead roles of the hippie couple working it all out in their Village pad.

In the rehearsal process I came up with a circular movement pattern based on the number 8. Each actor could move in consecutive circles or simply at different intervals just stand still as if in the middle of the two circles. Victor, who was familiar with fluid stage movement from working with Tom O'Horgan, led the dance in the opening section as the two actors took to the small rectangular platform stage at the Cino, pacing about as if they were in a cage, which in this case was meant to be a small apartment in the Village. There was only $50 for set expenses. We found a wooden door on the street and set it on milk crates, covering these as well as the stage with black enamel, adding hand-made shiny black vinyl-covered cushions to create a sofa, and covering an ottoman in the same vinyl. A small low-lying coffee table set in front of the sofa was utilized for coffee cups and drinks or for Jacque Lynn Colton as Ingrid – a character modeled somewhat after the Warhol actress Ingrid Superstar – to line up the contents of her shoulder bag, which included an assortment of pills, dexedrines, uppers and downers. For the back wall we put up a giant black-

The First N.Y. Theater Strategy Festival presents

robert heide's 'moon'

WITH

JAYNE HAYNES ~ ALLAN GOLDSTEIN
MARLENE FISHER ~ HERBERT KRUSE
JOHN GILMAN ~ PAUL LIEBER

○ CABARET THEATRE ~ DRINKS AVAILABLE ○

The Manhattan Theatre Club, Inc.
321 East 73rd Street
Reservations: 288-2500 (11a.m.-6p.m.)

JUNE 6-10 / 8:30
13-17 / 9:30

Poster for "Moon" in the first New York Theater Strategy Festival, at the Manhattan Theatre Club

and-white photo poster of a leering, shirtless Marlon Brando in *A Streetcar Named Desire*; later in the run replacing it with a similar poster featuring a sexy Marlon in a black leather jacket on his motorcycle in *The Wild One*. Both posters were bought at Lamston's dimestore on Sixth Avenue – and that is how we created a set for practically no money at the Cino. The actors brought in their own costumes and, of course, makeup. Lighting for this production was by Donald L. Brooks.

Joe Cino would introduce the show to the audience, sometimes wrapped in an American flag, by playing one of his favorite Kate Smith recordings, "When the Moon Comes Over the Mountain," which contains the lyric, "Each day is gray and dreary, but the night is bright and cheery." Recorded music was also used in the play – the Rolling Stones' "1000 Light Years from Home," the Dave Clark 5's "Why Do You Love Me?," "Darling Be Home Soon" by the Lovin' Spoonful, and "19th Nervous Breakdown" also by the Stones. At certain points in the play I slowed movement down to create intensity in a superrealistic way and to add tension. One scene, with rock music playing loudly, had the character Sam dancing to a disco beat, Ingrid isolated on the sofa popping pills, and Sally and Harold staring blankly outward. A few weeks after the last performance of this premiere production of *Moon*, Joe Cino, high on drugs, and after doing a ritualistic dance after the cafe had closed for the night, committed a harikari suicide with a knife, and died a few days later in Saint Vincent's Hospital.

I describe all of this in these notes after seeing a production of *Moon* in Boston in which the actors sat immobilized in chairs and spoke the lines seemingly without intent, rarely looked at one another, and only got up and moved when stage directions specifically indicated. At another production I saw, the director chose to repeat the Christopher scene twice, having the actor rushing about in a campy way and throwing away his lines in a hurry-up distracted manner. I thought in this case I was seeing someone else's play; and so realized that direction, movements, or deliberate non-movement at times were the key.

The characters that emerged in the writing of this play came directly out of my own life experiences in the Village. In the building I lived in (and still do as of this writing) were the actress Sally Kirkland (just above me), who was always rehearsing scenes for the Actors Studio with the likes of Rip Torn or Keir Dullea, and Zal Yanovsky of The Lovin' Spoonful (just below), running around in the nude in his apartment and sometimes even in the hallway – apartment doors were left open in the 1960s. Other characters in the building included Zolly's girlfriend, the gifted

Shakespearean actress Jackie Burroughs, who later performed my play *Why Tuesday Never Has a Blue Monday* on Canadian television, and Dick Higgins of the Fluxus movement, who lived in true bohemian style even though he was the heir to the Worcester steel mills fortune.

Moon was a hit in its original run at the Cino, and a return engagement opened on January 30, 1968 (the Caffè Cino at that time was being run by the actor Charles Stanley, the writer/ critic Michael Smith, and harpsichord manufacturer Wolfgang Zuckermann). The second cast had Linda Eskenas and Robert Frink as Sam and Sally and Lucy Silvay as Ingrid. Jim Jennings and John Gilman returned in their original roles, and there was a dreamy, color-filmed projection by Bill Stern which featured Linda dancing in the opening sequence. One weekend during this run Lucy Silvay was sick and was replaced with two different actresses, the Obie Award-winning Mari-Claire Charba and a neighbor of mine from across the hall, a social worker named Margaret Wilcox, both with scripts in hand. What made it all happen for this production was the extraordinary and artful lighting by Johnny Dodd. For the scene late in the play of the Christlike visitation of the upstairs neighbor (played by Gilman) with his freshly baked bread offering and dressed all in white – in contrast to the beatnik black costumes of the others – Dodd's lighting scheme reflected the artist character's lines, "I paint mostly circles, in blinding colors that hurt your eyes if you look at them too long," with intense, multi-colored circles of light projected on the stage and back wall. For Johnny the creative lighting was always of a high professional quality with no holds barred.

Ross Wetzsteon came to review *Moon* for *The Village Voice*. He wrote, "I found *Moon* hilarious – in fact, one of the most delightfully funny plays of the season. Linda Eskenas is brilliant and delicious as a pale, tense, post-teeny bopper, and the other cast members are excellent. I recommend it highly." Michael Smith edited a play collection entitled *The Best of Off-Off-Broadway* for E. P. Dutton in 1969, and included *Moon* along with plays by Sam Shepard, Maria Irene Fornés, Søren Agenoux, Donald Kvares, Ronald Tavel, and himself. This publication led to many productions across the country at colleges and theatres like Eric Krebs's George Street Playhouse in New Brunswick, New Jersey, which starred Richard Portnow, Ellen Gurin, Marlene Fisher, Frederick Forrest, and John Gilman (again); at the National Cathedral in Washington, D.C.; in Hollywood at the Actors Studio West; and at the Cherry Lane Theatre in the Village, where it was paired with my play *At War with the Mongols*. The play had a run as part of the first New York Theater Strategy Festival at the Manhattan Theater Club with Jayne Haynes and Paul Lieber. *Moon* was also published in an acting edition by Breakthrough Press, in *The Off-Off-Broadway Book* edited by Albert Poland and Bruce Mailman in 1972, and in *Return to the Caffe Cino* edited by Steve Susoyev and George Birimisa in 2007.

At War with the Mongols

Following the production of *Moon* at the George Street Playhouse in downtown New Brunswick, the producer, Eric Krebs, commissioned me to write a new play for his theatre. I went home and came up with *At War with the Mongols*. The two hippie characters Mick and Meg are in a sense a continuum of the Sam and Sally characters out of *Moon*; this time they are on an LSD trip imagining an invasion of the U.S. mainland by Mongol hordes. It was written for two actors who had been in *Moon*, Linda Eskenas and John Gilman. We find the couple hiding out in a beachfront shack. The situation was in part a carry-over image of the Vietnam War, which had everyone I knew in an uproar at rallies and sit-ins – today we might think of a possible attack from radical Muslim groups, ISIS, or other terrorists who could blow up a dance hall, movie theatre, New York skyscraper, or any place anywhere for that matter. The couple have brought along bags of Lay's potato chips and bottles of Coca-Cola as survival provisions and in the midst of their acid trip decide to have fun acting out commercials they have seen on television – "You can't eat just one!!" and "Coke is the real thing!!" – to allay their fears of the threat of destruction and death from the Mongols. Perhaps this has already happened, or all of it is a dream – or a figment of the imagination. The unknown comes into play, and the idea that if we have fun it may all go away – disappear as if by magic. And that is what happens. Glinda the Good descends out of nowhere as in *The Wizard of Oz* to take the couple "back home" where they will find safety in their own little love-nest. I intended all of this to happen as if in a comic-book dream. None of it is real – or is it?

During the run of this play in New Brunswick there were violent intermittent thunderstorms followed by floods, and at the same time race riots - just as in other New Jersey cities like Newark - so in the beginning of the run there were just small clusters of people in the audience. One elderly African-American man showed up at every performance. He told us he had never seen a play before in his life. Watching it he seemed to be astonished and mesmerized. This man showing up nightly was a great gift.

Robert Patrick and William M. Hoffman were also invited to bring their Cino plays to the George Street Playhouse; and they both came to New Brunswick to attend performances of *At War With the Mongols*. Billy, who was working as an editor for Hill & Wang in New York, decided to publish the play in his *New American Plays Volume 4*, and that was for me just great. Newspaper-style black-and-white comic-strip blocks illustrated the red, white, and blue cover of the volume, which included, in addition to mine, plays by Susan Yankowitz, Michael Smith, Emanuel Peluso, Ken Rubenstein, and Jim Magnuson. The Pop-comic illustration for *At War with the Mongols* depicts Mick (Gilman) with his thick blond locks shouting "Har! Har!" as he fires a machine gun at enemy Mongol soldiers wearing caps topped with Chinese Communist stars running in abject terror from the "Blap! Blap! Blap!" bullet-firing sound of the gun.

I had a terrific time directing my two Greenwich Village pals as Mick and Meg, and all in all the play was a great success. From there we were invited to do *Mongols* with the same twosome at the Cubiculo Theatre (on the West Side in Manhattan), where it attracted good reviews and audiences. *Mongols* was presented,

Audience gathering to see the double bill "Moon & Mongols" at the
Cherry Lane. Photo by Deborah Shatin.

with Gilman and Francine Middleton, in December 1970 at the
Old Reliable on East Third Street on a double bill with *The Bed.*
Later, a rich Middle Eastern businessman and his "kept woman,"
a talented student director and actress, produced an excellently
mounted production on the big stage at Marymount College
which I felt was near perfect. Elaine B. Shore, the star of a popular
television series, needed to spend some of the money she was
earning, and along with the great film director Otto Preminger
produced the play on a double bill with *Moon* for a three-week
run at the Cherry Lane Theatre under the banner-title *Moon &*
Mongols. Elaine had played Ingrid in *Moon* in Washington at the
National Cathedral and also at C. W. Post College, where *Moon*
had been on a double bill with Sam Shepard's *Melodrama Play.*

American Hamburger

In November 1976 Theater for the New City announced A Unique and Amazing Two-Weeks Festival – Village Writers on the Village – to commemorate the 200th year of the founding of the United States of America in 1776. With grants from the Ford Foundation and the New York State Council on the Arts, Crystal Field and George Bartenieff commissioned playwrights including Rosalyn Drexler, H. M. Koutoukas, Sally Ordway, Arthur Sainer, Harvey Fierstein, Ronald Tavel, Maria Irene Fornés, Joel Oppenheimer, Muriel Rukeyser, Harvey Tavel, Helen Duberstein, Victor Lipton, and myself to write plays with a specific connection to the history of Greenwich Village, to be performed at TNC's theatre in the Jane West Hotel. Needless to say, the ensuing productions were as varied as the writers. Harvey Fierstein, for instance, offered a play called *International Stud* that took place in the back room of a gay bar on the waterfront and was enacted almost totally in darkness. This play became one part of his successful trilogy of gay plays entitled *Torch Song Trilogy*. New York City had been the epicenter of many patriotic celebrations that year,

At the Theater for the New City, the 11th of November 1976 to the 24th Bartenieff - Field present A Festival of New Work

VILLAGE WRITERS on the VILLAGE

a Bicentennial Collage of Voices

PLAYS   SONGS   POEMS
MUSIC & DANCE

about famous & infamous CHARACTERS & EVENTS *from revolutionary times to today*

– to be interspersed with the finest SHORT PIECES by village writers of the past – Ex: POES *The Raven* - to be performed on a table top!, MELVILLE, O'NEILL, ODETS & *The private Life of Edna St. Vincent Millay* – to be performed by the finest company of actors, writers & singers.

All writers will be present at the performance of their work –

Karl Bissinger	Robert Heide	Aileen Paslof
Roslyn Drexler	Shirley Kaplan	Andrew Piotrowski
Helen Duberstein	H. M. Koutoukas	Arline Rothlein
Joan Durant	Chrise Maile	Muriel Rukeyser
Paul Dver	John Herbert McDowell	Arthur Sainer
Jane Eksman	Robert Nichols	Hugh Seidman
Harvey Fiersteen	Joel Oppenheimer	Ronald Tavel
Marie Irene Fornes	Sally Ordway	Dolores Walker
Aenlin Gray	Grace Paley	

Theater for the New City   Show begins at 8 PM.
113 Jane Street   For reservation call 691-2220
Admission by contribution
Thanks to the New York State Council on the Arts

highlighted by a visit from President Ronald Reagan and other U. S. and foreign dignitaries to watch the spectacular Parade of Tall Ships in the Hudson River, topped off by a spectacular fireworks display with the Statue of Liberty as a backdrop.

A critic from *The Village Voice* named David Finkle wrote: "Heide's *American Hamburger* and Allen Ginsberg's *Kaddish* are already a worthy part of Village literature." I was ecstatic to be thus linked with the great Ginsberg, whom I had known since the time when Beat poetry was coming of age. I first heard him read at the Gaslight Café on MacDougal Street along with Jack Kerouac, Ted Joans, Gregory Corso, Jack Micheline, Taylor Mead, and others.

There was another kind of American revolution going on in New York and other cities in the decade of the 1970s, a sexual revolution being acted out in bars with dark back rooms and cellars where groups of gay men congregated to indiscriminately play at sex, sex, and more sex. Along the waterfront in Greenwich Village were "the trucks" and the abandoned and dilapidated piers (former passenger terminals) where it all took place. Danger was the name of the game, and many wound up in the river following anonymous sexual encounters. Heterosexual couples too engaged in back-room antics in places like the Hell Fire Club and Studio 54. For just men it was the Anvil, the Mine Shaft, Dirty Dick's, the Eagle, Jack Rabbit's, or the Toilet on the wild, wild waterfront. The movie *Cruising* with Al Pacino depicted this nighttime world of men on the prowl and was filmed at some of these locations.

All this inspired me to write *American Hamburger,* wherein a conservative history teacher by day would at night head down to "the trucks" dressed in black leather, jeans, and boots to act out his fantasies. In the play he leaves the notorious Keller Bar and heads across the street to the trucks and onto a pier, where following a sexual encounter he is thrown into the river. An acquaintance of mine, Walter Giegold, who was one of Candy Darling's boyfriends and the kept man of the German munitions heir Arndt Krup, ended up in the river after a night of debauchery. He was missing for over a year when, after a persistent search led by director Ron Link, who had worked with Giegold on several plays and hired

Village Writers on the Village: (top to bottom) Robert
Heide, John Herbert McDowell, Amlin Gray,
Ronald Tavel, Harvey Tavel, Joan Durant, H. M.
Koutoukas, Helen Duberstein Lipton, Maria Irene
Fornes, Harvey Fierstein, and foreground, Arthur
Sainer

a detective agency, his body was discovered to have been buried
in an unmarked grave in New York's Potter's Field. The character
in my play whom I called A Village Tourist is as if in another
world and in another time zone, finding himself in Washington
Square Park in a state of panic and bewilderment with George
Washington, who led regimental troops in the square, and the poet
Maxwell Bodenheim, who wrote *My Life and Loves in Greenwich*

Village. After recounting his night on the prowl and drinking in Village bars, he comes to realize that he is now, like the gentlemen he has just met, a dead man who must join in with the other ghosts that are said to haunt and roam the Village to this day.

After complaining of being hungry, the three ghosts head over to the Village McDonald's on Third Street, ostensibly for a burger. Before leaving the Square Washington asks, "Is he a general, this McDonald?" and later, somewhat astonished, rephrases the question with "...so it's all hamburger then?"

After 1980 with the arrival of AIDS, it was time to straighten up and fly right. Death was knocking at the door. The good-time party was over, and the cruising on Christopher Street, the bathhouses, the discos with backrooms, after-hours all-night revelries at the river dives, and furtive, anonymous sexual encounters gradually became no more than a memory as time moved on.

When a book I co-wrote with John Gilman, *Greenwich Village, a Primo Guide to Eating, Drinking, and Making Merry in True Bohemia*, was about to go to press, my editor at St. Martin's, Jim Fitzgerald, decided it would be cool to include this Village play, and thus *American Hamburger* was published in a guidebook. The play had some Actors' Equity workshop productions, notably at the Actors Alliance at The Townhouse on West 60th Street. It also was produced by Andy Milligan, a filmmaker who had been a mainstay director at the Caffè Cino, on a double bill with *The Comeback* by Jack Gilhooley at The Troupe on West 39th Street. That production starred James Higgins, Jack Poggi, and Paul Lieber, who played the Village Tourist.

Increased Occupancy
Suburban Tremens

Maria Irene Fornés, Julie Bovasso, and Megan Terry formed the New York Theater Strategy originally as a women's playwriting group which applied for grants and awarded them directly to the

*Playwright members of New York Theatre Strategy, front row from
left: Robert Heide, Leonard Melfi, Julie Bovasso, Paul Foster; middle
row: Megan Terry, Charles Ludlam, Ed Bullins, Jean-Claude van
Itallie, Rochelle Owens, Murray Mednick, Ronald Tavel, Rosalyn
Drexler; on steps: John Ford Noonan, Ken Bernard, Tom Eyen (in
dark glasses), Maria Irene Fornés, William M. Hoffman*

playwrights, thus eliminating the middleman producers. Their first
action, after deciding to include male playwrights, which helped
in fundraising (with Murray Mednick and Ken Bernard installed
as first and second vice-presidents), was to produce a Festival of
Plays from the 1960s. Lynne Meadow hosted this production at
the Manhattan Theatre Club on East 74th Street. Theater Strategy
paid $700 per night and offered the playwrights $150 each to
mount either a one-act play or a short full-length play. The festival,
which ran from May 16 to June 24, 1973, was a great success
and included many hits from the Caffè Cino, including my play
Moon, Tom Eyen's play *The White Whore and the Bit Player*, and

David Starkweather's *The Family Joke*. Other playwrights in this festival included Robert Patrick, William M. Hoffman, Rochelle Owens, Ronald Tavel, John Ford Noonan, Terrence McNally, Rosalyn Drexler, the group's founders, Fornés, Bovasso, and Terry, Ed Bullins, Sam Shepard, Leonard Melfi, and others. In subsequent years the Strategy created a bridge from the 1960s to the 1970s by offering new plays, among them Eyen's *Neon Woman*, Owens's *He Wants Shih*, Tavel's *The Ovens of Anita Orange Juice*, H. M. Koutoukas's *Too Late for Yogurt*, Michael Smith's *Cowgirl Ecstasy*, and my own plays *Increased Occupancy* and *Suburban Tremens*. The production budgets for these plays were approximately $3,000 each depending on the number of actors in the casts. Many of them were produced at Westbeth Theater Center, and sets were often provided by the Strategy. Eventually the New York Theater Strategy was used as a producing tool for Irene Fornés's plays like *Fefu and Her Friends,* and in 1979 it ceased operating.

The opening of *Increased Occupancy*, written as a curtain-raiser for the longer work, *Suburban Tremens*, has a cityscape background with two characters on stage who see themselves as burgeoning artists attempting to live out a bohemian lifestyle in Greenwich Village. The Landlord enters the small loft space with the fixed intent of harassing the tenants. In a playful fun-fest tickling assault, the "artists" bring the landlord to the floor, where, laughing hysterically, he has a heart attack and dies. Placing his body in the hallway alongside some big black garbage bags, they return to the artwork they are creating together, happily splashing black paint onto a huge canvas. Standing in the hallway is an ominous figure in a bright orange jumpsuit – an exterminator with gas mask and spray gun who has come to kill roaches and trap vermin.

There is a parallel to this scene in *Suburban Tremens,* which takes place in a suburban enclave in New Jersey, when a drunken husband wearing a pig mask emerges from the basement and in a fit of rage violently attacks and rapes his terrified wife. In the process he kicks in the glowing television set, which blows up. A moment later he cries out and falls dead, leaving his wife screaming for help. My purpose in bringing forth the two separate incidents

Randolph Graff

Everett Quinton in "Increased Occupancy" at a benefit for the Actors Fund at Howl! Arts, October, 2016

of sudden heart attacks and the deaths of the landlord and suburban breadwinner husband was to provide an arc for the two plays. My intent in developing these two apocalyptic instances was to incorporate and create a kind of tragic-comical farce where everyone is in a distracted state, with each character – as in a Marx Brothers movie, where all logic ceases to exist and caution is thrown to the wind – paying no mind or attention to the other..

Ultimately both plays were produced under the umbrella-title *Suburban Tremens*, the longer play, in which all hell is breaking loose. The mother figure, Freda Stone, was played by the Obie Award-winning Regina David. She brought a piercing demonic reality to Freda, who is trying to maintain her sanity while everyone around her – son, daughter, husband – is falling apart. A hip drifter, Angel Dust, turns up, invited home by the teenage daughter, and a grieving neurotic neighbor, Mister Fedder, moves in on the scene following his own wife's suicide, driving her station wagon into a canal after imbibing several martinis. I should add here that Regina David, who also played the leading lady in my plays *Tropical Fever in Key West* and *Crisis of Identity*, was to my mind one of the best actresses at the time in New York, right alongside Kim Stanley and Geraldine Page. At some point Regina, originally known as Jean David, disappeared.

I had a good time directing these plays, and the entire cast could not have been better. Theo Barnes's smart, atypical, redundant, brilliantly conceived and executed suburban living room set, with overstuffed furniture and oversized matching lamps and an adjoining area for the son's room, was exactly right. While *Increased Occupancy* was inspired by my own life in New York City, *Suburban Tremens* was influenced by my New Jersey family, who after the race riots in Newark in 1968 decided, with many, many others, to move to the suburbs of South Jersey and other such protected enclaves where they felt they could be safe. My parents moved into a ranch house in Point Pleasant, while my sister, her husband, and four daughters moved into a new housing development in Brick Township. Owning your own home, driving the latest model car, and materialism with a vengeance was the name of the game in suburban living, and I felt lucky when I escaped to Greenwich Village, where I knew I could live a more creative life.

Tropical Fever in Key West – The Cake and An Old Tune

How a trip to a book fair at Disney World in Orlando, Florida, followed by visits to Miami, the Everglades, and Key West, led to the play *Tropical Fever in Key West* by Robert Heide, which was commissioned by George Bartenieff and Crystal Field and produced at Theater for the New City.

Tropical Fever in Key West is the rubric I used to cover two interrelated plays. *The Cake* is set in a house belonging to a well-known playwright, while the other, longer play, *An Old Tune*, takes place on the front lawn of a different Key West house, where a down-in-the-dumps retired couple sitting on metal lawn chairs, one an ex-band singer, the other the former owner of a birdseed company, are enjoying Happy Hour, drinking Red Parrot Vodka Zombies waiting for night to fall. They talk agitatedly of large free-roaming Florida alligators and the drunken falling-down playwright who lives across the way. After a while a young, attractive uniformed sailor walks into the scene, wanting to know where the famous playwright lives, and later a doctor looks in on the couple and, captivated, runs off with the sailor, leaving his patients again to ponder their existence over another highball. A critic from the *Christian Science Monitor*, referring to the doctor's exit with the sailor, wrote, ". . . and now we know what Mr. Heide is up to."

Michael Feingold, who has been for decades and still is as of this writing a theatre critic at *The Village Voice* (following in the footsteps of Jerry Tallmer and Michael Smith), wrote this in his review of January 3, 1984:

"Robert Heide's plays – tiny, sharp-edged creatures – emerge sporadically, after long intervals of silence. The wonder of the two new ones, which TNC is presenting under the overall title *Tropical Fever,* is that Heide's talent appears as fresh as if it had been swathed in felt between uses to keep it shiny. Something new has been added as well: where earlier pieces like *Moon* and *At War with the Mongols* conducted their tense psychological games in tight-mouthed ambiguity, these new ones, *The Cake* and *An Old Tune,* are warmer, more expansively revealing, and mellower about their characters. And at the same time, disconcertingly, they're more openly bitter about the dismal state of our culture and the ruts it digs people into.

"Both plays take place in Key West across the street from each other. In *The Cake* we are at the upscale villa of a famous, dissipated, aging writer, a character in whom Heide has amusingly melded some myths and some truths about several well-known American authors. The confrontation here is between the writer, who either is or is not played out; his new assistant, whom he either does or doesn't intend to make his lover and the new course of his creativity; and his current, alcohol-wrecked lover, who is apparently trying to destroy himself, the writer, and the new assistant in turn, and who either has – or has not – poisoned the birthday cake which he and the writer are munching cheerily as the curtain falls.

"In *An Old Tune,* we are on the downscale side of the street, where a worn-out New Jersey band singer and her birdseed wholesaler husband live in the emptiness of early retirement, trying vainly to buoy their spirits with drinking; pills from a malevolently cheery local doctor; and fantasies about dying, doing each other in, her glamorous past, and the recently deceased playwright across the street. The action

Book cover designed by Jon Glick for "Mickey Mouse—the Evolution, the Legend, the Phenomenon!" by Robert Heide and John Gilman, the official Mickey Mouse biography from Disney Editions, New York

here, seemingly more static than in the curtain-raiser, is also more violent when the characters intermittently rouse themselves to life.

"The play has the advantage of an excellent set by John Eric Broaddus (the second-act stage-set design is a comic masterpiece). The cast's chief visible asset, at present, is Regina David, who makes an infallibly funny pop-expressionist icon of the New Jersey wife. Over the years I've seen her play St. Mary of Egypt, Elsa Maxwell, a widow in a Marsha Norman play, and now this. As there's obviously nothing she can't do well, I'm looking forward to her *Hamlet*."

The inspiration for *Tropical Fever in Key West* came after a trip to Orlando with John Gilman, where he and I were to be part of a book fair and promotion for our co-authored book *Disneyana – Classic Collectibles 1928–1958* published by Hyperion Press. The focus of this lavishly illustrated coffee-table book was a man named Herman "Kay" Kamen, who in 1933 became Walt Disney's sole licensing and merchandising agent. Kamen's ingenious methods made the already famous Mickey Mouse a superstar, with his image on everything from a watch to toy trains, dolls, tin wind-ups, clothing, toothbrushes, comics, Big Little Books, jam, bread, milk, soda, chocolate candy bars, school pencilboxes, and just about anything else imaginable. (The Mickey Mouse wristwatch – and pocket watch and alarm clock – was a phenomenon, saving the Ingersoll company from bankruptcy in the Depression.) It was the genius of Kay Kamen that kept the Disney Studio afloat with the requisite cash needed to produce Mickey and Donald Duck and Goofy and Horace Horsecollar and Clarabelle Cow cartoon shorts, award-winning Silly Symphonies like *The Three Little Pigs*, and eventually the animated features *Pinocchio, Snow White and the Seven Dwarfs,* and *Fantasia.* Kamen's last national merchandising campaign was for *Cinderella* (1950). Tragically, he and his wife died in a plane crash in the Azores in 1949.

John and I were put up in a fancy house at Walt Disney World for a week, sold and signed books at the book fair daily, swam in the country club pool, and rode all the rides for free. We were assigned a spiffy new car with no time limits and decided to tour Art Deco Miami Beach and ogle the scary alligators in the Everglades. We drove on down to Key West, stopping frequently to eat conch fritters and home-made Key lime pie. I should add that since then we have written three more books about Mickey Mouse and Walt Disney, including *The Mickey Mouse Watch – From the Beginning of Time* and *Mickey Mouse – The Evolution, The Legend, The Phenomenon!* – the latter Mickey's official biography. We later wound up talking Disney on the Today Show with Katie Couric. I sported an original 1933 Ingersoll Mickey Mouse wristwatch, showing it off to Katie and her 40 million viewers.

Once in Key West we checked into an old-time gay guest house. With all the travel and the in and out of the air-conditioned car and then suddenly languishing in the hot tropical atmosphere, I found myself passing out. Quickly the two gentlemen hosts of the guesthouse took me to their doctor, who turned out to have been Tennessee Williams's doctor when the playwright was in town. He gave me all kinds of tests, including an electro-cardiogram, finally pronouncing that my heart was okay but declaring in his broad Southern accent, "You're sufferin' from exhaustion. Watcha been doing? You need to sit under a palm tree for a while." He talked about Tennessee's drinking and about his cousin, also a doctor, who had treated Elvis. "That boy was on so many drugs . . ."

Later John and I wandered around Key West, watching amazing pelicans diving into the water, perched on the piers, and soaring in flight. It was after we found Tennessee's house, unoccupied almost a year after his death, that we encountered the couple across the street on their lawn, waiting for the official start of Happy Hour, pouring drinks from their bar, a converted ironing board. They pointed to the writer's house, saying, "Oh, he was always falling down dead drunk on the stairs." I thought to myself, these people themselves are right out of a Tennessee Williams play. On the train trip back to New York I met a sailor who had also gone on a pilgrimage to visit the Williams house.

This trip to Key West later entered my mind as a play. The characters demanded to be written. I hoped that if it worked it might be seen as a tribute to Tennessee. *The Cake*, as it turned out, was a combination of my good friend Edward Albee and Tennessee himself, whom I had met with his sister Rose at the Broadway opening night party at Sardi's for Robert Patrick's play *Kennedy's Children*. "Would you like to meet my sister Rose?" he asked, a moment not to be forgotten. When Williams himself appeared onstage with Candy Darling, a good friend, in *Small Craft Warnings*, I got to hang out with him and Candy at bars on the Upper East Side. I always thought Candy, who was great in the play opposite the author, could have been a wonderful Blanche DuBois in *Streetcar*.

When it came time to cast *Tropical Fever*, an actor named John Uecker showed up at TNC to audition for the part of the playwright. It turned out he had been staying with and watching over Tennessee at the Hotel Elysée when the writer succumbed to a combination of too much alcohol, drugs, and medication including sleeping pills. Uecker did well in the part. He gave J. P. Dougherty a Panama hat belonging to Tennessee to wear as the doctor in the play. Regina David as the retired band singer was perfect; Mel Gussow, the *New York Times* critic, pronounced her performance "sublime." I felt all of the actors in this production were just perfect. The director, Sebastian Stuart, brought it all together and understood what the plays were about. An actor himself, he let the actors "do-their-own-thing," to use a Joe Cino phrase, and with that everyone seemed to come together in the sense of ensemble.

Crisis of Identity

This was the third and last play I did with the brilliant actress Regina David. I wrote this one particularly with Regina in mind. Her work motivated the other actors, who would become inspired by her total commitment. Previously she had won an Obie Award for her wild, way-out performance in Rochelle Owens play *Beclch* and played lead roles in several summer seasons at Drew University's Shakespeare Festival in Madison, New Jersey. It occurs to me now that *Suburban Tremens, Tropical Fever in Key West,* and *Crisis of Identity* might represent a trilogy of plays for a leading actress – and how lucky I was to have Regina playing in all three. In her acting she did not just inhabit the character she was playing but would somehow magically pull in and incorporate the audience and beyond. Like the master actor Charles Ludlam, she would glare at a person in the audience who coughed without missing a beat; or if someone out there was talking or whispering, she would take a moment, give forth a blank stare in silence, and then go on. Ludlam told me in an interview I did for the *New York Native* – it was his last interview before he died – that he learned about this breaking-the-fourth-wall/outside-moment technique from actresses like Lynn Fontanne, Katharine Cornell, and Helen Hayes. He enjoyed this kind of "great actress" moment and incorporated it often on stage at his Ridiculous Theatrical Company on Sheridan Square. In Jack Gelber's junkie-jazz play *The Connection* at the Living Theatre, which I saw many times, I witnessed one of these reality moments one night when a loud airplane flew overhead and the entire ensemble of actors and the jazz musicians as well turned their heads and – looking upward – waited for the plane to pass before getting on with the play.

Crisis of Identity was commissioned by Crystal Field and George Bartenieff for Theater for the New City, and with a good production budget, the actors Regina, Robert Frink, and Daryl Marsh worked perfectly together. The artist and set designer John Eric Broaddus created what was meant to be the penthouse apartment of a top business executive who is being investigated for corruption and also fears that his life is in danger. The penthouse was dense and murky, with only a glimmer of light peeking through an oversized Venetian blind, the dark set lending an ominous feeling as in some dark dream or Greek tragedy.

Our hero has hired a muscular young bodyguard for protection as well as companionship, treating him almost as an adopted son. Enter the wife, Beatrice, who talks about just coming back from the continent of Australia; soon it becomes clear that she has actually been in a rehab hospital where she was being treated for physical and mental problems related to alcoholism. Beginning to drink heavily again once back home, she flirts with the young man, performing a frenetic and seductive hula dance, thinking she might not have been to Australia at all but had just enjoyed a vacation in Hawaii.

When *Voice* critic and my theatre compatriot Michael Feingold came to review the play, he wrote about an Albee influence – mommy, daddy, and a handsome "adopted" young man, as in Edward's *The American Dream*. I intended *Crisis* as a familial Oedipal play wherein everything is enacted out of some deeper unconscious drive – in the man an undefined sexual frustration and desire for power and money, in the woman a need for sexual delusions. Deep down underneath, an Oedipal sensual libidinous need is waiting to break out into the open. A sense of desperation, unhappiness, and unfulfillment pervades all three characters.

In the end, in a bewildered state, they decide to order in a giant bucket of Colonel Sanders's Kentucky Fried Chicken, which they ravenously go at, joking and laughing, as if it were their last meal. In my play *American Hamburger* the ghosts of George Washington, Maxwell Bodenheim, and a Village tourist decide to go to McDonald's for a hamburger. In *At War with the Mongols* the hippie couple who are hiding out and on the run from a Mongol invasion of the United States take a break from the turmoil of this imaginary war and, stopping the action, drop acid and act out a television commercial, eating Lay's Potato Chips slowly, one by one, exaggeratedly drinking Coca-Cola at the same time. As in many commercials the sales pitch is not the product itself, be it food, a new car, or a bedroom set, but the direct sensual sexy appeal of the "pretty people" actors, hired to make viewers love the product so much that they go out and buy – and in a big hurry. Sam Shepard, a friend and colleague from the Caffè Cino and La Mama days, used real food as an element of his Pulitzer Prize-winning play *Buried Child* – shucking corn, and cutting up bunches of carrots – adding a touch of superrealism to the mystery of a work that primarily focuses on a son's return to his crazy dysfunctional family. When I saw this play again in a revival at the Signature Theatre on 42nd Street, Sam and I talked about the old days, and I was reminded of the use of food in our respective plays.

Short Plays

Shorter than short was the requirement for plays in many festivals and fund-raisers. Joe Cino once told me that as far as he was concerned, "The shorter the play the better." I wrote a short curtain-raiser called *Split Level* for the longer one-act *Moon* after *Moon* had been published and was being done in regional theatres and on college campuses around the country. *Split Level* is a play in which a gun-crazy suburban couple are hired to shoot a local politician, hoping the money earned for this assassination will pay off the mortgage for the split-level dream house they have moved into. Other of my short plays like *Hollywood Palms, East of the Sun, Zoe's Letter,* and *Statue* were written to help Ellen Stewart raise money to keep La Mama Experimental Theatre Club afloat. *Mother Suck* was performed at a theatre benefit at Art D'Lugoff's Village Gate by the brilliant Helen Hanft as a confused, terrified, crazed mother anxiously waiting in a Greyhound bus station for a reunion with her son, who has had a sex-change operation at Johns Hopkins Hospital. Under Ron Link's direction, Helen turned this monologue into an uproarious laugh riot. Working with Helen Hanft, the Queen of Off-Off-Broadway, who became a good friend, was a very special experience for me.

At Theater for the New City on Second Avenue, George

Bartenieff and Crystal Field commissioned plays and musicals by performers and writers including Helen Hanft, Barbara Garson, Remy Charlip, Al Carmines, Irene Fornés, Leonard Melfi, Amlin Gray, and Jean-Claude van Itallie for a festival for nuclear disarmament called Arts for Life. My contribution was *Mr. Nobody,* a short play about a group of people in a café in the East Village encountering a character (played by Robert Frink) completely covered in gauze and bandages whose face might have been burned off by radiation after an atomic test in Nevada. The other playwrights pondered the "what if" aspects of a nuclear attack.

Media Circus was my contribution to a "Funhouse Experience" directed by Tom O'Horgan at Here Arts Center called *Greed/ Flood...an Organic Virtual Reality about the Johnstown, Pennsylvania Flood.* In *Media Circus* a hysterical television anchor and weather woman are broadcasting more and more disastrous news and weather. O'Horgan described this event: "Everyone was too busy dancing to worry about the workers lost in the flood. Money is the 'suck' in success. Greed is not hunger, it's appetite. All theatre is political. The dam broke in America a long time ago."

Lupe

I first met Andy Warhol through the photographer Edward Wallowitch at Aldo's, a semi-upscale gay restaurant on Bleecker Street. Andy, in tie and jacket, was wearing his trademark white-silver Truman Capote wig. He seemed somewhat passive and shy as we shook hands. It soon became clear that Edward, whom I had met at Northwestern University, was having an affair with Andy.

I saw Andy again at Edward's brother John's floor-through basement apartment at 8 Barrow Street. John Wallowitch, a pianist, composer, cabaret performer, and man about town, had a salon where the likes of Eartha Kitt, Alice Ghostley, and Joanna Berretta would sing, with John pounding the ivories. One amusing song he both wrote and sang went, "Death – it's the latest – it's the end – take your life and chuck it. Death – it's the latest – let's transcend

– go and kick the bucket. Death – it's gonna get you in the end!" The swigging of martini after martini was the order of the day in that musical Greenwich Village pad in 1958.

After my initial encounters with Andy I lost touch, but at some point in 1965 he decided to film my play *The Bed* for one of his early experimental split-screen movies. Jonas Mekas's Film-Makers' Cinematheque premiered the movie at the 41st Street Theater on April 27, 1966.

I began then to spend time at Warhol's Silver Factory at 231 East 47th Street, where I enjoyed hanging out with Edie Sedgwick and Billy Linich-Name, who had been a close friend of mine before he began working for Andy. Bob Dylan was fascinated by the glamorous and beautiful Edie, who was becoming famous as the new Warhol superstar. Edie took me for rides in Dylan's limousine. We would stop along the way, between shopping sprees at Bloomingdales, Saks, and Best & Co., to have Bloody Marys at the Ginger Man, where she would sign her name to the checks. This was around the time Dylan put out the *Blonde on Blonde* album – one of the songs, "Just Like a Woman," was written for Edie. In a 1978 *Playboy* interview, Dylan said, "The closest I ever got to the sound I hear in my mind was on individual bands in that *Blonde on Blonde* album. It's that thin, that wild mercury sound – metallic and bright gold, with whatever that conjures up. That's my particular sound."

I was present at the Factory when Warhol filmed a "screen test" portrait of Bobby, as we called him, all in black, sitting in a chair and moping. Afterwards the sullen Dylan picked up a big silver silk-screen of Elvis Presley with gun in hand, saying to Andy, "I think I'll take this for payment, man," upon which he walked into the elevator and left. Andy's face turned tomato-soup red.

Andy was having trouble with Ron Tavel, who had written some of the films that Edie starred in, and asked me if I might want to be the new Factory film writer. I agreed. I had acted in two of his movies, *Dracula/Batman* and *Camp*, both starring Jack Smith, which was a lot of crazy fun. The idea of writing something for Edie appealed to me. Andy specified, "It has to be something where Edie commits suicide in the end." I went home and after reading Kenneth Anger's *Hollywood Babylon* account of the movie star Lupe Vélez, known in Hollywood as the "Mexican Spitfire," decided that was it and went ahead with the script full-speed. I had learned from mentor Andy that if it doesn't happen fast, it might not happen at all. The script was called *The Death of Lupe Vélez* but Andy decided to just call the film *Lupe*. He lavished a full-color film treatment for Edie; and she never looked more beautiful in a sheer, almost transparent negligee. Kenneth Anger shows Lupe planning a beautiful suicide death in her Hollywood Hills mansion. After writing to her lover, "Harold," who has left her pregnant, she covers her bed with tuberoses, swallows a bottle of Seconal sleeping pills, and waits to die. As Anger tells it the pills, mixing with a Mexicana-spicy dinner Lupe had eaten that night, causes her to vomit, with her head winding up in the toilet bowl – where later she was found dead. In Warhol's *Lupe* the last shot is of Edie with her head hanging over the toilet, which Anger wrote was the same one Hollywood gossip columnist Louella Parsons had sat on while interviewing Lupe the day before.

Lupe was the last film Edie made with Warhol. A day after the film was shot Andy asked me to meet him at the Kettle of Fish, a bar on MacDougal Street. When I got there he had not yet arrived, but Edie was at a table, drinking a Bloody Mary. When I sat down across from her she began sobbing, saying, "I tried to get close to him but he never…" At that moment Andy came in with a cardboard box containing a custom-made blue suede suit he had ordered at the Leather Man on Christopher Street. He dragged a tall stool over to our table and perched himself there, hovering over us. Neither Andy nor Edie said a word for some time. I stared out the window. Before long a limousine pulled up and in came Bob Dylan, all in black, his face half obscured by large dark glasses topped by his trademark frizz-curled Afro hair-do. Sitting down, he ordered a beer. There ensued more of the deadly, silent tension. Suddenly Dylan grabbed hold of Edie with a gruff "Let's split!" and out they went. Andy stared straight ahead and said nothing. Finally, he asked me to take him to 5 Cornelia Street, the tenement building where the Judson dancer and Warhol film star Freddie Herko (*Haircut,* also featuring Billy Name and John Daley) had leapt from a fifth-floor window to his death on the pavement below. Johnny Dodd, the lighting designer, and Michael Smith both lived in the apartment where Freddie performed his last ballet leap. Andy looked up at the window and said, "If only he'd told us – we could have filmed it." Then he added, "When do you think Edie will commit suicide? I hope she lets us know so we can at least film it."

My one disappointment in *Lupe* the film is that Edie could not memorize the lines in the script I had written for her so it all had to be done as an improvisation. In my scenario Lupe returns from the great beyond to ponder her life; but Andy decided to end the picture with her death as in Kenneth Anger's account, with her head in the toilet. In most of Andy's films after *Lupe* the dialogue was improvised. I guess I could lay claim to being the last Warhol screenwriter after the first, Ron Tavel, who had tried to bring some order into the madness.

I Shop: Andy Warhol

After Andy Warhol was shot by Valerie Solanas on June 3, 1968, just before the assassination of Robert Kennedy (June 6, 1968), everybody was in a state of shock. "How could this happen?" In the instance of Andy Warhol's shooting, with all the craziness and drugs happening around the ongoing Warhol scene and its cast of characters, one might say it was inevitable; but miraculously, near death, and with a top specialist surgeon on the case, Andy had a reprieve. He rebounded and returned to his work as an artist and filmmaker; but without a doubt he was from then on forever in pain.

When he was eventually released from the hospital we got together one afternoon at the Caffè Reggio on MacDougal Street, one of Andy's favorite Village coffeehouses. When he arrived I saw instantly how frail, pale, and in a state of shock he was. Speaking in a soft whisper he said, "You should write a play about this," meaning the shooting. This was the furthest thing from my mind at that time. I had been at the Museum of Modern Art the day Andy was shot. A crazed woman dressed in a shirt and men's trousers (not Valerie) aggressively shoved a pink paper flyer into my hand, stating, "The sweet assassin has shot the plastic man." In the flyer I read in horror about S.C.U.M., the Society for Cutting Up Men – Valerie's manifesto for women.

In later years I was asked by Barry Rowell, Catherine Porter, and Ralph Lewis of Peculiar Works to write something for an event called "Bang the Drum" they were producing to raise money for their site-specific theatre company. I decided it would be fun to write the short play I entitled *I Shop: Andy Warhol*. The cast of characters would be led by Andy, who had a life-long obsession (among many others) with shopping and collecting practically everything. I remember him clearly at flea markets, antique shows, and specialty shops and at stores like Fiorucci's buying his designer shirts and Italian blue jeans. It was always Buy! Buy! Buy! He would bring along Edie Sedgwick or the glamorous superstar of later years Candy Darling just for the fun of it. Dressing up and going out-on-the-town to openings and on to late-night disco at Studio 54 was what it was all about for Andy in those days.

In the playful format of *I Shop: Andy Warhol* I ignored the time framework as in effect one shop leads to another, just as the superstars came and went. Why not merge Edie with Candy, Bobby (Dylan) with Billy (Name)? Of course I could not help but create a character I called Vicki (a pseudonym for Valerie, of course) – what would it all mean if it wasn't for her? – an ominous character lurking in the background hoping for five – ten – or fifteen minutes of fame no matter what the cost. After seeing the play, my Caffè Cino cohorts and good friends William M. Hoffman and Doric Wilson said to me, "You sure got the Warhol Factory scene nailed" and "You got it right on." I was happy because I knew if it was bad or did not work, these two playwrights would let me know.

Do I miss Andy? Yes. But no matter what, he is still everywhere, to my mind a great American genius who changed everything.

The Other Robert Heide
An Afterword

Besides the 25 plays published herein the playwright has written extensively for a great variety of newspapers and periodicals such as the *New York Daily News*, *The Village Voice*, *Westview News*, *The Villager*, *Artdesk*, *Portfolio*, *Disney Magazines* and many other publications including the *New York Native* during the AIDS crisis. In the early days AIDS was known as GRID (gay-related immuno-deficiency), and the *Native* existed primarily to report on the new virulent plague that was then mysteriously taking away the lives of so many gay men. Heide conducted interviews with icons in Greenwich Village like Charles Ludlam of the Ridiculous Theatrical Company and the Caffe Cino playwright H. M. Koutoukas. To lighten and bring up the spirits of the readers he also contributed "camp" cover stories on stars like Lana Turner, Tallulah Bankhead, and Joan Crawford or gay men's idols like Rock Hudson, Tab Hunter, Tony Perkins, James Dean, or Guy Madison. At the *Village Voice* his interviews included the French film actress and Rothschild heiress Nicole Stephane, who starred in the classic Cocteau-Melville film *Les Enfants Terrible*. Ms. Stephane, who became lovers with Susan Sontag, spoke in the interview of the homosexuality in the film and the writings of her friend Jean Cocteau. At the *Voice* Robert Heide also created centerfold guides on everything from mod fashion to Mickey Mouse to Jersey City ice-cream parlors. Double-page centerfold spreads gradually evolved into full scale textual and photographic books focusing on American popular culture primarily in the Depression decade of the 1930s and including the 1940s and 1950s.

These books, co-authored with John Gilman, include *Dime-Store Dream Parade – Popular Culture 1925-1955* (E. P. Dutton); *Box-Office Buckaroos – The Cowboy Hero from the Wild West Show to the Silver Screen* and *Popular Art Deco – Depression Era Style and Design* (both Abbeville Press); *Home Front America – Popular Culture of the World War II Era* (Chronicle Books); *Starstruck – The Wonderful World of Movie Memorabilia* (Doubleday); *Disneyana – Classic Collectibles 1928-1958* and *The Mickey Mouse Watch – From the Beginning of Time* (both Hyperion); and *Mickey Mouse – The Evolution, The Legend, The Phenomenon!* (Disney Editions); *O' New Jersey –Daytripping, Back Roads, Eateries, and Funky Adventures* (three editions, St. Martin's Press); *New Jersey – Spirit of America* (Harry N. Abrams); *Backroads of New Jersey* (Voyageur Press); *Greenwich Village – A Primo Guide to Shopping, Eating, and Making Merry in True Bohemia* (St. Martin's Griffin).

Among many other television programs and films Robert Heide has appeared in *The Century – America's Time* (TV miniseries); *Andy Warhol's Factory People* (MTV documentary); *Lords of the Revolution* (VH1 Andy Warhol documentary); *Beautiful Darling* (Candy Darling documentary); *Superstar in a Housedress* (Jackie Curtis documentary); *Jack Smith and the Destruction of Atlantis* (documentary). His plays have been published in several anthologies including: *The Off Off Broadway Book*, edited by Albert Poland and Bruce Mailman (Bobbs-Merrill); *The Best of Off Off Broadway*, edited by Michael Smith (E. P. Dutton); *New American Plays, Volume IV*, edited by William M. Hoffman (Hill and Wang); *Return to the Caffe Cino*, edited by Steve Susoyev and George Birimisa (Moving Finger Press); and in numerous acting editions. Critical discussions of his plays are found in: *Caffe Cino – The Birthplace of Off-Off Broadway* by Wendell C. Stone (Southern Illinois University Press); *The Off Off Broadway Explosion* by David A. Crespy (Back Stage Books); *Playing Underground* by Stephen J. Bottoms (University of Michigan Press); and *Off-Off Broadway – the Second Wave: 1968-1980* by Christopher Olsen. Heide's personal and creative relationship with Andy Warhol is highlighted in *POP – The Genius of Andy Warhol* by Tony Scherman and David Dalton (Harper Collins); and *Factory Girl – Edie Sedgwick* by Nat Finkelstein and David Dalton.(VH1 Press)

ACKNOWLEDGMENTS

SPECIAL THANKS

Michael Townsend Smith – publisher, editor, colleague, playwright, and friend

John Wright Gilman – collaborator, co-editor, photo research, and life partner

Edward Franklin Albee – lifetime friend and mentor

THANKS ALSO TO:

Editors

Jim Fitzgerald, Doubleday & St. Martin's Press; Walton Rawls, Abbeville Press; Cyril Nelson, E. P. Dutton; Bob Miller, Hyperion; Wendy Lefkon, Disney Editions; Steve Susoyev, Moving Finger Press; Larry Ashmead and Craig Nelson, Harper & Row; Genevieve Morgan and Karen Silver, Chronicle Books; Ruth Peltason, Harry N. Abrams; George Capsis, Westview News

Writers

Sam Shepard
Jerry Tallmer
Mel Gussow
Frank O'Hara
Michael Feingold
Howard Smith
H. M. Koutoukas
Michael McGrinder
Jeff Weiss
Paul Foster
Robert Patrick
Tom Eyen
George Birimisa
David Carter
William M. Hoffman
Lanford Wilson
Doric Wilson
Story Talbot
Don Kvares
Terrence McNally
Diane DiPrima
Cynthia Carr
Rochelle Owens
John Guare
Ron Tavel
Charles Ludlam
David Starkweather
Jean Claude van Itallie
David Crespy
Erika Munk
Barbara Kahn
Magie Dominic
Martin Duberman
Legs McNeil
Victor Bockris
Timothy Bottoms
Wendell C. Stone
Michael & Suzanne
Wallis – Route 66
Torsten Otte & Mike
Deppe
James Kotsilibas
Davis
Blake Gopnik
Tony Scherman
David Dalton

Producers   Lee Paton Nagrin, New Playwrights; Joe Cino, Caffè
Cino; Ellen Stewart, Cafe La Mama; George Bartenieff and Crystal
Field, Theater for the New City; Julian Beck & Judith Malina, Jim
Spicer, Living Theater; Maxine Munt &Alfred Brooks, The Changing
Scene, Denver; Speedy, The Old Reliable Theater Tavern; Eric Krebs,
Ric Cuneo, Philip Cohen, Brecht West (George Street Playhouse);
Maria Irene Fornés, Julie Bovasso, New York Theater Strategy; Lynne
Meadow, Manhattan Theater Club; Casey Childs, Sally Plass, Primary
Stages; Barry Rowell, Katherine Porter, Ralph Lewis, Peculiar
Works Project; Carter Edwards, Jane Friedman, Howl! Arts; George
Chauncey, Ron Gregg, Yale University

AND TO THE FOLLOWING

Actors

Victor Lipari
Jim Jennings
Linda Eskenas
Gordon Ramsey
Marilyn Roberts
Jacque Lynn Colton
Lucy Silvay
Shirley Stoler

John Uecker
Agosto Machado
Chris Tanner
Everett Quinton
Jayne Haynes
Lise Beth Talbot
Carol Fox
Robert Frink
Regina David

Paul Lieber
Mark Simon
Helen Hanft
Myra Carter
Marian Seldes
Gillien Goll
Jonathan Frid
Stanley Bell
Frederick Forrest

Directors

Robert Dahdah
Ronald Bruce Link

Tom O'Horgan
Nick Cernovich
Tim Cusack

Ralph Lewis
Sebastian Stewart

At the Factory

Andy Warhol
Edie Sedgwick
Billy Name
Ultra Violet
Taylor Mead
Alan Midgette
Richard Bernstein
Freddie Herko
Candy Darling
Jackie Curtis

Holly Woodlawn
Brigid Berlin
Joe D'Allesandro
Paul America
Lou Reed
Gerard Malanga
Ingrid Superstar
Baby Jane Holzer
Eric Anderson
Jack Smith
Walter Dainwood

David Bourdon
Robert Olivio aka
   Ondine
Danny Fields
John Daley
Naomi Levine
Nico
Penelope Palmer
Ivy Nicholson
Sean Carillo
Bebe Hansen

Andy Warhol Film Project

At the Whitney: Callie Angell, Claire Henry, Tom Kalin
At the Warhol Museum: Geralyn Huxley, Curator of Film & Video

Friends

Stephen 'Hoop'
  Hooper
Kevin Geer
Jimmy Rado
Julie Reilly
Timothy Bissell
Lisa Jane Persky
Michael Riedel
Rochelle Oliver &
  Fritz Weaver
Peter Gilman (John's
  brother in France)
Travis Painter (John's
  cousin)
Kenneth Anger
Marianne Faithfull
Ali Anderson
Mel & Eunice
  Birnkrant
Frances Beatty,
  Feigen Gallery
Ray Johnson
Dorothy Podber
Wendy Lipkind
Joanne Beretta
Janet Capron
Peter Mintun
Peter Leiss
John Currie
Letitia Ferrer
Gerome Ragni
Mark Kostabi
Al Klingler
Natalia Padalino
John Patterson
Albert Poland
Countess Olivera
  Sajkovitch
Lady Hope Stansbury
Dwight Goss
Jamie Warhola

Larry Myers
Jeremiah Newton
The Harrises, Off-
  Off-Broadway's
  First Family – Ann
  and George; Fred,
  MaryLou, Jayne
  Anne, Eloise, Walter
  Michael, George Jr.
  aka Hibiscus
Dagon James
Celeste Holm
Charlotte Wilcox
Barbara Barondess
Allen Perry & Don
  Rollins
Liz Ryan
Blake Boyd
Jakob Holder
Larry Hassman
Carl Goldman
Robert Bryan
Jeffrey Geiger
August Ventura
Kyle Ericson
Rich Conaty, host of
  The Big Broacast
  on WFUV
Wheeler &
  Gwendolyn Dixon
Elizabeth Finkelstein
Joe Franklin
Quentin Crisp
Thomas Kiedrowski
Ron Lieberman
Clayton Patterson
Esther Robinson
Sally & Alyn Heim
Mari Claire Charba
Chris Kapp
Johnny Dodd
Michael Warren
  Powell

Andrea & David
  Rubin
David Sheward
David Kaufman &
  Ken Geist
Randy Graff
Arthur Fournier
Deborah Shatin &
  Lyle Hallowell
Craig Highberger
Craig Schneider
Craig Maier
Noam Dworman
Joyce Mandell
Steve Ross
Carol Overby
Farrar Lee Fitzgerald
  & Thomas George
  Lannon
Erik LaPrade
Seth Weine
Jay Reisberg
Bill Wilson
Ken Ketwig
Madeline Hoffer
Lucille Anunziata
The Wallowitch
  Family – John,
  Edward, Anna
  Mae, Paul
Wim Sonneveld
Joyce & Gordon
  Tretick – Show
  Business
Ned Rorem
Tom Duncan
Joyce Johnson
Robert Akeret
Sandy Turner
Alison Orlin
Eduardo Tirella
Doris Duke

Theatre Study Teachers

Alvina Krause at Northwestern University; Stella Adler; Uta Hagen,
HB Studio; Harold Clurman, Horton Foote, Estelle Parsons at the
Actors Studio

Neighbors — The House on Christopher Street

Marion Burger	James Zulauf	Jackie Burroughs
Margaret Wilcox	John Schline	Dick Higgins
Mary Goldie	Zalman (Zolly)	Sally Kirkland
Nena Chavarria	Yanovsky of the	
Lisa Pelikan	Lovin' Spoonful	

Family

Olga and Ludwig (parents); Evelyn (sister); Walter (brother); Carol
Tooker (niece); Jesse Tooker (grandnephew)

Childhood

The gang on Franklin Terrace, Irvington, NJ - Norma Edgar, Richard
Edgar, Dolores Borowski, Peggy Miller, Norman Rhinehartson, Lois
Hausman, Robert Roberts, Arnold Martin, Billy Burlew, and special
thanks to our primo English teacher Elsie Kennard at the Florence
Avenue Grade School

Photographers

Edward Wallowitch, George Bonanno, Nat Finkelstein, Stephen Shore,
James D. Gossage, Cesar Geraldo, Timothy Bissell, John Eric Broaddus,
Deborah Shatin, Randolph Graff, Dan McCoy, and unidentified others

CPSIA information can be obtained
at www.ICGtesting.com
Printed in the USA
FSOW02n0355120917
38413FS